*If a man is to write a panegyric,
he may keep vices out of sight;
but if he professes to write a* LIFE
he must represent it really as it was.

DR. SAMUEL JOHNSON

Biographies

The Haunted Palace: A Life of Edgar Allan Poe
Oscar Wilde and the Yellow Nineties
Wingless Victory (D'Annunzio and Duse)
The Immortal Lovers (Elizabeth Barrett and Robert Browning)
The Saint and the Devil (Joan of Arc and Gilles de Rais)
The Life of the Heart (George Sand and Her Times)
American Giant (Walt Whitman and His Times)
Poor Splendid Wings (The Rossettis and Their Circle)
The Romantic Rebels (Byron, Shelley and Keats)
Farewell the Banner (Coleridge and the Wordsworths)

Novels

The Last Love of Camille
The Eagle and the Rock
The Sentimentalist
Gallows Hill
Pagan Interval
The Golden Round
The Ardent Flame

Translation

The Decameron of Giovanni Boccaccio

History

Puritan City: The Story of Salem
The Land of the Italian People

Art Monograph

Ruotolo: Man and Artist

Jean-Jacques Rousseau

Conscience of an Era

Frances Winwar

Random House   New York

FIRST PRINTING

Grateful acknowledgment is made for permission to quote from other books, as follows: To McGraw-Hill Book Company, Inc., for *Boswell on the Grand Tour, Germany and Switzerland, 1764,* edited by Frederick A. Pottle, Copyright, 1928, 1953, by Yale University; To Houghton Mifflin Company for *Portrait of a Golden Age: Intimate Papers of the Second Viscount Palmerston, Courtier under George III,* compiled and edited by Brian Connell; and to Librairie Hachette for translation of material from *La Vie Privée de J. J. Rousseau* by René Trintzius, 1938.

To George W. Alger

Contents

Part Three

Part Four

Part Five

Part One

1. *Beginnings*

No man is born hero or angel but it is not denied him to rise
to greatness nor even to the fulfillment of himself as that ultimate achievement of humankind—a man.

If Suzanne, wife of the amateur fiddler, dancing master and
skilled watchmaker, Isaac Rousseau, pondered those thoughts,
the pangs of labor, seven years after the birth of her first son,
François, drove them from her mind. She had been in the
throes for hours and since she was approaching her fortieth
year, the midwife and the neighboring gossips who had gathered, as they always did on such occasions, partly to offer help,
but chiefly for the secret pleasure of witnessing, rather than
performing, the miracle of birth, began to exchange worried
glances.

It was a fair June day, the twenty-eighth of the year 1712.[1]
The boy François had been entrusted to the care of Isaac's sister, Theodora Bernard, while Isaac himself, who proudly let

no one forget that he was a Citizen of Geneva, the New Zion, worked on his watches and settled the affairs of his small world among his patrons and cronies.

He had had his adventures, Isaac Rousseau—a sentimental, romantic individual, even before romanticism. Dissatisfied with his too quiet existence, and ambitious to make a name and perhaps a fortune, he left his shop, his wife and child one day, and sailed away to Istanbul. But then, he was only one of the many in his position seeking betterment abroad. The fabulous, rediscovered East lured and he answered its beckoning. Who knows? Fame, riches and the Grand Turk's own houris might be waiting on the farther shore. Whether or not he found them and whether, as Jean-Jacques not yet conceived would later have it, Isaac became watchmaker extraordinary to the Grand Turk's seraglio, he seemed so well satisfied with his place and environment that Suzanne became alarmed at his prolonged stay.

As it was, she had her troubles at home. An extraordinarily attractive woman, well-formed, with large, flashing dark eyes and refined features, a beauty whom Isaac prided himself on snatching from a host of admirers—she found it increasingly difficult to walk the safe road without being ambushed by some aspirant to her favors, the most persistent being none other than Monsieur de la Closure, the Résident de France himself. The neighbors, of course, kept a constant alert, which they would have done in any case on a woman in her position. But Suzanne had early acquired a reputation for being more emancipated than the rest of her sex. Had she not as a young girl donned men's clothes to see the show which a group of traveling quacks had put on in the market place to sell their nostrums? What self-respecting young lady would have done such a thing? And was she not always talking about republics and the New Geneva as if she were a man? Did she not spend more time on reading than on cooking, sewing and embroidering— occupations much more suited to a housewife? Worse, she would often sing, accompanying herself on a two-headed theorbo; and did she not dabble with paintbox and colors, like the foreign visitors from across the Channel?

In spite of her neighbors' qualms Suzanne virtuously kept to the strait and narrow, looked after François who was always up to mischief, and compensated for her mateless life by devouring the romances of Mademoiselle de Scudéry, especially the breath-taking vicissitudes of *Artamène or the Grand Cyrus*— the whole ten volumes. Although, as everybody knew, Cyrus was in reality Louis XIV, and Sapho, the heroine, Mademoiselle de Scudéry herself, the sentimental yet impassioned episodes accomplished their magic on the lonely Suzanne. More effective still was another favorite, *Astrée,* the pastoral romance by Honoré d'Urfé which for nearly a century had been dampening the handkerchiefs of the female population of Europe, particularly of England where the translation of the work had been enjoying printing after printing without ceasing to find new hordes of readers.

There is no record of whether Suzanne read the more ponderous volumes in the small but choice library which she had inherited from an uncle, a minister. But there were, among her favorites on the shelf, Nani's *History of Venice* and the works of Fontenelle, including his *Dialogues of the Dead.* Though few, the books were such as stirred the imagination and induced a love of reading. One may doubt, however, that Suzanne proceeded very far in Le Sueur's *Discourse on Universal History* and his *History of the Church and the Empire.*

Meanwhile since François, lacking the curb of a father, was beginning to reveal wild and irresponsible traits and since Isaac, despite his years of absence, was no closer to fortune than before, Suzanne urged him to return to Geneva, particularly because he seemed to have forgotten wife and child. It was not, however, because of the Grand Turk's ravishing houris, but from an unaccountable access of sanctity. It was so remarkable that it inspired his religious Superior, Pastor de Pera, to send him back to the ministers of Geneva as a special envoy.

Whether or not Isaac's return proved fruitful to the New

Zion, history does not say, but it brought an increase to the Rousseau family in Suzanne's second and belated pregnancy. They had been a prolific breed, the Rousseaus, Isaac himself being one of fifteen children. Alas, the infant born of the ardors of the couple's reunion cost Suzanne her life. Although the labor itself had been difficult, the child was well-formed and the mother appeared to recuperate normally. A week later, however, Suzanne was dead of puerperal fever. So the infant was severed from his closest tie when he was most in need of it.

"I was born nearly dead," wrote Jean-Jacques Rousseau years later. "They had little hope of saving me . . . But a sister of my father's, a wise and good woman, took such good care of me that she saved my life." [2] He said nothing of forebears, nor did he trace the family line to some ancient nobleman who might glorify the plain name of Rousseau. He stated simply: "I was born in Geneva in 1712, of Isaac Rousseau, Citizen, and Suzanne Bernard, Citizeness. A very meager patrimony, to be divided among fifteen children, had reduced my father's portion almost to nothing, and he had for his livelihood only his skill as watchmaker, in which he was indeed very proficient. My mother, the daughter of the minister, Bernard, was richer: she had wisdom and she had beauty." [3]

The wise and good woman who had cared for the infant was Aunt Theodora, a being no less fallible and no better than is common humanity. There had been no scandal in her life so great that a tolerant community could not readily pardon, both for the frequency of its occurrence and for the fact that, in the end, it hurt no one. Simply, Theodora Rousseau had fallen in love with Suzanne's brother, Gabriel Bernard. Since they were too impulsive and too much in love for prudence, they did not wait for the minister to bless their union, so that their first child came into the world with remarkable celerity—scarcely a week after their marriage.

His antecedents, such as they were, satisfied the later famous Rousseau, but not his admirers, who ransacked the archives to find some title of nobility, some flower of heraldry to attach to the name. They did not succeed until a quarter of a century or so ago, when the tenacious scholar Monsieur Eugène Ritter came up with a certain Didier Rousseau, a native of Montléry-les-Paris, France, who in 1549 had fled the religious inquisitors of his native land to find in Geneva the freedom to think and to worship as he chose. This Didier may or may not be the Deucalion of the Rousseau clan from which Jean-Jacques sprang. Certainly his principles and his love of liberty, not to mention the intellectual latitude that both imply, were as true of the adult Jean-Jacques as of his putative ancestor.

Meanwhile, as important as Tante Theodora in the boy's life was *"ma mie Jacqueline,"* as he called the simple, devoted young servant who looked after him, took him out on his walks and was to remain close to him until past her eightieth year.

With his brother François, however, perhaps because of the difference in their years and because the lad was early apprenticed to his father's trade and therefore seldom had time for play, Jean-Jacques had little communion. As it was, François, undisciplined in his ways, had also a streak of wildness in his nature that made him intolerant of restraint. Consequently, taking to heart the wisdom of not sparing the rod in order not to spoil the child, Papa Rousseau, a mild man unless aroused by what he believed to be a just cause, endeavored to improve the scapegrace by means of punishment. One day Jean-Jacques happened to come into the shop while the rod was being applied. Horrified, he flung himself between his irate father and his howling brother, clasped the victim in his arms and making a bulwark of his body, received the blows on his own back and shoulders. In the struggle François fell to the ground, Jean-Jacques still protecting him with his body. Isaac, incensed, redoubled his blows, but seeing that Jean-Jacques would not let his brother go, flung aside the rod and returned to his work.

François did not improve despite such protective measures. He took less and less interest in the art of watchmaking and finally abandoned it altogether. For a while he drifted from one trade to another, absconding from each in turn. Inevitably he fell into dissipated ways among individuals as shiftless as himself, and finally vanished altogether, leaving no more trace than a pebble disappearing in the engulfing ocean. Isaac received only one letter from the prodigal and that from Germany. Then he had no further news, either from him or of him. His fate remained a mystery which neither his father, his relatives nor anyone else took the pains to determine.

What François suffered in parental neglect Isaac made up for by the love he lavished on his younger son. "No king's offspring could have been better cared for, nor with greater zeal, than was I during my early years," Jean-Jacques wrote of those days, not without a hint of complacency.[4] The reason was obvious. Suzanne had been deeply loved by Isaac, and in the boy he saw her features. Jean-Jacques was flesh of her flesh, the fruit of their love. In the boy he also saw unfolding a sensitive, promising young mind, which he himself would nurture and help to bring to fruition.

"I felt before I thought; this is the common lot of humanity. But I experienced it more than anyone else," Jean-Jacques declared further. Indeed, even as a child there had been that quality about him which made women and even men take him to their hearts. It was a sort of spell he cast, of tenderness and need, which turned him into the eternal orphan in search of a mother, or at least of a figurative womb, in which to shelter his naked sensibilities. This was Jean-Jacques, the love-hungry waif, who to the end of his days was to seek in the closeness of friendship with, for the most part mature women, the security of a dependent and often self-abasing love.

He was to develop his capacity for feeling to the ultimate of an art. He was to extol it and turn it into such virtue that generations yet to come would be infused with it as by the breath of a new divinity. For the present, however, with or without the guidance of his well-meaning parent, he turned himself out to pasture in the literature of sentimentality. In later life he could not recollect when or how he had learned to read. He remembered only his magical response to his discovery of the printed word. From then on he became addicted to it and with his father, as omnivorous a reader as himself, he would course through the library that Suzanne had left behind.

They would begin their reading after supper, choosing the books at random—now Plutarch, now *The Worlds* of Fontenelle, Ovid's *Metamorphoses,* the *Discourses* of Bossuet. They were perhaps too sophisticated a diet for so young a reader, but the mind of a child, like the stomach of an ostrich, can digest anything. Happily there were also Molière's comedies and the various romances that had given Suzanne the thrills which life had not provided. Father and son would take turns reading aloud to each other and the ritual, together with the works that had been so dear to Suzanne, gave Isaac the illusion of her presence and to the boy a rueful longing for the mother he had never known. Often the two would become so absorbed in their book that they would lose all sense of time. On at least one occasion it took the twittering of the swallows to remind them that it was morning. "Let's go to bed," said the shame-faced father, closing the book. "I am a bigger child than you."

Isaac doted on his young son, who was as unlike François as if they had been born of different parents. Somehow with the older boy everything had gone wrong. Was it because he had lost his mother when he most needed her and that Isaac had been too much absorbed in his grief to care for him? Or had it been some original flaw in the lad, some blight in the seed? Whose fault? His? Suzanne's? Or was it perhaps that they had been too much in love with each other to really care for the child?

In any case the mistakes they had made with François, Isaac was not going to repeat with Jean-Jacques. Whereas the first-born had been left from childhood to roam the streets as he pleased, Jean-Jacques was not allowed to mingle with the other children, nor to go out without Jacqueline, Isaac himself or some other attendant. Nevertheless Jean-Jacques recalled that he was no better, if no worse, than the rest of the children of

Adam. A gourmand by nature, he did not hesitate to filch any fruit, bonbon or other tempting morsel within his reach. He occasionally lied, but he was never destructive. Once only he indulged in a piece of mischief—but that had been partly the fault of Madame Clot, the shrew of the neighborhood, who was always at her door giving a piece of her mind to someone or other. One day, when she had gone to hear the sermon, Jean-Jacques, passing her house, saw that she had left her earthenware cooking pot outside the door. The temptation was too strong, the memory of her loud shrewishness too recent. Lifting up his smock, the young rogue directed his jet into the *marmite*. One speculates on Madame Clot's astonishment at finding on her return a bouillon she had not made.

It was with Aunt Theodora, the wife of his uncle Gabriel Bernard, that the boy spent most of his time. Uncle Gabriel, an engineer, was still at the beginning of his career, which was to culminate in his distinguished service under Prince Eugène of Savoy, the famous victor at the battles of Oudenard and Malplaquet.

Aunt Theodora, gentle, kind and accomplished, treated her nephew as tenderly as her own son, Abraham, sensing in the boy latent qualities that would bear watching. She marveled at the extraordinary sensibility that held him in a spell whenever she sang to him his favorites from among the many airs and ballads that she knew by heart. She had a thin thread of a voice, fine as the silk that sped in and out of the fabric in her embroidery frame, and of a sweetness that went to the heart of the listening child.

Sitting at her feet or standing beside her, he would fix his eyes upon her pleasant face framed in its black hair with a flattened, hooklike curl at the temples. He felt a sense of peace, of well-being, with her, a happiness which came as much from her as from her songs. One in particular, a simple pastoral, moved him to tears and kept that power over him until long after all other enchantments had faded.

Tirsis, je n'ose
Écouter ton chalumeau
   Sous l'ormeau;
   Car on en cause
Déjà dans notre hameau.

Un coeur s'expose
   À trop s'engager
   Avec un berger
Et toujours l'épine est sous la rose.
   Tirsis, je n'ose
Écouter ton chalumeau.

I dare not, Thyrsis,
   Hearken to your reed
   In the elm's shade,
   For ah, indeed,
They speak of it already
   In our glade.

Rash is the heart
   That on a shepherd boy
   Bestows its joy,
For every rose conceals a thorny smart.
   I dare not, Thyrsis,
   Hearken to your reed.

Thus early the child was learning a rueful fact of life: that all beauty, all pleasure, has its price in eventual pain. Melancholy, that bittersweet ingredient which lends such zest to sentimentality, was beginning to work its charm on a mind all too disposed to it by nature. His father still kept him at home, perhaps justly apprehensive of the dubious benefits of exposing the too sensitive lad to a pack of young Hottentots at school. As it was, Jean-Jacques, without benefit of regular schooling, was farther advanced than many a boy of his years, certainly far more than his cousin Abraham who had no taste but for the

woods and fields and boyish pranks. He learned geography
from a globe, still under the guidance of his father, and he
awakened to the immensity of the heavens by means of another
globe that showed the celestial bodies and the constellations.
The marvels of earth and heaven enlarged his imagination and
filled him with awe. Then, as if Isaac felt that the boy was soaring too high, he would bring him back gently with the words:
"Jean-Jacques, come. Let us talk about your mother."

"Well, then, *mon père,* we are going to cry," the child
warned.

"Ah, give her back to me," moaned Isaac. "Comfort me for
her loss. Fill the emptiness she has left in my soul. Would I
love you so much if you were only *my* child?" [5] Then the two,
the lonely man and the agitated boy, would talk and weep together.

So, in that atmosphere surcharged with emotion, but coun-
teracted by the more terrestrial life at the house of his Aunt
Bernard where Jean-Jacques had a companion close to his own
age in his cousin Abraham, the boy grew, following more or
less his own will and fancy. He read, he studied, but most of all
he roamed about field and wood, amid that nature which was
to be perhaps his most lasting love and the deepest and broad-
est influence in his life. Concentrated and all-absorbing, his
memory retained visual images, sounds, odors, the minute flowering weeds at his feet, the changing cloud palaces overhead,
and all effortlessly and with delight. No one looked after him
particularly at this stage, not even Jacqueline. It was a free,
happy life which included Isaac and his harmless sentimentalities and his aunt, with her songs and ballads after the day's
duties were done. Then, too, there were the enchanted adventures which his reading provided. So, until his tenth year, life
flowed pleasantly on toward a future that expanded to equally
agreeable horizons.

Sometimes he would go to his father's shop. "I think I see
my father now, living by the work of his hands and nourishing

his soul on the sublimest truths," he was to write in the dedication of his *Discours sur l'origine de l'inégalité.* "I see, lying
with the tools of his craft, Tacitus, Plutarch and Grotius. And
I see by his side a son he doted on, receiving instruction from
the best of fathers—with too little fruit, alas!"

Then, suddenly, in that feline way fate has of tripping one
up when one least expects it, Isaac got into trouble. It had
been the remotest thing from his mind, which was set on the
pleasure of a day's hunting on the outskirts of Geneva. He had
started out, gun on shoulder and pouch slung across his back. A
June dawn was smiling on his venture; the activities in field
and wood promised well. He had just entered a field when its
owner, Pierre Gautier, a retired captain of the Chevalier
Gardes du Corps of the King of Poland, blocked his way, with
the words: "Be so good as to spare our meadows."

Somehow this plain, perhaps ironically polite request on the
part of the Chevalier rang a false note in the Citizen of Geneva,
who, in a fury because he knew himself in the wrong, struck him
across the cheek. After such outrage there remained only one
way of healing wounded honor. "Come. Let us get out of the
city limits and we'll settle this with the sword," proposed Isaac
Rousseau.

The Chevalier looked him up and down. "With people like
you," he said, "I am accustomed to using the stick."

The Citizen of Geneva, infuriated by the insult, went at him
like a game cock. "Listen here!" he cried, drawing his *épée.*
"I'll have you know that I am Rousseau! I am Rousseau!"

At this provocation the Chevalier had no choice but to un-
sheathe his own weapon and accept the challenge. The two
went at each other with a will, Isaac reiterating at the top of
his lungs, like a battle cry: "I am Rousseau! I am Rousseau!"

The police, too late to stop the fray, received orders to arrest
the disturbers of the peace. As even in the Republic of Geneva,
where equality ostensibly prevailed, the administrators of justice made a distinction between the watchmaker Rousseau and

the Chevalier Gautier, it was the artisan whom they decided to sentence to prison.

Isaac, who was well liked, was soon informed that the gendarmes were on their way to seize him. Having too great a love of freedom, particularly his own, he made a bundle of his indispensable possessions and, leaving Jean-Jacques with the Bernards, left for Nyon, smarting at the injustice of which he was the victim. Was there not an article in the Law of Geneva that specified imprisonment both for the offender and the offended whenever the peace was disturbed? What sort of justice was this, then, which could condemn the innocent and exonerate the guilty rich? But he was Rousseau and he would not crawl— never, no matter what the advantage—and this was one of the principles he instilled in his son Jean-Jacques. He was Rousseau, the master of his own destiny. From that day he exiled himself from his beloved Genevans. Now, like them when they had repelled the attack of the powerful Duke of Savoy in 1602, he might have sung in thanksgiving the words of the 124th Psalm: "If it had not been the Lord who was on our side . . . then they had swallowed us up quick . . ."

Some years later Isaac married again and as Jean-Jacques recalled, "He was to die in the arms of a second wife, but with the name of the first upon his lips and her image in the depths of his heart." [6] Meanwhile at Nyon, Isaac had set up shop again and out of his earnings contributed to the Bernards for his son's support.

Jean-Jacques' life was soon to change when, with his cousin Abraham he was sent off to Bossey, a few leagues from Geneva, and enrolled at the boarding school of the minister, Monsieur Lambercier, to learn Latin, deportment and other accomplishments. It was the first time that the boys had been sent from home and they allied themselves more closely against the contingencies that might arise in the new environment. As it happened, they need not have feared. The minister, an easygoing man in his middle years, performed his duties with a minimum of effort from long familiarity with his flock, preached according to their understanding, gave his daily reading of the Bible and otherwise served his parishioners as guide and counselor in the inevitable problems of life.

The minister Lambercier and his sister had come to Bossey not long since. If the church members had been dismayed that the new pastor always preached sitting down, habit soon accustomed them to the novelty. If in his sermons he often taxed them with being stupid, prejudiced and uncouth, they tolerated his reprimands and endeavored to improve. Though a preacher, he was still a man and they had learned enough charity to know that no son of Adam is perfect. Still, the Lamberciers had had to face their ordeal before arriving at their present acceptance.

Like all close communities Bossey had its laws and its codes, together with the self-appointed guardians of public morals. Not long after the Lamberciers' advent in their midst, it came to be known, probably through one of the domestics, that it was the minister's habit to go to his sister's room in the morning while she was still in bed, to bring her a cup of coffee and kiss her good-day. Certainly there could be nothing sinful in a brother's kissing his sister, and no one thought anything of it till a man of God, the curé of Pontverre, began shaking his head and hinting at incest. After all, Mademoiselle Lambercier was no old spinster but a healthy woman of thirty, a woman, indeed, who might have been considered handsome.

Once the spark of suspicion had been kindled, unintentionally or through malice on the part of the curé, it had the effect that he surely must have anticipated. In no time at all the whole town was aflame with moral indignation, demanding that the unnatural couple be brought to justice. So great was the clamor that in 1713 the Petit Conseil of Geneva held an inquest to determine whether the Lamberciers, brother and sister, were guilty of the crime imputed to them, to wit: whether the said Lambercier, a minister of God, had indulged in various indecent familiarities with his sister and whether the said sister had become pregnant and been brought to bed with a child.

In the course of the inquest the brother was thoroughly examined by a group of men, while Mademoiselle Lambercier went through the same ordeal at the not too gentle hands of a covey of women. In the end the inquest, on the information brought to it, judged that there had been no proof whatsoever that Mademoiselle Lambercier had been guilty of incest, but only of occasional eccentric behavior which was charitably attributed to the fact that she had had no access to the great world. As for the minister, her brother, he was merely admonished to act with more prudence and propriety. What seemed most extraordinary in this trial was the stern admonishment which the judges at the inquest addressed to the accusers at its close.

All these matters and other doings at Bossey had long been forgotten by the time Jean-Jacques and Abraham joined the flock in the care of the Lamberciers. There was little excitement but much curiosity about the new arrivals, the established incumbents eyeing the novices, the novices sizing up the bullies they might have to take on. What most concerned Mademoiselle Lambercier was the problem of new sleeping arrangements which would have to be made in the already overcrowded school.

Since Jean-Jacques and his cousin were the youngest pupils, Mademoiselle Lambercier had them share her bed with her at night. Certainly it was not unusual throughout Europe for whole families to occupy the vast matrimonial beds in those days, and the custom still holds in remote districts, not only in Switzerland but in France, Spain and Italy. Still, the boys were on the brink of adolescence and Jean-Jacques, precocious and always susceptible to the tenderness of women, derived a guilty thrill from the contact. He yearned to please Mademoiselle Lambercier, to be noticed by her, and nothing troubled him so much as to catch an expression of displeasure on her face.

One day, some unspecified peccadillo of his determined

Mademoiselle Lambercier to teach him a salutary lesson. So far she had never punished him except by a look or a reprimand. This time she employed the switch—as she thought, to good effect. Strangely enough, what she meant to be a painful chastisement served instead to awaken the boy's eroticism. "For I had found in the pain, even in the shame of it, a mingling of sensuality which left me with more desire than fear for its immediate repetition by the same hand. Indeed, since some precocious sexual instinct was doubtless part of it all, a similar punishment administered by her brother would not have seemed at all agreeable." [7]

The truth of this observation he experienced not long thereafter when a comb of Mademoiselle Lambercier's was found lacking a number of its teeth. For some reason this act of vandalism was attributed to Jean-Jacques who firmly maintained his innocence. No one believed him. Worse, he was punished for it with a severe flogging from the not too gentle hand of Mademoiselle Lambercier's brother. This time there was no pleasure in it, but on the contrary a dumb resentment accompanied by a rebellious brooding at the injustice of it all. As it happened, Abraham had also received a flogging for wetting his mattress, and that night, when they went to bed in the room which they were now sharing—Mademoiselle Lambercier having thought it prudent to forbid them her couch—they sympathized with each other's hurts and inveighed against the tyranny of adults in general and Executioner Lambercier in particular. In a burst of Roman indignation the two victims, their arms about each other, inveighed against their tyrant, shouting at the top of their lungs: *"Carnifex! Carnifex! Carnifex!"*

Whether the chaste spinster was wiser and more observant than she seemed, or whether certain facts were brought to her attention by her brother, she never flogged Jean-Jacques again, contenting herself with delegating the punishment to other hands. "Who would believe," queried the reminiscent old man of the *Confessions,* "that this childhood punishment, suffered at the age of eight [8] at the hands of a spinster of thirty, was to determine my tastes, my desires, my passions, my very self for the rest of my life? . . . Endowed from my very birth with a blood burning with sensuality, I preserved myself from all stain till the age when even the coldest and tardiest come to maturity.[9]

Though he held his adolescent blood in check he was to give full rein to his imagination, converting every woman to a Mademoiselle Lambercier, desirable but unattainable, in a sublimation which, while it kindled his eroticism, also spiritualized it beyond consummation.

His cousin Abraham seemed to keep very much in the background through it all, except for one exciting enterprise which the two undertook together. One morning they and the rest of the boys had been summoned outdoors to celebrate the planting of a walnut tree by the august Monsieur Lambercier himself. Two of the students had the honor of being chosen its godfathers; the rest, Jean-Jacques and Abraham among them, performed the humble task of holding the tree upright in the hollow while its roots were being covered and the soil trampled solid about them. A circular trench was then dug to supply the tree with water. During this ceremony, accompanied by triumphal songs, the two cousins were so moved that they decided they must have a tree of their own, complete with the *aqueduc* that was to nourish its roots.

Their desire grew each day as they witnessed the ceremony of the watering. Finally they procured themselves a young willow and planted it a few feet away from Monsieur Lambercier's walnut. But how to nourish it? The water had to be fetched in buckets and from a considerable distance. They had an ingenious idea. Why not an aqueduct, to link their willow with the walnut? Eagerly they dug a connecting ditch from the basin to their tree, and waited for the daily watering. Their plan worked out marvelously. Unfortunately Monsieur Lambercier saw his tree, Peter, robbed to save the boys' Paul. Affronted by their ruse to water their willow, he ordered everything demolished at once, making the morning air ring with his incensed cries of: "An aqueduct! An aqueduct!"

The carefree days were to end in the autumn of 1724, but not before an exciting event. The King of Sardinia, with the Prince and Princess of Piedmont, was journeying through Switzerland and passing sufficiently close to Bossey for the Lamberciers to set out with their pupils to take a look at royalty. The King himself was just passing their group when all of a sudden Mademoiselle Lambercier stumbled, fell on her face, and as her skirts flew up in the impetus of the fall, revealed her most private rondures to the gaze of the startled sovereign.

2. *Adolescence*

September of 1724 found Jean-Jacques with his cousin Abraham once more at Geneva. Certainly the two years of schooling at the Lamberciers' did not constitute a complete education but unfortunately it was all that the Bernards and Isaac Rousseau could afford. Isaac continued to pay for his son's keep from Nyon, but it was as much as he could do to maintain himself and his shop as well. When Jean-Jacques would be a little older he planned to apprentice him to some useful trade.

Meanwhile in their new freedom the two cousins gamboled like lambs in a meadow, without the restraint of a shepherd. Uncle Bernard was too much involved in plans and drawings for his engineering, and Aunt Theodora too busy with prayers and psalm-singing to look after them, since now she had taken a pietistic turn. Therefore the boys roamed the streets together, making an oddly assorted pair—Abraham tall and lanky, with the face of a baked apple according to Jean-

Jacques, who, in contrast, was small and slight, with delicate features, large liquid dark eyes which he had inherited from his mother, a charming mouth making a perfect Cupid's bow, and a broad, high forehead. Their disparity was too much for the neighborhood gamins who, the moment they caught sight of them, would start yelling "Barna Bredanna! Barna Bredanna!" their nickname for Abraham.

The poor boy bore the mockery with patience, but it was more than Jean-Jacques could bear. With imprudent chivalry he finally challenged the young bullies to a fight. One of them accepted. They fought and Jean-Jacques was beaten, even though Abraham did his best to help. Still, the moral victory was his. He had fought injustice. He had made his protest. What did it matter that the physically stronger had won? It would not always be so. His boldness cost him dear, however, for the bullies ganged together and made it impossible for the two cousins to go out except when their tormentors were at school.

They managed nevertheless to see the marionette show of a roving Italian impresario, Gamba-Corta—Short-Leg. They were so enthralled by those droll wooden figures, far more real than the people who stood about laughing at their antics, that they decided they must have a marionette theater of their own. In no time they were making wooden figures and cutting and sewing the costumes for them. They also fashioned drums, cages, flutes and all the equipment of a small theater. Since their miniature actors must talk, the cousins concocted comedies and staged them before the household, themselves speaking the lines in the breaking voice of adolescence. Then one day they introduced an extraordinary novelty for a marionette theater, which usually dealt in buffoonery and low pranks. They preached a sermon for the edification of the whole family. Of them all, Uncle Bernard was the most amazed on hearing the words and rhetorical flourishes of his Sunday homilies so skillfully aped.

Besides these domestic amusements and far more exhilarating to the growing boys were the rambles through the woods on the outskirts of Geneva. It was here that Jean-Jacques first acquired his love of nature, from his delight in the minute herbs and grasses to his wonder at the grandeur and profusion of creation. But he could not go on idling, though to his receptive mind every impression, every excitement provided substance for future speculation, no matter how casually he obtained it. Still the harvest was as yet far off and both his Uncle Bernard in Geneva and Isaac Rousseau at Nyon decided it was time Jean-Jacques learned some useful trade. Moreover, his aunt was beginning to have qualms over the influence the carefree, lazy boy would have upon her Abraham, already too much in his clever cousin's shadow to do justice to himself.

Jean-Jacques was nearing thirteen when, after much speculation on what he was fit for, the Bernards decided to send him to Monsieur Masseron, the *greffier* or town scribe. Uncle Bernard extolled the virtues of the youth, who, he informed the *greffier,* was personable, intelligent, eager to learn. "He knows a great deal, a great deal," he assured Masseron. In his eagerness to place the boy he overdid his praise to such a degree that Masseron, who expected a prodigy, was naturally disappointed at finding a mere adolescent with all the awkwardness of his years. Well, perhaps looks were not everything. He put Jean-Jacques to work at once but, already predisposed to dislike him, he found nothing in him to commend. "Your uncle promised me a pleasing lad and he sent me an ass," he complained. "He told me you knew everything and you know nothing, nothing at all." The clerks jeered at him and assured him he was only fit to handle a file.

Jean-Jacques went home, shamed and humiliated. His head was full of a thousand things which would have been far beyond the comprehension of those boors, Masseron included. Still, it was evidently necessary to have some trade or profession to earn one's bread. He therefore meekly agreed to have himself apprenticed to an engraver. On the twenty-sixth of April, 1725, two months before his thirteenth birthday, he pledged himself to Abel Du Commun, who in turn agreed to teach his profession to the youth Rousseau, "concealing nothing of the said profession, nor any part thereof from him; to feed and to give sleeping room to the said apprentice, and also to raise and instruct him in the fear of God and of good morals, as is befitting the head of a family." And all this in consideration of the payment made to him, Du Commun, of three hundred livres and two gold louis.

Certainly this drastic change of milieu—indeed, of social position—could not but have come as a harsh reality to the erstwhile hero out of Plutarch; for, even discounting the fancies of an active imagination, the disparity between his life at the Bernards' and his present state created a gulf beyond bridging. He had known tenderness and understanding with his father. He had, through his own eager curiosity, already set out on his quest of the true, the good and the beautiful, though without consciously knowing what he sought. Suddenly he found himself in bond, for five years of his life, to a man whom he could neither like nor respect, a gross, violent boor of twenty who felt that the only way to inculcate the trade he had to teach was by applying the lash, which he enjoyed doing, with or without provocation. It was a far different experience from the same punishment at Mademoiselle Lambercier's hands. Here the only feelings pain aroused were wrath, resentment and contempt for the boor at whose hands he suffered. Here, too, because Du Commun was inclined to stint in the rations for his apprentices, Jean-Jacques took to helping himself without scruple to anything edible within reach.

Ordinarily he had adhered to a noble Roman's regard for truth, thanks to the inspiring examples from his reading. Now he lied in an unconscious rebellion against his state. He lied about what he had or had not stolen to appease his hunger. He lied to save himself a whipping. He lied for the sake of lying. Once he went so far as to steal, not from need but for profit, when he raided a neighbor's asparagus bed so that a confederate could sell the booty and both share in the returns. Where now the noble Aristides? Where the nobler Brutus? Jean-Jacques knew he was doing wrong. He also knew that if caught he would be punished without mercy. Unconsciously his misdeeds were his revenge against his situation. Certainly he had never stolen, least of all food in his father's house, though even from early childhood he had not been free of gluttony. There had been a certain fine roast on one occasion, which, with his father's guests, he had watched as it turned appetizingly on the spit. As he was being sent to bed without his supper for some mischief, he said good-bye to each guest in turn and then, ruefully turning toward the spit, he bowed and added: "Good-bye, Roast!" Amused at his sally the guests pleaded for his pardon and Jean-Jacques was permitted to share in the feast. Such pleasantries, however, would not have been appreciated at Du Commun's where, alas, very rude discipline was applied.

Jean-Jacques had one hunger, however, which he could appease, thanks to the woman, La Tribu, who kept a bookshop of sorts in a cubbyhole fronting the street, and a commerce of a more private nature in the back room. Jean-Jacques became one of the most assiduous frequenters of the shop, borrowing the volumes indiscriminately: history, romance, poetry, drama, anything which for a day, for a few hours, would transport him to a realm far away from the Du Communs and the other bullies of the world. No sooner had he finished one book when he laid down his money for another. La Tribu, sizing up the burgeoning adolescent with his wide eyes and delicate yet sensual mouth, began to bring out certain special volumes to tempt his natural curiosity with their salty text and inciting pictures. From some instinctive pudicity he resisted the lure and so never penetrated the alcove at the back of La Tribu's shop for the more recondite mysteries she had to unveil. As for the kind of literature to which she would have initiated him, he read none of it, according to his admission, until past his thirtieth year.

He was an already acutely susceptible adolescent, however, and though still innocent and abnormally shy, aware of mysteries which life had yet to unveil. He was thrust closer to them shortly, as it happened, when Du Commun married and brought his wife to live in his already cramped quarters. Inevitably the secrets of the alcove became guilty revelations to the wakeful apprentice, a thin partition away.

He became restless, surly and discontented. Du Commun complained of him to the Bernards, who already had become disaffected with the boy. He seldom spent an evening with them. Even on Sundays, forgetful of church and the holy day, he would set out on excursions to the country with his rough friends and would not be seen again till nightfall. Once he got to the town gates after they had been closed. Since it was the first time, he was punished but also forgiven, on his promise that it would not happen again. But alas, a boy's temptations in the freedom of nature, among companions as lively and carefree as himself, made him lose all sense of time. Again he had to sleep under the stars, outside the city gates, while the Bernards, fretful and incensed, waited for him at home, shaking their heads over their unruly charge, who would surely come to a bad end, or disappear like that other scapegrace, his brother François.

During his apprenticeship Jean-Jacques went to visit his father several times at Nyon, where Isaac had succeeded in establishing himself and in making new friends. The liking which the people of Nyon felt for the father extended also to his personable son, who in the prevalently feminine circles strutted about like a young cockerel, conscious as he was of the attraction he had for young and old. There was a Madame de Vulson in particular who made much of him, but it was Mademoiselle Vulson, her daughter, who at the ripe age of twenty-two chose the twelve-year-old for her cavalier, though as a front for a more serious intrigue. Jean-Jacques' head began to spin for, child though he was, he took the matter seriously, so seriously indeed that his transports and jealous scenes kept the Vulson circle constantly amused.

Nevertheless, while the precocious gallant was playing the jealous Othello with Mademoiselle Vulson, he was carrying on a simultaneous and less innocent love affair with a curiously perverse Mademoiselle Goton, whom he still remembered vividly enough in his old age to leave an unforgettable portrait of her, with her curious face and her strange, knowing eyes, with her imperious ways that dominated him at once and her irresistible blend of boldness and modesty. "She allowed herself to take the greatest liberties with me yet without permitting me to take a single one with her. She treated me exactly like a child . . ." The inference here, as understood by Rousseau specialists, is that the little Goton gave him some of the treatment that he had enjoyed at the hands of Mademoiselle Lambercier.

Between the two, the avid young libertine gave free rein to his imagination and succeeded in deriving a different sort of pleasure from each, while at the same time establishing a limit for the one love and the other. Mademoiselle Vulson, though adored, was not desired because beyond desire, like the chatelaine whose favor the medieval knight carried with him to battle. She gave him standing, for indeed he must be someone, to obtain the consideration of one so much older than himself and for whom so many sighed. "I loved her like a brother but I was jealous of her like a lover. Of Mademoiselle Goton I would have been as jealous as a Turk, as a maniac, as a tiger if I had as much as imagined that she could have given another the treatment she granted me—for this was indeed a grace which had to be begged for on bended knee." [1] Ah, Mademoiselle Lambercier! Did she ever know what latent passion her disciplinary flogging had aroused?

One day, to Jean-Jacques' great joy and greater pride, Mademoiselle Vulson came to Geneva. To see him, of course, for what other reason could have brought her there, especially after the fervid exchange of letters that had bridged their separation? His pride knew no limit. Mademoiselle Vulson, a grown woman, had come all those miles to be in the city where her young lover lived. For two days he was out of his head with joy and manly pride. Ah, she must indeed love him. It is true she spent most of her time going from shop to shop in the elegant little city, buying all manner of things as if she were stocking up for a lifetime. But he could not blame her for that. The important, the inebriating fact was that she had come all that distance to be with him.

The parting was exquisitely tender, not without tears and, on the young lover's part, with cries that made the welkin ring. Anxiously he waited for her to write him, but the days passed without a word from Mademoiselle Vulson. A week later she sent him bonbons and a pair of gloves. Alas for a young lover's dreams! Together with the sweets came the shattering information that Mademoiselle Vulson was now Madame and that she had come to Geneva not to be with her young adorer but to buy her trousseau. The blow was shattering to the boy's pride, though little Goton offered her kind of consolation. Still he fumed and brooded. He turned morose. He became disaffected with life in general and his situation in particular. Geneva was a place of torture. The Bernards were tyrants, Du Commun was a jailer, a monster and executioner. The marvel and excitement of his dawning manhood were debased and well-nigh extinguished in Du Commun's miserable dungeon.

In revulsion he abandoned his reading; he neglected his Latin studies, which he had till then pursued; he abandoned the ancients whom he had venerated, even the heroic Romans after whom he had patterned himself. Although he had always had a taste as well as an aptitude for drawing, and could employ the engraver's burin to advantage, he soon wearied of its limited use in watchmaking and in moments of leisure amused himself by engraving small medals, in imitation of those awarded for merit. There, in the dingy shop, he formed a kind of order of chivalry among the apprentices, and decorated each with one of his medals on which he had proudly engraved the arms of the Genevan Republic. Alas, when Du Commun surprised him one day fashioning such a medal, he raised a hue and cry that his devil of an apprentice was counterfeiting the money of the Republic. That time Jean-Jacques suffered the most merciless beating of his life. At last his spirit rebelled. Nothing could be worse than his situation. Brutal treatment here, disaffection at the Bernards'. He must do something about it if he would not ruin his life.

The solution came earlier than he expected. One evening he was sauntering back toward the town gates with his friends, a good half-hour before closing he thought, when to his dismay he heard the drum roll and the shrilling of the retreat. He quickened his step, he raced in a sweat and out of breath. He was within a few paces of the drawbridge which was about to be raised. He shouted in a voice strangled by anxiety. Too late. It happened to be the night when a certain punctilious Minutoli was in charge, whom not even the Archangel Gabriel would have prevailed upon to raise the bridge an instant beyond the time he had set for it. The sight of the two sides of the bridge rising in the air like the horns of the Devil himself, with their augury of God only knew what evils, decided the desperate boy. With a cry he flung himself face down upon the ground, in an agony which his carefree companions, who looked upon the adventure as a lark, could not understand. That night, while the others were sleeping under the stars, Jean-Jacques took stock of himself and his situation. His aunt and uncle had their own son to think about, and he knew that they considered him a bad influence for the docile Abraham. No use returning to them, even if they would consent to take him back. The alternative? His bench at Du Commun's and the brutishness, the tyranny and, most certainly, the beatings. Then and there Jean-Jacques resolved to leave Geneva.

At dawn, when the drawbridge was lowered and his comrades were hastening to return to the city, he told them that he would not be going with them, but bade them tell his cousin Abraham to meet him at a certain place the following day. The lad was still very much attached to Jean-Jacques, despite his mother's efforts to alienate him from his influence. Abraham, she said, belonged to the upper classes, whereas Jean-Jacques was now no better than a waif of Saint-Gervais. However, with the loyalty of boyhood Abraham kept the appointment. Sensing that perhaps he would be seeing Jean-Jacques for the last time, he tucked away in his clothes a little sword which the older boy had always coveted. He also made a bundle of a few articles that Jean-Jacques might need on his journey. At the appointed place they said their good-byes. Before they parted Jean-Jacques accepted the sword, but later the creature of sentiment ruefully reflected that Abraham had resigned himself to their parting without too many tears. As for his aunt, she would probably feel relieved of a burden. She knew what was afoot by her son's mysterious behavior; but she did nothing to prevent Jean-Jacques' going. In the end it would mean one care less for her and perhaps a salutary lesson to that irresponsible youth. On that pious note she dismissed Jean-Jacques from her mind.

Meanwhile in that budding March of 1728, with all nature stirring awake from the torpid winter, Jean-Jacques felt an exhilaration that reduced to insignificance worries that would have bowed a less exalted head. Here he was, not quite sixteen, with his mind full of books and romantic dreams but with a trade only half learned and no means of earning a livelihood. Still, others in his situation and with half his intelligence had made a name for themselves. He was a pretty youth—he had had sufficient testimony of that from the women—and circumstances might favor him. From that slim thread he spun an iridescent web, imagining himself in a grand chateau, the favorite of the seigneur and the chatelaine, the lover of the demoiselle, the friend of her brother, and the protector of the people. Extraordinary how he envisioned so early the romantic tableau of *La nouvelle Héloïse*.

Reality, alas, proved less rosy. He did succeed in getting a bite to eat and even in finding shelter in the environs of the city; but until he reached the territory of Savoy he found no true hospitality. There, at Confignon, he somehow learned of the curé, Monsieur de Pontverre—a name long familiar to the young republican for its part in the history of Geneva. Attracted by the association and pressed by his need, Jean-Jacques presented himself at Monsieur de Pontverre's door.

If the good curé had at first received his young guest from charity he was soon welcoming him for his intelligence. Though obviously needy the youth had breeding and knowledge and he spoke well, especially when defending Protestant Geneva, against which Monsieur de Pontverre had fulminated in a number of heated pamphlets. Jean-Jacques on his part was curious to know just how formidable this *Gentilhomme de la Cuillère*—this Gentleman of the Spoon—would prove against his own arguments. Certainly he, Jean-Jacques, would show him one Genevan who would not be swallowed in that fashion. Meanwhile he ate the good curé's food and drank his Frangi wine, making it clear to himself, if not to his host, that not all the heady vintage in his cellar could swerve him from his own religion, no matter how enticingly that good man represented Mother Church. Still, the fact that such a thought had occurred to him was not without significance. He knew that many conversions occurred—but *he* was a Genevan. Besides, he concluded, when he set out toward his destiny with his pack on his back, what is a little compliance if it makes another person happy? "God calls you," the curé had said while speeding him on his way. "Go to Annecy. There you will find a good, charitable woman whom the King's kindness has placed in a position to rescue others from the error into which she herself has lapsed." [2]

The words of the curé evoked the image of a snowy-haired matriarch in nunlike gown and wimple, a pious smile upon her face and comforting words on her lips. It was exactly the symbol of motherhood which the orphan had created for himself. Though he felt humiliated to go with others as needy as himself to receive her bounty, and though Annecy was more than a day's journey from Confignon, he set out nonetheless, impelled as much by the spirit of adventure as by the promise of aid at the end of the road.

He was not one to do anything in a hurry. By his leisurely pace one might have thought him on a pleasure jaunt. His head full of extravagant dreams, he wandered along the burgeoning countryside, past handsome estates with here and there an old chateau that summoned up wimpled damsels and lovelorn troubadours. Often the pangs of hunger, intruding upon his romantic speculations, made him lift his voice in song and, indeed, he sang charmingly. But alas, no golden head appeared at the high turret window, no voice responded to his singing except perhaps the growling of some mastiff roused from its sated dozing.

At last, three days after leaving Confignon, he arrived at Annecy. He had with him a letter from Monsieur de Pontverre for Madame de Warens. He wrote another on his own account in his best calligraphy, employing the elegant phrases culled from his reading. Then, enclosing his within Monsieur de Pontverre's, he set out for the chateau of Madame de Warens.

It was Palm Sunday, the twenty-first day of March, 1728. The countryside was bursting with bloom, like his hopes. When he arrived at the Warens chateau he learned that the chatelaine had just left to go to church. He started off at once in the direction indicated and soon caught up with her and her retinue on a path behind the main house. A brook ran babbling along one side; a garden wall bounded the other. When he first saw her she was standing with her back toward him, at the door of the Church of the Cordeliers. Impulsively he called out her name. She turned around. The boy was tongue-tied. He had expected a meek grandmother, white-haired and seamed with wrinkles. He saw a fresh face, glowing and rosy, a pair of sparkling blue eyes and—an extraordinary observation under the circumstances—the contours of an enchanting bosom. "Nothing escaped the eyes of the young proselyte; for I became hers at once, certain that a religion preached by such a missionary could not fail to lead me to heaven." [3]

Madame de Warens eyed him appraisingly, then turned to the letters, the curé's and his, which he had thrust into her hand. She read them both, his own twice, as he noticed.

"Ah, my child," she said. "There you are, so young and already wandering about the world. What a pity! Well, go to my house and wait for me," she added. "Tell them to give you something to eat. I'll talk to you after Mass."

For the boy it was as if the sky had opened. He went back to the chateau and waited, scarcely believing his good fortune. An hour ago he had been a vagabond, sometimes given a crust, oftener sent away with a harsh word. Now, pleased with the world after a generous breakfast, he was waiting for the gracious chatelaine, in her very house. What might not come of the good curé's kind words on his behalf? Madame de Warens might see how intelligent he was and how well he could write. He might become her secretary. Indeed, he would do anything to be near her.

Yet why was she not a Protestant? Why had she abjured and become a Catholic, as he soon found out? Where was the lord of the house, Monsieur de Warens? Had she any children? What bliss to have been the child of such a mother! How had she come to live at Annecy?

Madame de Warens satisfied the flattering curiosity of the sixteen-year-old. She was born Françoise Louise Eléonore Delatour du Pil, of an ancient and noble family of Vevey. Her mother had died when Françoise was a year old, a fact which the already adoring youth found a fateful bond. Had he not been orphaned almost from birth? The similarity of their early misfortunes at once spun an invisible filament of sympathy between them, a kinship of affliction which instantly bound them as no identity of joy could have done. She was barely thirteen when she had been given in marriage to a nobleman, Sebastian-Isaac de Loys de Warens, on the twenty-second of September, 1713. It would have been a good match, she said, if her husband had not been so much older than herself, or if God had blessed them with children. In reality the groom was only twenty-five years old when they married, and though of a noble family he had no title, so that Madame la Baronne de Loys de Warens was really self-ennobled, thanks to her impudence and her change of locale.

The tale she told was one to kindle chivalrous ardor in the coldest heart, let alone that of an already enraptured youth. Unworthy Monsieur de Warens not to prize such a jewel! The truth of the matter, however, was that Madame de Warens owed her husband her talents and her education, which had transformed a simple girl from the Pays de Vaud into an accomplished young matron able to shine in the most aristocratic circles.

Whatever her true situation may have been with Monsieur de Warens, it eventually became sufficiently intolerable for her to take drastic action. She learned that the King, Victor-Amédée, would soon be at Evian. Leaving house and husband, she set out on a venture that had its hazards but also its glimmer of hope. Victor-Amédée was a zealous Catholic. He was also a benevolent monarch. Seizing the propitious moment Madame de Warens obtained an audience, flung herself at the feet of the King and begged to be taken under his protection. King Amédée could not remain cold to such a fervent suppliant. On her conversion to Catholicism he put her under his protection and also bestowed upon her a pension of fifteen hundred Piedmontese livres.

The abjuration itself provided a grand and crowded spectacle. The lovely convert, escorted by a detachment of royal guards was brought to Annecy where, at the Convent of the Visitation, she flung herself at the feet of the Bishop of Geneva, fervently declaring: "Into Thy hands, O Lord, I commend my spirit." Many cried: "A miracle!"

With unspiritual practicality, however, Madame de Warens had also seen to it that on quitting Monsieur de Warens she did not also relinquish a number of little luxuries. There was a gold-headed cane, for instance, that she liked to display on her promenades. There were her jewels and other adornments —her fingers even now were loaded with rings—and there was the family silver. For a heaven-bent lady she had still enough of the practical in her to make Monsieur de Warens marvel and rage. She had been such a sweet, innocent child when he married her.

All that had occurred in 1726, two years before the arrival of her young pensioner. Since that period she had done her duty, providing converts for the Church. As Jean-Jacques in his naïveté saw it, the good lady was employed in an edifying work. Certainly no one so beautiful and so kind could have had any but the most selfless of motives in doing what she did. All day long there was a constant coming and going— young and old, traveling men and beggars, mostly the latter, who seemed more zealous to receive the good lady's alms than the comfort of her religion. Her goodness, her gentleness and her dedicated altruism touched the youth's heart, already smitten by her tender affection toward himself. Ah, to have had such a mother! For him she shone, a saint on earth, dedicated to saving souls. How could he have known that for every convert she made she received her price and that he himself was marked as one of her redeemed lambs?

At Geneva, meanwhile, Isaac Rousseau had been making belated efforts to recover his runaway son, though the spur was as much the hope of avoiding payment of an indemnity of twenty-five écus, claimed by Du Commun for his absconded apprentice, as his own concern for Jean-Jacques. Madame de Warens had sent him a reassuring letter at the boy's request; but Isaac had ignored it, choosing rather to think the worst of the situation. Gallantly Jean-Jacques came to Madame's defense and berated his father roundly. "Examine yourself and see whether you have no cause to reproach yourself—I don't say with regard to me but toward Madame de Warens who took the trouble to write to you in such a way that it left you no reason whatsoever to fail to answer. . . . For the past six months have I required anything of you but to show some little appreciation to Madame de Warens for the many favors, the many kindnesses with which her goodness overwhelms me unceasingly? What have you done? You have neglected to show her even the most elementary considerations of politeness and good breeding. Were you doing it solely to afflict me? . . . You were dealing with a lady beloved for a thousand reasons and worthy of respect for a thousand virtues, besides which she is not of a rank or station that can be despised. Indeed, I have always noted that whenever she has had the honor of writing to the greatest lords of the Court, even to the King, her letters have been answered with the greatest exactitude. What reasons therefore can you give to justify your silence?" [4]

He would not close the letter without giving his father something else to think about. Since the beginning of the year, he said, he had sunk into a state of extraordinary lassitude. "My chest is affected and it looks as if it will soon degenerate into phthysis. Only the goodness and care of Madame de Warens can sustain me and prolong my days. . . ." [5]

Isaac was genuinely alarmed. A certain Sabran of Geneva was leaving with his wife to go on a journey and since he would be passing through Annecy, Isaac commissioned him to send him back his son. Sabran soon appeared at the table of the charitable Baronne de Warens where he gorged himself, while Jean-Jacques, as much from adoration of his hostess as from despair of perhaps having to leave her, ate hardly a crumb. But the Baronne had no intention of surrendering her lamb already marked for the fold of Mother Church. Still, she could not keep the youth with her much longer without inconvenience to her good works and her reputation.

Sabran offered a solution. Why not send Jean-Jacques to some benevolent institution to be prepared for a vocation? He had heard of an excellent one in Turin, especially dedicated to preparing proselytes for the Church. He himself would be passing through the city. As for the expenses of the trip, surely Madame la Baronne could easily prevail upon His Grandeur, Monseigneur the Bishop, to provide the money, considering the worthy purpose for which it would be used. Madame de Warens listened with interest but allowed herself time to think the matter over. Meanwhile Sabran, conveniently forgetting his promise to Isaac Rousseau to send him back his son, took the matter into his own hands and proceeded to arrange everything with the Bishop.

The youth was torn by conflicting desires. Madame de Warens was so kind, so beautiful, so unselfish. He had never been so happy as during those few weeks with her. If he obeyed his heart only, he would refuse to leave her but throw himself at her feet instead, swearing to dedicate himself to her service forever. Still, the adventure of the journey, the prospect of another country, also lured him. As for Madame de Warens, she made her choice on the side of prudence. Le Petit was still too young.

"Poor little one," she said, stroking his hair at parting. "You must go where God calls you. But when you grow up you will remember me." [6] As a memento she gave him a ribbon trimmed with silver for his sword.

With pack once again upon his shoulders, Jean-Jacques set out with Sabran and his wife, comforting himself that whatever he was doing he did in obedience to his lady's wishes. She had advised him to go. He had obeyed, his heart beating with love and, he had to admit it, also with the exhilaration of freedom. He had never been out of Switzerland until his flight and he had never crossed the Alps. He got into the spirit of the adventure and was soon enjoying the sun and sky, the open road and freedom.

He had barely been gone a day when Isaac Rousseau arrived at Annecy with a fellow watchmaker, a certain Monsieur Rivat, to seize the truant and to take him home. Since the bird had flown, Isaac Rousseau enjoyed only the satisfaction of an interview with Madame la Baronne. Certainly Jean-Jacques, who could not afford to travel except on foot, had not gone so far that Isaac and Monsieur Rivat could not easily have overtaken him on their horses. Strangely enough, their lack of initiative, if not their indifference, rankled with Jean-Jacques. "My brother had been lost through such negligence, so thoroughly lost that no one ever knew what became of him." [7] Still, if the two men had found him and taken him back home, who knows what might have been his destiny? As it was, Isaac Rousseau had recently married again at Nyon, and now found himself supporting not only his wife but a horde of relatives who followed in her train. Suzanne had left a small capital, the income of which he, Isaac, could utilize as long as his sons were not under his care. Unconsciously, perhaps also from necessity, he made no great effort to have them with him. Indeed, he had already given up hope of François.

From his father's behavior Jean-Jacques derived a moral maxim—"To avoid situations which place our duties in opposition to our interests, and which reveal our advantage in the disadvantage of another . . ." [8] Years were to pass, however, before he could act on this altruistic maxim. At present it was expedient to make the best of his situation while waiting for whatever opportunities life flung in his path.

It was an odd little group, the hardy Sabran, straight as a grenadier in the lead, his graying black hair in an old-fashioned queue, his voice shouting orders like a martinet—unless he happened to be in the presence of any dignitary of the Church, whereupon, with consummate art, he whined with the pietism of a mendicant friar, or, when it suited his ends, thundered an edifying sermon, for he fancied himself a preacher. Indeed, he never failed in his effect, especially when he delivered the Latin homily he had learned by heart and which he delivered in and out of season, often many times a day. What did it matter that few of the simple folk who listened understood a word of it? The very mystery worked in his favor. Indeed, it paid off remarkably well.

As Jean-Jacques observed, Sabran never lacked money if he heard the jingle of it in other people's purses. Madame Sabran, however, puzzled the youth. By day she was a meek, tranquil woman who ambled along scarcely uttering a word; but a great change would come over her at night, when her noisy insomnia would awaken Jean-Jacques, who always shared the couple's room at the inns. It took him a while to discover what really ailed Sabran's sizzling spouse, under the spell of Madame de Warens, which, like a starstudded curtain of gauze, enchanted and mitigated the grossness of reality.

The thought of her engaged his mind and stirred his imagination. Had he not wept at their touching farewell? And had she not said to him: "When you grow up you will remember me"? He was no child. More perceptive of nuances than many another of his age, he built upon those words what she had intended him to build—and more. It was no mere fancy on his part. She had bade him come back to her when he was a man. "I looked upon myself as the work, the pupil, the friend, the lover, almost, of Madame de Warens." [9] Like a knight, he was setting out to face the world, to fight the dragons, to conquer the enemies of good, with the name of his chosen lady engraved in his heart. True, Madame de Warens need not have hastened him off to Turin. Surely she had done it for his own good. (Why was it that one's own good almost always derived from doing what one least desired?)

An element of vanity with a generous admixture of self-pity helped the unhappy Jean-Jacques to transform his expedition to a joyful venture. He was young, he was free; he could do what he chose with his life. Would he not soon be crossing the Alps? He saw himself as another Hannibal. Still, what a pity that he had no army, no elephant—for that matter, not even a donkey. But he was eager, he enjoyed good health and his imagination supplied what he lacked. Everything along the way he transformed to suit his mood. There was no incident, a green fruit plucked, a drink of icy water from a spring, an unknown plant or familiar flower, that did not add to the carefree joy of the traveler, for like his father he had the lust of wandering. He also dined well, for Sabran, who cherished his stomach, feasted like a prince. It was almost with regret that, after a week's trudging and climbing Jean-Jacques found himself at the gates of Turin.

But what a disillusioning arrival. No sooner had he left the Sabrans than he discovered that he was absolutely penniless, with nothing of his own but the clothes upon his back. Madame Sabran had managed to appropriate everything, even the ribbon that Madame de Warens had given him for his sword. The sword itself would have gone the way of the ribbon had he not stubbornly resisted. It was a high price to pay for the Sabrans' company. But he was in Turin. He still had his sword, if without its ribbon. Fortunately he also had a few letters which would help to open some doors for him in that foreign country.

3. *The neophyte*

Jean-Jacques had never been in a city as vast as Turin or as rich in history and its monuments. The grand Cathedral of St. John the Baptist, in the early cruciform style, had been completed in 1498. Statues of the great and figures of the Madonna, the works of Guarini, still adorned it, while a special chapel, completed in 1694, contained the miraculous *sudario,* said to be the shroud in which Joseph of Arimathea had wrapped the body of Jesus Christ. There was also the domed church of San Filippo Neri, begun in 1672 and still abuilding; and there were, besides, numerous historical monuments—the Palazzo Madama, erected in the thirteenth century for William of Montferrat; the University, a recent building which contained a great library and many Roman antiquities. Amadeus, the First Duke of Savoy, had made Turin his chief town. For many years it housed the ducal family. The Church, through Leo X, then raised the bishopric of Metropolitan rank. Like all towns in those restless times it had suffered its vicissitudes: the French occupying it from 1536 to 1562; the plague killing eight thousand of its citizens in 1630. It was now more than ever an important city, as much for its development as for its position in relation to the Pass over the Alps.

The defrauded young traveler, for the present more concerned over his penniless situation than interested in architectural treasures, lost no time in presenting his various credentials, which unaccountably had escaped the Sabrans. "I had some letters, I delivered them; and immediately I was conducted to the hospice for neophytes, to be instructed in the religion for which they were selling me my subsistence." [1]

So, tersely, and as if anxious to have done with the unpleasant business as quickly as possible, the old autobiographer, keeping his promise to show his fellows a man in all the truth of nature, betrays uneasiness through his very brashness. True, the lad was homeless, hungry, miserably dressed. As he stood before the heavy door barred with iron, imagining himself on the other side, shut off from the world, an abjurer of his own religion, he must surely have had his moment of conscience. He could have faced about and fled from what in the eyes of all Genevans would have been the barter of his faith, his honor, for a mess of pottage. It was not as if there were no other resource, for any good-hearted housewife of Turin, taken by his need and his charming face, would have given him a crust and cheese. Or he could have offered to perform some task—chop wood or fetch water for pay or barter.

He found it more expedient to join the group of oddly assorted male and female aspirants to the Faith, who were soon led through separate doors to what appeared to be a vast auditorium with an altar surmounted by a huge crucifix occupying one wall. While waiting for what was to follow, a Slav—one of a pair passing themselves off as a Moor and a Jew, for the greater effect of their conversion, no doubt—confided to Jean-Jacques that he and his comrade lived by embracing the Faith in Spain and Italy, or wherever else it was to their profit to do so. However, even such a confession did not turn away from his contemplated abjuration the youth who had once seen himself in the heroes of Greece and Rome. On the contrary, he spent a good part of the time, while waiting for the ceremony, in scrutinizing the female proselytes in the hope of finding a charming face among them. But as they had been recruited from the streets where they ordinarily plied their trade, he had no success, though there was a girl among them, of about his own age, whose mischievous eyes sought his, and whom he glimpsed again and again during the several months it took for the devoted missionaries to prepare their converts for Mother Church. Despite his efforts to approach the fair neophyte she was so besieged by an overzealous missionary wrestling for her soul that the bold youth had no success in his repeated ruses to approach her alone.

A strangely corrupt atmosphere hung over the hospice of Lo Spirito Santo, despite its sincerely benevolent purposes. The amalgam of vagabonds and strays from every part of Europe, housed under one roof, often for months during the period of indoctrination, generated intimacies and situations that had more to do with the Devil than with God. Jean-Jacques, despite his adolescent explorations with the precocious Mademoiselle Goton and the mature Vulson, had still retained an ingenuous innocence about sexual matters which had so far preserved him. He trusted everyone and saw in every kindness toward himself only an expression of benevolence, common to man toward his fellows. He therefore accepted without a thought the many kindnesses of the so-called Moor, who had befriended him. Despite his frightening features and gingerbread complexion he seemed a good sort of person, with whom the boy established a friendly communication through the lingua franca in which the Moor was able to make himself understood. He seemed to take pleasure in the boy's company and did him many little kindnesses.

Jean-Jacques was grateful for his attentions but he would

have preferred a less demonstrative affection. It was one thing to allow oneself to be kissed and fondled by a little Goton. It was quite another to receive the same attentions from the Moor, with his burning eyes and the ugly scar of an old wound on his cheek. "The poor man has taken a liking to me, though it is rather lively. It would be wrong to rebuff him," Jean-Jacques reflected.

The Moor, however, passing from kisses to more overt caresses, made his intentions so unmistakably explicit one morning when they happened to be alone in the auditorium, that the youth took fright and with a cry leapt back, freeing himself from the seducer. Out on the balcony, whither he had fled, more terrified and troubled than he had ever been, he tried to repress a mounting nausea. In his innocence and shock he could not keep the Moor's strange behavior to himself. He told the old hospice housekeeper about it; the man must surely be sick. The good woman called the Moor a cursed dog, a vile beast, and advised Jean-Jacques to keep his mouth shut. That, however, was what Jean-Jacques could least accomplish. The following morning one of the administrators gave him a stern lecture. He, Jean-Jacques, was tarnishing the good name of the institution. What fuss to be making over so little! He thereupon instructed the youth on the facts of life, which he should long since have known, and ended by saying that though this was a forbidden sin, like lechery, it was no worse and certainly no more harmful. Why stir up such a storm about the matter? After all, the intention was rather flattering. So why take it amiss that someone had found him desirable? "He told me without any circumlocution that in his youth he had received a similar honor and that, being surprised in a position wherein he could not offer any resistance, he found that it had not been such a terrible thing, after all. . . . He imagined that the reason for my reluctance was fear that it might be painful, but he assured me it was a vain fear and that there was nothing to be alarmed about." [2]

He spoke of it so casually that Jean-Jacques was scandalized, particularly since there was a third party, another ecclesiastic, at the interview, who seemed as little affected as if they had been having the most ordinary of conversations. Well, there must be something wrong with himself to have taken the whole business so seriously, he concluded. Evidently it was a common practice in the world. He had simply not learned of it sooner. "Without knowing any more about the matter, my aversion to the thing extended to its apologist . . . He darted a look at me that was hardly caressing and from then on he spared no occasion to make my stay at the hospice as disagreeable as possible." [3]

In spite of the unpleasantness Jean-Jacques stayed on, manifesting a weakness of moral fiber that was to influence his actions at crucial periods of his life. The days passed and then the weeks. He saw the "Moor" baptized with great pomp— for it was not every day that such a heathen saw the light. He was dressed in white from head to toe and the contrast between his dark features and the garment of innocence afforded the onlookers a sight that was both an allegory and a dramatic triumph.

Jean-Jacques' conversion, to believe his apologia long after the fact, had not been as precipitate as it seemed. Indeed, it had taken a whole month, according to his statement, before he too put on the white garment and was solemnly led to the Church of St. John for his abjuration and his reinvestiture in a gray gown trimmed with white Brandenburgs. In the procession were two men, each carrying a copper bowl, one before and one behind, to receive the contributions of the edified populace. Since Jean-Jacques was not a Jew or a Moor, and was therefore less deserving of reward for his conversion, he was not allowed to keep his gown, which certainly would have been very useful. Also, the charitable alms proved disappointingly meager.

After the procession he was commanded to appear before the Inquisition to clear himself of heresy. It was a solemn and, to him, a terrifying ceremony, though not so terrible as his being asked point-blank by the Inquisitor if his mother was damned. The lad had enough presence of mind to answer that he hoped God had enlightened her in the hour of death.

What were his thoughts when he reflected on his abjuration? How did he reconcile within himself the fact that it had taken the heathen Moor far longer to abjure than it had taken him, Jean-Jacques Rousseau, Citizen of Geneva and a Protestant? On this matter the records are merciless, thanks to Gaberel's *Histoire de l'église de Genève*: "Jean-Jacques Rousseau of Geneva (Calvinist) entered the hospice at the age of sixteen, the 12th of April, 1728. He abjured the errors of the sect on the 21st; and on the 23rd of the same month Holy Baptism was administered to him, his godfather being Sieur André Ferrero and his godmother Françoise Christine Rora (or Rovea)." [4]

He had money in his pocket, however—only twenty livres, but a treasure to him who had not had a denier. Now, if only he could find work to do, or a gracious benefactress like Madame de Warens . . . Meanwhile he wandered about the city, enjoying the sights: the changing of the Guard, the processions always thronging the streets. He mingled with the crowds, following wherever they led, even to the Royal Palace where he was filled with awe that he, the waif Jean-Jacques, should find himself amid all that splendor. His imagination made him a king in an instant. Once back upon the streets he counted his sous; for a while he would not starve. He lived on *giunca,* a kind of curdled milk, and crisp breadsticks, cheese, fruit and red wine. By dint of inquiring he also found lodging at the house of a soldier's wife who charged a sou for a night's shelter. She had recently married, he was told, though she had five children. Everybody slept in the same room—wife, husband, infants, lodgers. Jean-Jacques, sated, free as a lark and with still a little money in his pocket, enjoyed the sleep of the blessed. On the morrow he went wandering as usual, stopping off at the Royal Palace to listen to the Mass, which was really a concert, so fine were the King's singers and musicians.

One morning, along the Contra Nova, he caught a glimpse of a pretty young woman through the glass of a shop window. Before he knew it he was standing before her, drawn by her sparkling black pupils that were at once a light and a promise. Cherubino was at her feet at once. His tongue loosened at once by her radiance as by his desire, he poured out his brief story, extolled his talents as an engraver and asked for the privilege of using them in her service. With unusual tact for one so young—she was hardly four or five years older than himself—she fed him while listening to his tale, which he rendered as pathetic as possible. She heard him sympathetically and called him a brave lad, adding that no good Christian could be indifferent to his story.

Without more ado she sent a servant to fetch the necessary tools from a neighboring goldsmith and set Jean-Jacques to engraving her fine silver plates. Needless to say, in the light of her beautiful eyes, he lingered as long as possible over the work. As it happened, her husband, Signor Basile, was then traveling on business. The situation would have been idyllic, were it not for one of the employees, a sullen fellow who set himself up as a sort of Cerberus to guard Madame Basile's honor. Everything would have been so agreeable if the fellow had not been so suspicious, for he played the flute delightfully.

Still, in spite of Cerberus, Cherubino adroitly managed often to find himself alone with Madame Basile, for he was perceptive enough to notice that she enjoyed his company as much as he enjoyed hers. However, it was more a pantomime of love than love itself, for Madame Basile was too chaste a woman to encourage him, while Jean-Jacques knew too little of love to interpret explicitly the sighs that ruffled her fichu and, in its rise and fall, revealed tormenting glimpses of her firm, pearly breasts. He was annoyed that she treated him like a child, caring for his linen, exhorting him to cleanliness and sermonizing him like the most devoted of mothers—the last relationship he wanted, at least from her. Burning with desire and yet too respectful to make it known, he would simply sit tongue-tied at her feet, adoring.

One day she had left the door of her room ajar as she sat sewing by the window. Jean-Jacques saw her and for a moment stood there, undecided. Impulsively he fell on his knees and waited, his eyes fixed upon her. He had never felt so troubled, not even in the presence of Madame de Warens. Then he noticed that Madame Basile had caught sight of him in the mirror. She was beckoning him to come to her. Trembling he rose, went to her and fell upon his knees at her feet. She saw the confusion, the agitation that made him quiver and stammer incoherently. She let him kneel there, without a word, while she went on embroidering as he sighed in bliss and frustration. What kindled him even more than his adolescent desires was the sight of *her* struggle, *her* emotion and the stubborn lowering of her lids so that she would not read his passion and succumb. Then they heard the sound of a door opening in the adjoining room.

"Get up quickly! It is the maid," she whispered.

He seized the hand that she had lifted in warning, kissed it passionately and started to his feet. Their love progressed no further. She was too chaste. He was too young. Soon Signor Basile returned and in not too happy a temper, thanks to the information relayed him by his vigilant assistant. Suspiciously he eyed the suit of clothes, the handsome hat of the young jackanapes—all that finery bought by his wife with his money.

"You'll not fail to make your way with the women," Cerberus flung at him sarcastically.

It was not to be in the house of Madame Basile, however, for her husband was not slow in giving the pretty page his *congé* —though not before Madame Basile had recommended him to her friend, the Comtesse de Vercellis. Now, for the first time, Jean-Jacques felt the humiliation of having to wear livery. It was a fine house, finer than Madame Basile's, but it was also a sad and somber place, frequented by monks, especially now that Madame de Vercellis, who had cancer of the breast, knew that she had not long to live.

She was a woman of keen, though cold, intelligence, so restrained and self-controlled that no one ever heard her breathe a sigh or utter a word of complaint, despite her pain. Recognizing the boy's intelligence, she made him her secretary and they would spend hours together writing letters. She was a charitable woman, doing good for its own sake and with such stoical objectivity that the sentimental Jean-Jacques was shocked. What good is charity if there is no real sympathy in it, but only a sense of duty? However, he saw with approval that she thought of her friends and dependents in making out her testament. After that, as if in relief, she broke wind. "Good," she said. "A woman who can break wind is not dead yet." With those words she died.

What was Jean-Jacques' disappointment at the reading of the will to learn that though she had made provision for everyone she knew, there was not the least mention of the needy youth for whom she had often betrayed a kindly affection. Why had she shown such curiosity about him and asked so many questions, especially about Madame de Warens, if she had not meant to include his name among the others? He felt the omission so deeply that long afterward he was to rationalize it to his advantage: he had not fawned upon her and courted her like her rogue of a nephew, her heir, and her scheming domestics. Also there had been a plot against him. Why else had the nephew and servants kept him from seeing the poor lady when they knew her to be dying? "And I had wept sincere tears in her room, without her or the others being aware of it." [5] Woe to an ungrateful world where even genuine tears are not appreciated.

However, Comte de la Roque (her nephew) saw to it that Jean-Jacques was given thirty livres and that he kept the fine new suit he was wearing, despite the protests of the officious head of the establishment, Monsieur Lorenzi, who was all for ripping it off his back. Nevertheless, despite his finery, he was out of employment. Packing up his few belongings he added to them a rose-colored ribbon shot with silver, which had taken his fancy—a trifle, surely, that no one would miss. Unfortunately it was discovered in his baggage by the prying Lorenzi. What was that ribbon doing among his things? Where did he get it? Who had given it to him? Confused and ashamed and very much frightened, Jean-Jacques declared that Marion, Madame de Vercellis' maid, had given it to him. The girl was sent for at once. She was fresh, pretty, her cheeks still rosy from the air of her native mountains. She was also modest and truthful. Before Comte de la Roque, the household and all those who had heard of the theft, Marion was confronted with the ribbon, and also with Jean-Jacques' reiterated charge that she had given it to him.

At first she was so taken aback that she could only stare at him without uttering a word. When she found speech, it was only to deny that she had ever seen the ribbon. At Jean-Jacques' insistence she stared at him, her very innocence in her eyes, pleading with him not to ruin the reputation of a poor, innocent girl who had never harmed anybody. Tormented by his own guilt, he still perversely insisted that she had given him the ribbon and with righteous indignation charged her openly with the theft. At this she could only weep. Then quietly she said: "Ah, Rousseau, I always thought you were a good fellow. You are making me very unhappy, but I should not like to be in your place."

Her meek denial stood no chance whatever with the crowd, inflamed by Rousseau's vehement charges. In the end Comte de la Roque sent them both away, saying that the guilty conscience of the culprit would be vengeance enough for the innocent. It was no vain prediction, as Rousseau later proved whenever he relived this shameful incident of his careless youth.

On finding himself once again without employment but with Comte de la Roque's thirty livres in his pocket, Rousseau went back to his old lodgings at Madame Basile's. He felt rich and therefore saw no need to seek another place. He was sick of wearing livery; he would never be a lackey again. He was free at last. Somehow this freedom gave him no joy, no sense of that exhilaration which could turn a dull day, an empty pocket, into sunshine and riches. "I was restless, distrait, a dreamer. I wept, I sighed, I longed for a happiness which I could not conceive, yet whose privation I felt nonetheless." [6] Cherubino lacked only a composer to set his adolescent flames to music.

Meanwhile, however, the torments were real and inconvenient enough. Pricked with desires he could not subdue, he summoned up the naughty games with the lascivious little Goton and so sharpened his urges. In his idleness he took to wandering along dark alleys, scarcely knowing what he sought, yet compelled to seek. He knew of a special place, at the end of a courtyard. In it there was a well to which the young servant girls would come to fetch water. He loved to stand at a distance to watch them. Soon watching alone was not enough. He had to show them what a man he was. Surveying the terrain, he found that at the end of the square there was a slight incline leading to *caves,* or cellars, which offered a safe hiding place for anyone who wished to make a quick exit. Emboldened by his discovery he took his stand as usual at a point of vantage where the girls could not fail to see him and, undoing his breeches, offered them the spectacle of his manliness. Sensible girls that they were, some pretended not to see him, others tittered, but a few felt affronted and made an outcry. The youth fled toward the cellars, the girls at his heels, and he did not stop running till he came to a safe hiding place. There, in the semidarkness he waited, backing into the tunnels as far as he could and counting on the dimness underground to conceal him.

Suddenly he was brought short by a wall and stood flat against it, hardly daring to breathe, for the girls, still pursuing, were coming closer, as he could hear by their shrieking. What alarmed him, however, was the reverberant thunder of an angry man's voice, and a walking light coming closer. He would have crawled through a crack in that wall, had he been able. The man, a brute with a ferocious mustache and a huge saber, collared him without ceremony, while his reinforcement of some half dozen crones, each armed with a broom handle, seemed to be waiting only for the signal to have at him.

"What are you doing here?" roared the man with the saber.

Instantly Jean-Jacques' imagination and his dramatic instinct came to his rescue. What was he doing there? Why, sir, what could he be doing? Did the gentleman not see that he was deranged? Ah, pity on his youth and affliction! Did Monsieur not perceive the gravity of his mental state? Ah, unlucky victim that he was! Even now his wicked relatives were on his trail to seize him and shut him up in a madhouse. Ah, Monsieur, he was a lost man if his identity were known! He was only a stranger here, but he was of noble lineage. Let the good gentleman release him. Some day—who knows?—the unhappy victim of destiny might be able to reward him.

Half convinced, half amused, the sabered gentleman let him go with a warning. A few days later chance, which sometimes enjoys a joke, brought about another encounter between the sabered one and Jean-Jacques, who was taking a walk with a young abbé. "I am a prince! I am a prince!" the man ridiculed, imitating Jean-Jacques' tone. "And I—I am a cullion. But don't let Your Highness cross my path again, or—!"

Jean-Jacques did not wait for him to finish the sentence. Oddly enough he was grateful to the man for his discretion and resolved to improve his ways.

4. *Maman*

He had an incentive toward amelioration in a Savoyard abbé, Monsieur Gaime, who was at the time preceptor to the children of the Comte de Mellarède. Jean-Jacques hoped through him to find a similar connection and while waiting was much in the abbé's company. Together they would climb the lofty Monte, from whose crest they could see the River Po winding down below, and on their left the great chain of the Alps, dominated by the huge, diaphanous ghost of Mount Viso. There, in that rarefied atmosphere, the abbé would speak simply of the pure, good life and its rewards, giving the youth counsel without preachment, which would have alienated the rebel. The seeds fell on the hard soil of young manhood, but were preserved there, to germinate like those grains found in ancient sarcophagi, when conditions favored. The immediate effect of the abbé's words was one of purification, which strengthened the youth's good intentions. But alas, the atmosphere of the cruder world below soon dissipated them.

Jean-Jacques' situation became desperate. He had no money left; his clothes needed renewing; and though Monsieur Gaime's words were edifying to his spirit, his stomach grumbled from unwilling fasting while his pride flinched at the state of his garments. In his need he had made several attempts to see the Comte de la Roque, who had shown him many kindnesses; but the servants, who often have a snobbery which their masters lack, would not let him in. Then one day the count sent for him.

Certainly Jean-Jacques lost no time in answering the summons. He was taken immediately to the count, who received him cordially, saying, with a hint of self-commendation, that he was one man who kept his promises. He had said that he would find a worthy place for Jean-Jacques. Well, he had found it in a fine house where the youth would have the opportunity of bettering himself and of becoming somebody. It was for him, Jean-Jacques, to make the effort.

As the count spoke the youth's imagination soared, lifting him to an empyrean altitude from which the world of reality looked small indeed. At last his opportunity had come. Once on his way, there was no limit to his rise. He had been crawling too long. He must now give impetus to his wings. Alas, upon further explication the count hurled him down to earth again. True, the Comte de Gouvon at whose palace Rousseau's services were required was premier equerry to the Queen, as well as head of the powerful house of Solar. Through Gouvon's influence what could an ambitious youth not attain? At first, of course, Jean-Jacques would be little more than a domestic. He might also have to wear livery. But a youth as intelligent as he would advance quickly, thanks to the interest that his master would assuredly take in him. Jean-Jacques listened in cruel disappointment. Livery. A lackey. That was what he would be. Always a lackey.

The gracious welcome accorded him by the Comte de Gou-

von won him over at once. There was no artificiality in the
dignified old man, who could unbend to be human, even
affable, to the young stranger. In an aside to De la Roque he
remarked, loud enough for Jean-Jacques to overhear, that he
had an agreeable physiognomy, which also promised intelligence and wit.

"My child," the Comte addressed him, "in all enterprises
the beginning is always hard. In your case it won't be too
difficult. Be good and try to be agreeable to everybody. That,
for the present, will be your only task. For the rest, be of good
cheer. They want to take care of you." [1] Soon the Comte de
Gouvon introduced him to his daughter-in-law, the Marquise
de Breil, and then to his son, the Abbé de Gouvon. Jean-
Jacques was not displeased. Indeed, he puffed himself up a
little. Such, surely, was not the welcome generally accorded a
mere lackey.

Soon he was ensconced in the household, with the domestics,
it is true, but unlike them he was spared having to wear the
ornate but hated livery. For the moment Jean-Jacques' ever
vigilant self-esteem was appeased. Then, just as he had begun to
congratulate himself on his luck and indulge his imagination
by reviving his old dream of being the bosom friend of the
son of the house and the favored lover of the daughter, he
was awakened with a jolt. Young Comte de Favria, the old
man's grandson, had him, Jean-Jacques, sit in the back seat of
his carriage like a lackey whenever he went driving. Jean-
Jacques' pride smarted but he dared not protest. He was well
treated, after all, and except for the letters he had to write for
his masters, and the pictures he would cut out for young De
Favria, he had most of the day to himself. The old count, who
looked after his protégé, knew him well enough to sense the
hurt to his pride at that exhibition of his social inferiority in
De Favria's carriage and tactfully put an end to it.

If the masters of the household, or the servants, speculated
on what the youth did with the better part of the day when
his duties were over, they could not have conceived that he

spent it discussing lofty and edifying themes with the Abbé Gaime. Intellectually acquisitive by nature, aware also that his education had been far from adequate, Jean-Jacques lost no opportunity for his improvement. He still read omnivorously and listened intelligently whenever there was something to be gained. His retentive memory was the magpie nest, himself the acquisitive bird. The basic structure of learning had been built in the important childhood years with the help of his father. His meager but sound schooling added to it. The chief contribution he provided through his extraordinary awareness, which missed nothing and profited from everything.

Sometimes the magpie store served even to raise him above what society called his betters. Yes, there was a sting to that, and it pricked even more painfully whenever a member of the family, like the beautiful Mademoiselle de Breil, made him feel it. She was of his own age, with a beauty made striking by the extreme whiteness of her skin and the blackness of her hair and eyes. For all the attention she gave his adoring looks and devoted courtesy, he might have been part of the pattern of the rug at her feet, too familiar to be worthy of notice. However, her indifference did not keep him from noting her slim waist, the sheen of her raven hair and ah! the pearliness of her breast and shoulders. The precocious sensualist coveted, the poet in him adored, the lackey venerated that beauty which he desired but could never reach. Still, Mademoiselle de Breil might have given him a glance—no more than she gave the lackey who stood behind her chair. But no. She seemed to be unaware that he, Jean-Jacques, was there at all. Only once had she looked up to glance at him in surprise when he had adroitly turned against Monsieur her brother an insult which that gentleman had directed toward him.

The following day, however, he was to enjoy a signal triumph at a very formal dinner when the maître d'hôtel presided in full regalia, sword at his side and hat on his head. During the conversation someone had brought up the subject of the Solar family device on the armorial bearings: *Tel fiert qui ne tue pas.* As it happened, there was no one in all that fine company who could account for the *t* in the word *fiert.* It was a mistake, said one, for the word did not require a *t.* It was the old spelling, said another. The old count noticed that Jean-Jacques was smiling, without daring to interrupt the conversation of the masters, and ordered him to speak up. Jean-Jacques needed no urging. The word *fiert* was Old French, he explained. It did not derive from *ferus* or *fierce,* but from the word *ferit* meaning *he strikes* or *wounds.*

With immense satisfaction and not a little pride, Jean-Jacques noted the amazement of the company. There they were, rich, titled, some like the abbé, even learned; but he alone, the lackey, had for once lorded it over them, all through his intellect. His real triumph came when he saw the approbation in the glance which Mademoiselle de Breil exchanged with the abbé her grandfather, who honored him with words of praise immediately echoed by the whole company. "It was one of those very rare moments which restore things to their natural order and vindicate genuine merit, degraded by outrageous fortune," he later commented with obvious satisfaction.[2]

He also enjoyed a more immediate victory. Suddenly awakened, Mademoiselle de Breil, deigning for the first time to turn her eyes upon him, asked him to pour her a drink of water. Overcome by her request Jean-Jacques obeyed with such enthusiasm that he not only filled her glass but also her plate and allowed a generous overflow for her lap as well. She was too self-possessed to make an outcry, as another would have done. Also, it may well be that his mute adoration had not remained wholly unobserved, for there is no lily so chaste that it fails to respond to the rays of the sun. At any rate an incident which would have sent another lackey packing did not earn him the least reprimand. Indeed, Jean-Jacques became a favorite of the household. The Abbé Gaime still pursued with him his elevated conversations on the equally elevated Monte. At home the son of the house, the Abbé de

Gouvon, whom the family destined for a bishopric, taught Jean-Jacques Italian and perfected his Latin. The Abbé de Gouvon had returned after a number of years in Italy, much affected by the elegant preciosities of the Della Cruscan school; therefore he penned delicate verses in Petrarch's tongue and passable hexameters in Virgil's. Under his tutelage as under Abbé Gaime's, the youth's mind expanded as well as his heart. Almost the dream he had dreamed of being the bosom friend of a noble youth, and the lover of his sister, had come true. How could he not hope when Mademoiselle de Breil continued to treat him kindly, while her brother made him little gifts, among them an exquisite toy, known as Hieron's fountain, which spurted shimmering jets of water like the finest which Turin had to show?

However, in Jean-Jacques' nature virtue and its opposite were never too far apart. As it happened, he met a distant relative, a certain Mussard, nicknamed Strangler, and another character called Bâcle, who immediately became the destroyers wrestling for the soul of the redeemed. They were not evil or shiftless, for Mussard was a miniaturist while Bâcle had for a brief time served his apprenticeship at the clockmaker's, with Rousseau. To the restless youth they represented freedom and the romance of a gay, wandering life, like that of the minstrels of old. Indeed, Bâcle would have outdone any trouper with his gay sallies and buffooneries. Jean-Jacques, rediscovering his ancient fellow apprentice, now felt that he could not live without him. He spent his free hours with him, and Bâcle even had the effrontery of seeking him out at the palace. But soon Bâcle would be on his way to Geneva. Alas, what a loss, lamented Jean-Jacques. To profit by the time still left before Bâcle's departure, Jean-Jacques would quit the palace without leave to spend every available moment with his friend. In vain the Comte de Gouvon, who frowned upon the friendship, had the gates barred against Bâcle. He only succeeded in putting up another barrier between himself and the infatuated Rousseau. Good-bye to the sage teachings of the venerable Gaime. Farewell to Jean-Jacques' aspirations toward the heights pointed out to him by young Gouvon. *Vale* to whatever tender and chivalrous emotion Mademoiselle de Breil had awakened in his heart.

At that particular time when spring was bursting out along the highroads he panted for freedom and the carefree life of the vagabond. Bâcle would be trudging his exhilarated way to Savoy. Nothing would deter him, Jean-Jacques, from taking the enchanted road. For enchanted it was to the youth whose blood was as tumultuous as the freshets bursting their winter bonds. April! It was April, just a year ago, on Palm Sunday that he had first been bewitched by Madame de Warens, by Maman. It was fate, yes, which was now conducting him to her again. Had she not said: "When you grow up you will remember me"? He had grown up. Was he not a man seeking his way in the world? It was fate. What else could be guiding his steps toward the place where he had spent the happiest days of his life? It was fate—and in his conviction that there lay his destiny, he could salve his conscience for not having even troubled to say good-bye to the kind old count, who had been so good to him, nor to thank sufficiently the Abbé Gaime, who had promised to say a favorable word for him to Monsieur de Bernex, the Bishop of Annecy, Maman's spiritual counselor.

Meanwhile Jean-Jacques, with the young vagabond trudging beside him, felt free as a creature of the air. This was certainly the life for him, and the future smiled ahead. What did it matter that after a few days neither had a copper in his pocket? They had wits and used them whenever they saw idling groups at inns and public places. Then Bâcle would open the floodgates of his charlatanry while Jean-Jacques demonstrated Hieron's wonderful fountain before the gapers. The people marveled, they were amused for a few moments and some even dropped a sou or more—but not enough to provide for two hearty young appetites. Finally they broke the fountain, but by that time they had become so bored with it that they felt more relief than regret.

On nearing Chambéry the fickle Jean-Jacques began to find the once irresistible Bâcle a burden, in spite of the pledge of eternal friendship they had sworn. He could not—rather, he would not—take his companion to Maman, whom he regarded with more than proprietary interest. Bâcle, however, to whom life had taught a few hard lessons, among them that it is foolish to believe that even a sworn friendship can last forever, decided to follow his own road, especially when he noted that the closer they drew to Annecy, the cooler his sworn brother became. Well, he would make things easier for the ungrateful youth. As they neared the town gate Bâcle stopped short. "So here you are in your city," he said. Then clasping Jean-Jacques briefly by the hand he bade him farewell and with a bow and a pirouette tripped out of his life.

Jean-Jacques, who for all his sensibility had little to spare for other people's concerns, bore the loss of his friend with extraordinary equanimity, if not with relief, though he was by no means in the happiest state of mind. What if Maman should not be at Annecy? She had so many interests which frequently took her from home. Worse, what if she had forgotten Petit or—unthinkable disaster—if she had already found someone else to take his place?

With trembling steps and quaking heart he walked in the direction of the chateau, seeing everything as through a haze and stopping at intervals to catch his breath. Again and again the dread thought recurred: what if she had changed toward him and he would be thrown upon himself, alone, worse than alone in the world? But he was instantly comforted by the fact that she had answered the letter which he had sent her from the count's. Was it dread of being abandoned, of starving to death if his resources failed, that threw him into such panic? No! No! He defied such fears like a Spartan. He had never begged for bread, and he never would.

Still, he was mightily relieved when he learned that Madame de Warens was at home. The moment he saw her he flung himself at her feet and seizing her hands kissed them with fervor while studying her face which, he noted, showed not the least surprise at seeing him returning so soon. "Poor little one," she said caressingly, "so you're back again? But I knew you were too young for that enterprise. Still I am relieved that at least it did not turn out as badly as I had feared." [3]

At her insistence Jean-Jacques discreetly recounted his vicissitudes, wisely omitting his questionable adventures with the young laundresses at the fountain and his encounter with their mustachioed champion. The tender relationship was resumed as if it had never been interrupted. Indeed, Jean-Jacques' fugue, as he noted, had turned out to his advantage, for after a few minutes' deliberation between Maman and the chambermaid, it was decided that he sleep in the chateau. It was not to be just for the night, he learned, when his few belongings were taken to his quarters, but for as long as he chose to remain with Maman. The chambermaid may have made some observation on the arrangement for to his great joy he heard Maman declare: "Let them say what they please. But since Providence has sent him back to me, I am determined never to abandon him."

He soon had his own apartment, not in the main building which was old but stately, but in a chamber in a private pavilion, giving out on the passage where he had first met Madame de Warens, that joyful Palm Sunday of 1728. The family circle had increased, he noted, for there was Claude Anet, twenty-three years old, always hovering about to take Madame's orders. A page? A secretary? An overseer? A lover? Cherubino was consumed with jealousy, though he little knew how justifiably. Priests and monks were constantly about as before, but in greater numbers and on an extraordinarily familiar footing. There was Abbé Léonard, who scarcely left her side, who called her Sister and seemed to enjoy such a degree of intimacy that Jean-Jacques naturally called him "Uncle," though jealousy consumed him. It was Monsieur Gros, however, the headmaster of the seminary at Annecy, whom she favored with the especially intimate pleasure of helping to lace her stays, a ceremony at which Petit, as Maman still called him, often assisted, torn between pleasure and jealousy. There was Maman, her arms and lovely throat exposed, in her lacy camisole and petticoats, unable to stand still for a moment, while Monsieur Gros pulled at the strings from the back, following her steps as best he could, and calling after her: "Madame! Madame! Please be still a minute!" Claude Anet, her sensitive young manager, would leave the room in anguish.

Such libertinage in Monsieur Gros, but especially in Madame de Warens, was hardly consonant with the apologia for her youthful ebullience which she had made to François Magny in her girlhood: "It may be my youth dazzles me and makes me see things in a false light. I assure you, however, that I feel little attachment to my possessions; I go about with an indifference that sometimes surprises me. That is a very special grace which I must render up to God, for in the ordinary progress of our lives we have . . . but a brief span in which to enjoy those things that lure us and flatter us. I would consider myself very fortunate if I could continue feeling as I do in this regard, so that when the end comes I may have the resolution to sunder without regret the ties that might still bind me to this earth . . . which I think of as a thorny road that, God willing, will lead me to a happier and lasting state. . . ." [4]

Life at Annecy was far from the sumptuous ceremonial at which Jean-Jacques had so briefly assisted at the Comte de Gouvon's in Turin. The chateau, however, was open to everyone: the varied and numerous ecclesiastics, the passing stranger, the field hand and the mendicant. There was no show of silver at the great table. Indeed, Maman owned few sumptuous pieces, but there was always plenty for all, and no one was ever turned away. She herself ate very little, but the table ceremonial was long and tedious because of her extraordinarily delicate stomach. The very smell of food nauseated her and it often took a full thirty minutes before she could swallow the first morsel—an unusual delicateness, considering her embonpoint. Jean-Jacques found the procedure not at all disturbing, for during the time it took Maman to finish her meal he himself had consumed two dinners, thanks to his always hearty appetite.

It was an ideal situation for Jean-Jacques, like that of a hero in a fairy tale. He had his share of vicissitudes for his years; but what hardships would he not have endured to find himself in his present state? He was cherished, he was fed. There was Mademoiselle Merceret, Maman's companion, to ogle discreetly, and Maman to adore. Often he would sit for hours at her feet, trembling inexplicably but saying nothing, only gazing at her and indulging in vague caresses, as much for a mother as for a mistress. Then he would leave her abruptly, seclude himself in some corner and weave fantastic dreams wherein he lived what he had imagined. Sometimes he would wander about her private apartment, touching every object that belonged to her, kissing the armchair, the bedcurtains, even the floor which her feet had touched, and he would lie there ecstatic in his imagined pleasures.

As for Madame de Warens, physically and sentimentally involved with Claude Anet, she indulged only her frustrated maternal feelings toward Petit, the very name she had given him making the present relationship clear—*present* because she well knew that *la fatalité,* that most obliging of forces, would in time bring about what she knew to be inevitable. Perhaps to make the waiting period easier, or from really maternal solicitude, she sent Petit to one of her relatives, Monsieur d'Aubonne, who had the distinction of popularizing the lottery in Turin. How that feat qualified him to pass judgment on the qualities and aptitudes of an individual as complex as Jean-Jacques, only Madame de Warens knew. In any case, after an interview with the youth Monsieur d'Aubonne pronounced him fit to make, at the very most, a village curate. Though Maman had better judgment, she nevertheless sent Petit to the seminary of Annecy, run by the Missionary Fathers.

Jean-Jacques, removed from his easy and delightful life, and imprisoned with other young martyrs to duty in a cell of the huge rectangular building pierced with long narrow windows like those of a dungeon, felt to the full the happiness he had lost and turned resentful—against meddling Monsieur d'Aubonne, against adults in general, even a little against Maman, who in spite of her love for him had allowed herself to be swayed by Monsieur d'Aubonne's counsel. Now Claude Anet had her all to himself. Jealousy gnawed him. It gave him little comfort to learn that Maman had used her influence to obtain for him the gentlest and kindest of the Missionaries, the Abbé Gâtier, to be his own special instructor. He carried his resentment to the end by attributing to that innocent soul some scandalous act for which the poor man, according to him, had been imprisoned, defamed and finally banished. No doubt all this had happened, but only in Rousseau's retributive imagination. One can only wonder what long-smoldering spite Jean-Jacques had nurtured all those years.

One pleasure which the youth enjoyed to the full at the mission was the organ playing and the singing. He had a passion for music, dating back to his childhood and the songs of his aunt. The dearest treasure he took with him to the seminary was a volume of Clérambault's cantatas, among them *Alphée et Aréthuse*, a special favorite. Often of an evening Maman would sit at the clavecin and play while he sang in a pleasing voice, following the score, which somehow he was able to make out despite the fact that his musical education had been rudimentary. Though he lodged at the seminary he was free to go to the chateau, a brief walk away—an arrangement which suited him perfectly, for he could dream of Maman in absence and, keyed up by anticipation, come to her in a glow of love. If only Claude Anet had not been made a third party in the relationship, Jean-Jacques would have been at the peak of happiness. At least so he thought. As it was, jealousy added its zest.

Detecting a new talent in Petit, Maman decided to cultivate it. On Sundays at the Cathedral a young man named Nicoloz

but generally known as Le Maître conducted the musical services. Nothing would do but that Le Maître come to the chateau to give them all lessons and to enliven their evenings with
musicales. Every member of the household would be called
upon to lend his or her voice—Jean-Jacques, Claude Anet, the
chambermaid and the cook, anyone who was not deaf and
dumb. Cherubino Rousseau shone at these evenings. New con-
vertees, pretty young women like Esther Giraud, who was
twenty-seven, and Mademoiselle Graffenried, not quite twenty
then, added their particular charm for Jean-Jacques—not
to mention Mademoiselle Galley, who was just nineteen, only
a year older than himself. Surrounded by so much feminine
charm, Jean-Jacques lost his head completely and was convinced that each and every one of the women was in love with
him. Perversely, he did not allow himself to be moved by
even the handsomest of them. After all, there was not a single
demoiselle among them, and none but a fair aristocrat would
do for him.

Meanwhile the time passed pleasantly enough, what with his
various though desultory studies and the ferment of activity
at home. Every day some new craze turned Maman's head. One
morning she was all for planting flax in her fields. Another day
she was busy with pestle and mortar, pounding herbs for her
private pharmacopoeia. Next, she had her herbals spread out
on the table as she carefully pressed the new specimens between
the pages. There was no limit to her interests or her ambitions, nor to her relationships. One day she doted on Claude
Anet. The next she had eyes and sweet words only for Petit.
The day after, it might be the turn of some stranger who
happened to knock at her door. As it was, the porter had no
peace, what with the beggars and newly converted.

One Sunday a great clamor and a sudden glare sent Madame
de Warens and her people outdoors. The Convent of the Cordeliers, close by the chateau, was burning and the roof of the
Warens house had already caught fire. The servants began mov-
ing out the furniture, but there was little hope that much of it

would be saved. Jean-Jacques with the rest helped to rescue the most precious pieces and, as if endowed with a superior power, he found himself lifting out through the window burdens that ordinarily would have required superhuman strength. The crowd gathered, to watch if not to help, and together with the curious had come Monseigneur de Bernex. On seeing what was happening he fell upon his knees in the garden and began to pray, Maman following his example. Jean-Jacques, descending and leaving the house, joined the kneeling suppliants.

Seconds later, as if swept by that wave of fervor, all were prostrate in prayer. There was little hope that the chateau would be saved since the wind was sweeping the flames over it. Suddenly the wind changed, veering away from the house. The fire which had started was soon put out and but for minor damages the building was safe. In their excitement the people began crying: "A miracle!" The word was taken up by the crowd and the wonder, repeated throughout Annecy, established the miraculous powers of Monseigneur de Bernex. Jean-Jacques was more convinced than any of them except perhaps for Maman, who had the exaggeratedly acute sensibilities of a most devout convert. Indeed, she once told Monsieur de Conzié, for nearly two years following her abjuration she had never been able to go to bed "without getting gooseflesh all over." Everything had changed once she had been converted. She undertook nothing without first consulting Heaven. Thus, when she formed her company for the exploitation of hemp, she placed the enterprise under the auspices of the Most Holy Virgin. Such sanctity, however, did not interfere with her easy morality nor her pleasures, innocent or otherwise. The Virgin's mantle was ample enough to cover them all.

Jean-Jacques shared her sensibility and in the matter of the rescue of the house from fire was convinced that there had been divine intervention, thanks to the prayers of Monseigneur de Bernex. A few years after Monseigneur's death his fellow Antonines began to collect material to serve toward his beatification. Jean-Jacques, at their request, told them what he knew of the miraculous shifting of the wind in answer to Monseigneur's beseeching. "I saw the Bishop pray," he said, "and while he prayed, I saw the wind change its direction." Later he had qualms because he had added that the shifting of the wind was surely a miracle.

Despite the odor of sanctity about the Warens chateau, there was a freedom, if not a license, that would have scandalized the sponsors who paid Madame so well for her converts. One February evening in 1730, while the household was seated around the fire, there came a knock at the door. A few minutes later the maid Perrine, who had taken a lantern and gone to open, came back followed by a short, heavy-set youth who limped a little, and who introduced himself as a musician. The word was an open sesame in that music-loving household, where even the turnspit and the scullery maid took part in the concerts. The fact that the stranger had added "from Paris" to his qualifications made him even more welcome.

Venture de Villeneuve was his euphonious name, which rang like a password to adventure and derring-do. Jean-Jacques succumbed instantly to his charm. He talked readily and well, with an air about him at once quixotic and poetic, witty and at times risqué, though not enough to alarm Maman. He might have been a young knight or a rogue, a saint or a madman. Certainly he was original enough to bring a novel excitement into a relationship that had been settling down to unromantic domesticity. Paris! If only he, Jean-Jacques, could go to that glorious city! Fascinated by that romantic adventurer, the youth could think of nothing but freedom, the highroad, France. Life with Maman, which until then had been pure enchantment, lost much of its glow. Once again the temptation to decamp, to go freely wherever he chose, seized him, in spite of the delightful life he had been living at the chateau.

Winter melted into spring and the April buds were like fingers pointing toward the highroad. As it happened, that same month Le Maître, who had quarreled with the Venerable Chapter of Annecy and sought to drown his troubles in wine, decided for his salvation to leave town and establish himself in a more sympathetic environment. Packing his belongings, he included among them the music of the Chapter, leaving not even the chants for the oncoming Easter service. As grief, even more than happiness, needs a confidant, *Petit Chat* went to Madame de Warens to pour out his unhappiness and to say good-bye. She was sympathetic, though in an offhand way, for at the moment she had a travel project of her own. However, she had Jean-Jacques and Claude Anet help Le Maître with the heavy bundle of music. The two hired a donkey and placed the burden on its back. The prospect of Le Maître's departure, however, stirred the *"bougeotte"* in Jean-Jacques. Maman, who had other concerns on her mind, encouraged it, and the two young men set out together for Lyon, where they would wait for the case of music to arrive.

At Lyon they had, of course, to wander about the city, to visit friends and see the sights. The Comte de Lyon, Abbé Dortan, received them, as did others of lesser note. Most of their pleasure, however, consisted in wandering about, which for Jean-Jacques was a favorite pastime. *Petit Chat,* however, did not have Rousseau's endurance. One day, whether from fatigue or excitement, he had an epileptic seizure and collapsed in the middle of the street, contorting himself and frothing at the mouth. Jean-Jacques, terrified, did not know what to do and, losing his head as the crowd grew in size and excitement, he slipped through its ranks, ran to the corner, turned it and disappeared. Wrote Jean-Jacques, years later: "Were there many other such confessions for me to make, I would abandon the work I have begun." [5]

Part Two

5. *Vaussore de Villeneuve*

On his return to Annecy, penniless and exhausted but full of eager anticipation of the welcome Maman would give her *cher Petit,* Jean-Jacques was disappointed to find her gone. Only Anne-Marie Merceret, the young housekeeper, was at the chateau and, as he found, in no pleasant mood. Madame la Baronne had set out for Paris on some important business and with her were Claude Anet and Monsieur d'Aubonne. Anne-Marie could not say when Madame would be coming back, but she had been gone for quite a while and she should soon be returning. At least Anne-Marie hoped so, for she had decided to go home to Fribourg. That seemed a good idea to the wanderer. Since Maman's homecoming was at best uncertain, he offered to escort Merceret, which would give him the opportunity to vist her father on the way and perhaps furnish his own empty pockets. Meanwhile at night he shared the bed of Venture de Villeneuve, who, equally inconvenienced by

Maman's thoughtless absence, had managed to find lodgings at a shoemaker's.

Why had Madame de Warens gone to Paris? Jean-Jacques did not know the reason, though he surmised that something out of the ordinary had taken her there. As it happened, Conte de Maffei, Ambassador to the King of Sardinia, was in Paris at that time. Did Madame de Warens have some special request for the royal patron? Certainly Monsieur d'Aubonne had entrusted her with a private petition on his own account, reckoning hopefully on her charm and influence. Nothing, however, came of the trip and the intrigue, for both Madame de Warens and Monsieur d'Aubonne left Paris disappointed and in a bad temper.

Jean-Jacques passed the time in pleasant idling while waiting for Merceret to set out for Fribourg. What charming adventures one had, simply doing nothing. There was that beautiful morning on the first day of July, 1730, when he had got up at the first glimmer and gone off to the woods to enjoy the sunrise. Everywhere grass and flowers had sprung and the shrubs were in flower. Though at that season the birds, too busy with their broods, had no time to sing, still for Jean-Jacques the air was filled with music as if the songsters, making their adieus to spring, were hymning the birth of a fair summer day. Nothing was lacking to the enchantment. Ah, but he was mistaken. Another sound, of fresh, girlish voices and laughter, charmed him more than the birds had done. With the voices came also the dull thud of hoofs not too far away. He waited for the riders to approach—two fair amazons, Mademoiselle Graffenried and her friend, Mademoiselle Galley. Jean-Jacques found himself on one side of the stream while the equestriennes were on the other. Though they were both charming young ladies, they were not accomplished horsewomen, a fact which their mounts evidently recognized, for both horses refused to cross the water.

Mademoiselle Graffenried, a convert who had often come to visit Maman, made bold enough to ask the youth to help them, which Jean-Jacques was more than eager to do. They were going to the old chateau of Toune, which belonged to the Galleys, and if their horses did not behave any better they surely would never get there. The gallant knight needed no coaxing. Seizing Mademoiselle Galley's mount by the bridle, he pulled the animal toward the other side while he himself stood in water up to his middle. Then he drew forward Mademoiselle Graffenried's horse, bowed and would have gone on his way. "No, no!" said the damsel, who would not be out-done in courtesy. "You are not going to get away from us like that. You got drenched on our account and in all conscience we should see to it that you dry out. You must come along with us. We declare you our prisoner."

His heart pounding, Jean-Jacques turned to Mademoiselle Galley. "Yes, yes," she said. "You are our prisoner. Go, mount behind her."

"But, Mademoiselle, I have not the honor of being known to your mother. What would she say—?"

"Her mother's not at Toune," said Mademoiselle Graffen-ried. "We're alone. We're returning tonight and you'll come along with us."

Jean-Jacques need no coaxing. He leapt upon the horse as he was told. "Your heart is beating so fast," said Mademoiselle Galley.

"It's the galloping," he said.

"My heart is beating hard too," she said. "I am not an ex-pert horsewoman and I'm a little frightened. Hold me about the waist."

Jean-Jacques promptly obeyed, encircling her closer than necessary. Had he moved his hands a little higher he would have felt her breasts, but he did not dare unclasp his itching hands. Yet though so close to bliss with Mademoiselle Galley, he must not ignore Mademoiselle Graffenried, to whom he cast eloquently languishing glances from his advantageous post. He enjoyed the torment of his double desire and his struggle to keep an even balance between the two temptations. Mademoiselle Graffenried, for her part, was not displeased with her effect upon the youth. She was a hot-blooded young woman, who had early won a certain reputation in her native Berne, which eventually had led to her leaving it for Annecy, where her particular talents were just being discovered.

It was early morning when they arrived at Toune with hearty appetites and in excellent spirits. They breakfasted at the grange, played with the farmer's children, spread Jean-Jacques' drenched clothing in the sun to dry and proceeded to the important business of preparing dinner. To their dismay, they found that among the provisions they had sent on from the city there was no wine—and Jean-Jacques had counted so much upon it to give him the boldness which, certainly, the occasion and the proximity of two such charming temptresses would demand. The girls also seemed disappointed, perhaps for the same reason, surmised the precocious Don Juan. They sent out for some, but none could be obtained, the peasants of the district being so abstemious—and so poor.

Their gay young spirits, however, enlivened the day better than any wine. They ate with an appetite that needed no whetting and for the dessert they went out into the orchard. Agile as a monkey—for Jean-Jacques, though slight of body, was nimble and strong—he climbed a cherry tree and from the branches flung down the clusters to the two girls, who were holding out their aprons. The young rake, from his point of vantage, enjoyed what glimpses he could catch of Mademoiselle Galley's turgid breasts. The delightful hollow between them, revealed by her low-necked gown, tempted him to mischief. Plucking an especially luscious cluster, he took aim and hit the target, to the hilarity of them all. "If only my lips were cherries," sighed the young voluptuary. "How gladly would I place them *there!*"

Through the rest of the day they gave way to their high spirits, laughing, chatting, romping, taking innocent liberties, and though the aroused manhood of Jean-Jacques demanded a more direct fulfillment, he contented himself with kissing—

just once—Mademoiselle Galley's hand. But what a kiss it was. Later they returned to the grange. They were alone. In her modesty Mademoiselle Galley kept her eyes lowered but Jean-Jacques knew from his own troubled emotions what she must be feeling. Trembling, but without uttering a word, he took her hand and pressed his lips upon it, gazing at her as he did so. Her eyes had a gentle look, not the reproach or annoyance he had feared. After a few seconds she slowly withdrew her hand. He almost hated Mademoiselle Graffenried for having come into the room at that moment.

How sordid his life suddenly seemed that night when he went to the cobbler's to share Venture's pallet. He had become disaffected with his companion of late for various reasons, one of which outweighed them all, though the matter involved was insubstantial enough. They had been discussing poetry one day, and Venture, who set himself up as a *littérateur* of sorts, explained to him the mystery of the rhymed couplet. Jean-Jacques suddenly discovered a new talent in himself when, with great ease, he produced a couplet. Venture who believed in sharing, immediately appropriated it and went about collecting praise that he had not earned. As for Jean-Jacques, he had his first experience of the literary world.

Meanwhile he waited impatiently for Maman's return and the resumption of the happy life, free from care and filled with a thousand pleasant nothings. Merceret, however, impatient to leave, would not wait any longer for her mistress. If Jean-Jacques wished to join her, let him make up his mind. He did, seeing that there was nothing else for him to do. He needed a new character, however, to enable him to make his way in the world. Packing his flute, his music and his few possessions, the self-styled musician, Vaussore de Villeneuve, reputedly late from Paris, set out ambitiously to challenge fortune. To make the journey pleasanter, and also out of regard for Jean-Jacques', or rather Villeneuve's, empty pockets, Merceret sent her baggage ahead, defrayed his small expenses and agreed to make a good part of the journey on foot. Generously

Jean-Jacques let her pay the way. The girl had always been a little in love with him, or at least so he assumed; for did she not adopt his turns of speech and his mannerisms? Besides, he was already too well versed in the ways of women not to know when he had made an impression.

As they proceeded he was flattered to note that Merceret had for him all the delicacy and consideration that he should have had for her, and his vanity puffed itself up. After all, Vaussore de Villeneuve, music master and author of a couplet good enough to be stolen, was no mere nobody. Let him but have the opportunity and he would show the world.

Meanwhile the two ate together at the inns and slept, chastely, as Jean-Jacques would have the world know, in the same bed, following the accepted arrangements at the inns. According to his own declaration, however, even if he had been tempted he would not have known how to go about the matter. "I could not imagine how a girl and a youth happened to sleep together. I thought it would take centuries to set about this terrible arrangement. If poor Merceret had thought to gain some return for defraying my expenses, she was disappointed." [1]

Why this reserve on the part of such an easily inflammable youth? First of all, Merceret, though an organist's daughter, very pretty and with a charming voice, was not an aristocrat. Had she been Mademoiselle Galley or Graffenried, Jean-Jacques might have proved bold. Perhaps. The act itself, the very thought of which inflamed his imagination and stirred his blood, was not without its psychic and physical reservations, thanks to Mademoiselle Lambercier, the depraved little Goton and the indulgent Vulson, who had created too many labyrinthine perils within for him to risk surrendering himself to what nevertheless he craved, only to betray some humiliating incompetence. This fear, more than any other consideration, kept him chaste.

As they were nearing Geneva he felt suddenly moved, almost heartsick. Not trusting himself to revisit the places so evocative of his childhood, he stood half fainting on the Pont du Rhône, overcoming with difficulty a strange physical malaise. Stronger still, however, was his pride in his city. "As the noble image of liberty was uplifting my soul, those of equality, of unity, the mildness of its customs, moved me nearly to tears, awakening a keen regret that I should have lost all these benefits." [2]

On the way to Nyon, which the travelers had to pass, Jean-Jacques wondered whether he should stop to see his father and his second wife. What! Could he be so near him and not see him? He would not forgive himself to his dying day. Leaving Merceret at the inn, he set out, eager for the meeting yet ill at ease, fearing the reproaches his father would surely make on his footloose wandering, on his still clinging to Madame de Warens. His fears were needless. Isaac Rousseau flung his arms about his son—How he had grown! What a handsome lad!—and wept for joy, a pleasure in which Jean-Jacques readily joined him. Still uneasy about his son's attachment to Madame de Warens, Isaac became even more alarmed on learning of his plan to become a musician. That was indeed folly! A musician! That, certainly, was the swiftest way to perdition. Fortunately his wife, a good sort of woman though too honeyed for Jean-Jacques' taste, interrupted them to invite the youth to stay to dinner. He could not, he said. There was Mademoiselle Merceret, whom he was escorting to Fribourg, waiting for him at the inn. Madame Rousseau tightened her lips and threw her husband a knowing look. A girl waiting for him at the inn? Was he going to marry her? Well, perhaps he would stop by on the way back?

It was not solely to Isaac Rousseau and his wife that the idea of Jean-Jacques' marriage occurred. Merceret herself had alluded to it, at first in jest, then more and more overtly. What a delightful place, Fribourg! Jean-Jacques would love it. Her father was well off, a musician, too, an organist. They could all live so happily together and then when her parent died—God spare him for many years!—Jean-Jacques would inherit his business.

Jean-Jacques granted it was a pleasant prospect, which his love of music rendered even enchanting, but his wise unwisdom rejected it. Something quite different it was that he wanted, though he did not know exactly what. At present it was perhaps only the freedom to wander about as he chose, to gather with apparent shiftlessness a harvest for the future. Besides, there was always Maman in the background, who would have to be consulted on such a step on the part of Petit. At any rate he left Merceret without a qualm and not even the gratitude she had naturally expected for the money she had furnished for his journey.

Soon he was off on the road again, enjoying his freedom and doubling his pleasure by thinking of the sacrifices he had made for it—the devotion of an adoring wife in Merceret and the comfortable life of an organmaker and musician—for he still persisted in following that calling. Indeed, at Lausanne, where he settled for a while, he had the boldness to arrange a concert. Gathering together an assortment of musicians to form an orchestra, Vaussore de Villeneuve, late of Paris (which Jean-Jacques had never seen), decided that as a special attraction he would give one of his own compositions. In the meantime he found lodgings with a simple fellow called Perrotet, at five *écus blancs,* which also included dinner and a good supper. Such was young Vaussore's persuasive charm that not only did Perrotet lodge his guest on trust but he also scurried about to find him pupils. The musicians of the little Lausanne orchestra were all as gullible as himself. With incredible effrontery Jean-Jacques handed out to the musicians the various parts which he had carefully copied—after having first submitted them to a certain Monsieur de Treytorens, professor of law, an amateur who enjoyed having musicales in his own parlor. As a finale Jean-Jacques had boldly tacked on as his own a little minuet which had been having a vogue throughout the country.

What did he play? And what was the cantata of his own composition which was sung at the same time? Was it *Alphée*? One does not know. Whatever it was, the cantata and the concert failed of the desired effect. Not a single musical aspirant came knocking at his door. No gracious hostess sent for him to conduct a musicale for her guests. Worse, he heard ringing in his ears, long after the event, the outspoken comments of the audience:

"It is absolutely unbearable."

"What mad stuff!"

"A regular Devil's Sabbath!"

The worst sting of all was the repeated assurance by certain sarcastic connoisseurs that his minuet was indeed charming, that it would go echoing around the country, that indeed it would make him famous. One good soul, a member of the orchestra, imagining what Rousseau must be suffering in shame and humiliation, came to see him the following morning. Jean-Jacques, always expansive, unburdened himself, pledging the Job's comforter to secrecy, with the inevitable result. By evening all of Lausanne knew the truth, though to Rousseau's amazement no one took advantage of it. He realized, however, that his future at Lausanne was doomed. He was summoned to just one house next morning, where a little vixen maliciously treated herself to the pleasure of showing him a heap of music of which he could not read a note—whereupon she triumphantly sang from the score.

With no hope of gain from the citizens of Lausanne and without Merceret to pay his expenses, Jean-Jacques lived like the birds of the air on whatever Providence threw in his way. Meanwhile his lean face assumed a poetic languor. One thing alone had given him satisfaction, the success of the final minuet at his concert. But that, too, was not without its drop of gall. Lies, shifts, cunning—but he had somehow to survive till he found himself, for he knew there was a self to find when he could think beyond the expediencies of the moment. At present he was a minor Venture de Villeneuve and the impersonation had at least the virtue of providing him with an occasional lodging and a meal. He also acquired various knowledge. For instance, he learned that it was more rewarding for the penniless to apply at the poorer inns for shelter and perhaps a bite to eat. At the grander places one was rudely turned away. Profiting by his experience he continued lodging for a while longer with Perrotet until he decided on his next move.

Frequently now he found himself thinking of Maman, though he corresponded with Mademoiselle Graffenried while admitting that it was Mademoiselle Galley who made his heart beat faster. But he knew that he was not in love with either of the girls. Little by little he grew tired of the correspondence and put an end to it by failing to inform Mademoiselle Graffenried of his too frequent geographical changes, not to mention the emotional ones.

Still his thoughts reverted to Annecy and toward "poor Maman" with a tenderness not unmixed with pity—perhaps for the guilt he felt in the disloyalty of having found any other woman even worthy of a single quickened heartbeat. Her spell, especially in times of misfortune, was more potent than ever. He had only to think of her to be comforted—and how much he needed that comfort now! As if to bring himself closer to her he set out on a dedicated pilgrimage to Vevey where she was born. In the state of exaltation into which he flung himself, he was a votary and Vevey held the shrine. Over and over he repeated Maman's name as he walked through the streets, and the longing to see her, to fling himself at her feet, became an intoxication which was in itself a fulfillment. Though he longed to find the house of her birth, where she had spent her girlhood, he did not dare to inquire. To mention the enchanted name would have been profanation, besides revealing the secret of his heart. It might even have compromised her or—worse—he might have learned some scandal. So he wandered about the city, stopping to worship at all likely shrines. Meanwhile, in his typical fashion, he gave little thought to any concern she might be having over his wandering and, particularly, his silence.

Since Vevey was only four leagues from the Lake of Geneva, so rich in associations—his childhood, Mademoiselle Vulson who, he remembered with emotion, had had the first fruits of his heart—he could not possibly fail to revisit it. So the pilgrim of sentiment walked along its shores reliving the tender moments of his boyhood. Ah, the bliss of a life on those enchanted shores! A modest house, an orchard no greater than one's needs, a small garden, a milch cow, a little boat and, for company, a trusted friend and a loving woman. With nature and all its beauty round about, what more could one desire? For the moment, alas, such bliss was attainable only in his imagination, and that, as he was obliged to admit, was serving him little toward the most elementary needs of food and shelter.

There is no road so dark, however, that does not lead to light. His situation could not be worse; it must therefore improve. He thought of the Church and on Sundays he now began going to hear Mass at Assens, not two leagues from Lausanne, setting out in the company of fellow Catholics. They were a varied group, mostly humble folk, but among them Jean-Jacques found a Parisian—a real Parisian from Paris—who took it for granted that he too, Jean-Jacques, was from that magical city. It was a compliment which he could not mar by a denial. Meanwhile he succeeded in obtaining a few pupils at Neufchâtel and it was there that he spent the winter, earning enough to allow him to pay his debt to Perrotet.

Since settled life had no spice, he seasoned his work with occasional excursions on his free days and particularly on Sundays. Every place has its zest for anyone who has the capacity to enjoy it; but for the dreamy youth it was still nature that most enraptured him. Occasionally he sought distraction at some inn where he would drink his glass of wine and spend a pleasant hour in the always interesting company. One day, finding himself at Boudry and with a hearty appetite, he went into a *cabaret* to dine. The company comprised the usual group of habitués and traveling guests, except for an exotic and imposing personage who certainly would have created a stir even in a metropolis. He was an outlandish figure with his furred bonnet and his rippling beard set off by the purple of his flowing gown. But even without such accoutrements the man's physical majesty would have commanded attention. Jean-Jacques was immediately fascinated as the stranger, supplementing picturesque gesture to the peculiar jargon he was speaking, tried in vain to make himself understood by the company. It was a hodgepodge of tongues, as Jean-Jacques detected, with something that sounded like Italian predominating, the whole punctuated by gestures which to the unimaginative gathering remained as recondite as the resplendent stranger's words. Smitten by the majesty and obvious opulence of the man, Jean-Jacques offered himself at once as his interpreter.

The stranger, according to his own description, was Father Athanasius Paulus, Archimandrite of the Holy Sepulchre of Jerusalem. The very title, in its imposing majesty, would have subdued the most skeptical. Added to the dignity and impressiveness of the man, it was awesome indeed. Everyone was suitably reverential, most of all Jean-Jacques, who had never before stood within the light of such majesty. Archimandrite of Jerusalem. The title rolled with the awesomeness of thunder. Yet that magnificent presence held within it a selfless and tender heart for, despite his elevated rank, the Archimandrite had the noble humility to beg—yes, beg—for alms to ransom the unfortunate Christian slaves in Palestine. Jean-Jacques would have fallen at his feet in admiration. He did better. He offered himself as the exalted one's interpreter for the rest of the holy man's pilgrimage. After all it was spring, and again the irresistible month of April, which bade plants to grow and youth to wander. Jean-Jacques obeyed. How could he not, in the wake of so resplendent a bird? He had other vouchers besides the Archimandrite's external splendor. In his own hands he held the letters patent signed by the Czar and the

Czarina of Russia, who had given the Archimandrite their blessing and, most assuredly, approval of a more tangible nature.

Certainly Father Athanasius Paulus did not look as if he had ever fasted unduly, and the appetite with which he cleared his plate at the inn argued for a robust digestion. How splendidly he was dressed! With something of self-approval Jean-Jacques glanced down at his own violet habit which he had recently bought, almost as if he had had foreknowledge of his new office. Indeed he had a new office: the Archimandrite had engaged him as his secretary and interpreter, for outside of his Greek, Turkish and lingua franca he knew no other language. Since the charmed youth asked for nothing and Father Athanasius promised much, they made no formal agreement about terms. Jean-Jacques could not have been happier. Here was a worthy occupation for him at last, and his effervescent imagination began blowing gaudy bubbles of fame, adventure and romance.

The Archimandrite had soon accomplished his purpose at Boudry and with his purple-clad secretary-interpreter in his wake, set out for greener fields and pastures new to provide for his suffering sheep in Palestine. The takings were not bad, especially now that he had the eloquence of his interpreter to serve him. He prudently did not stay long at any place—only the time it took to make his plea for the Christians held in bondage, to collect the offerings, to spend the night at some inn—and then on to the next town. Curious and patient scholars have traced the peripatetic pair through Bâle, Berne, Fribourg, Soleure. Fribourg proved extraordinarily responsive, for not only was Father Athanasius lodged and fed with his companion for a month, but he also garnered a fine harvest of charity; enough, indeed, to provide not only himself but also his secretary-interpreter with a mount. It was an easy and agreeable life, always active, always changing and, if one considered its purposes from the Archimandrite's point of view, a very rewarding one. Jean-Jacques found him a most agreeable companion, as eagerly footloose as himself and prepared for any situation. He also had a talent for turning everything to his purposes, even such a trivial accident as his cutting his finger while cracking hazelnuts at dessert one day. "Behold, gentlemen," he addressed the other guests. "Behold, this is Pelasgian blood!" Who else there could have boasted of such ancient lineage?

Something must have come to the attention of the Fribourg council to warn it against further encouragement of the Archimandrite in his pious quests, for suddenly his patent was revoked and he was invited to ply his charitable mission elsewhere. Nothing daunted, the resplendent Archimandrite went on to Berne, accompanied by his purple secretary and a new and eloquent harangue which he, the secretary, had composed. Its delivery by Father Athanasius netted them ten écus. But alas, as they continued on their journey, the sheep proved more skeptical and the fields less green, and as Archimandrite and secretary moved disconsolately on, the vision of Jerusalem grew dimmer and dimmer in the eyes of the neophyte. At Soleure Father Athanasius and Jean-Jacques Rousseau parted company, the former richer by a few écus, the latter no poorer than he had been and with freedom and the world again before him. If only Monsieur de Bonac, the French Ambassador, had not looked so closely into the credentials of Father Athanasius, uncovering the false Archimandrite and, in Jean-Jacques, the equally false Parisian, Vaussore de Villeneuve! As it happened Monsieur l'Ambassadeur, the Marquis de Bonac, had served in his capacity at the Porte and knew all there was to know of the Holy Sepulchre and those who were in any way connected with it. It took him only a few seconds of his private interview with Father Athanasius to unmask him—for the Ambassador needed no interpreter.

When the penitent fraud issued from the private chamber Jean-Jacques, ready to follow at his heels, was conducted instead before the Ambassador. He knew he would be questioned but then that would be no hardship for there was nothing he liked better than talking about himself. Who was he? A Parisian, Vaussore de Villeneuve, he lied. The Marquis de Bonac was an urbane gentleman and in his position of Ambassador did not lose his humanity.

"Well, who *are* you?" he repeated, not deceived by Jean-Jacques' reiteration of his euphonious pseudonym. "The truth, now!"

Jean-Jacques looked about him. The place was too public. If Monsieur the Ambassador would give him a private hearing . . . Impressed by such extraordinary delicacy the Ambassador conducted the youth to his private office and shut the door behind him. Jean-Jacques, bursting with eagerness to tell his *petite histoire,* fell upon his knees in penitential enthusiasm and poured out the flood of his narrative—"for a continual need to unburden myself always brought my heart to my lips." [3] He told the truth more or less this time, for Monsieur de Bonac was not one to deceive with impunity. Besides, in his sudden zeal for reformation Jean-Jacques determined to wash himself clean of sin and start upon a new life.

The Ambassador had seen at once the real Jean-Jacques beneath the surface of the vagabond and dealt with him accordingly. First of all he had him sunder all relations with his Archimandrite, which Jean-Jacques did, though reluctantly, for his heart, always eager to attach itself to someone, had already twined its tendrils of affection around that luxuriant stock.

Sending for his little bundle which the Archimandrite was holding for him, he acceded—for what choice had he?—to the Ambassador's wishes. Jean-Jacques of the *Confessions,* wishing to build up the young vagabond for posterity, indulged in an agreeable fantasy that had nothing to do with the truth, which was, simply, that Monsieur de Bonac gave him a fatherly lecture and sent him on his way with nothing more than his good wishes.

How could Rousseau of the *Confessions,* melted to tears by the youth's plight, refuse him deserved if tardy reward? Monsieur le Marquis de Bonac was not as devoid of heart as cold fact would indicate. Indeed, how could he have listened to that charming lad's story without helping him? Accordingly the events were restaged with suitable soft music and the introduction of Madame de Bonac, to whom the Ambassador had immediately presented his young friend so that she, too, could add her tears of sentiment to Rousseau's. The outcome was such as a fairy-tale adventurer would have dreamed. Madame de Bonac took him to her heart—metaphorically, that is—and, saying that under no circumstances should he be allowed to fall into the clutches of that evil man again, she suggested that Jean-Jacques stay at the *hôtel*. A few minutes later, his little bundle retrieved from the wicked Archimandrite, Jean-Jacques was lodged like a truly important person with the Secretary of the Embassy, Monsieur de la Martinière.

A challenge to greatness was not lacking. As Monsieur de la Martinière conducted the youth to his chamber he said: "In the time of the Comte du Luc this room was occupied by a famous man of the same name as your own. You have only to take his place in every way, so that some day the world will speak of Rousseau the First and Rousseau the Second." [4]

The words of Monsieur de la Martinière, if he ever uttered them, were not lost upon Jean-Jacques. After reading the books of Jean Baptiste Rousseau, who had slept in that room, he was fired with zeal to emulate him and produced a cantata in verse, in praise of Madame de Bonac—not, however, without the ulterior motive that Monsieur l'Ambassadeur might detect in the work a potential assistant to the Embassy. Extraordinary for Jean-Jacques, this time he did not fall in love. Perhaps Madame de Bonac was too old. Perhaps Monsieur l'Ambassadeur, splendid in his office, was too formidable a rival. Perhaps, too, Jean-Jacques was beginning to grow up.

6. *Jean-Jacques adrift*

Jean-Jacques was not long at the Ambassador's, though with every need provided for and with much leisure for himself, he might have wished the post permanent, according to his own definition of permanence. But there was the road, the irresistible road and this time with Paris as the destination—Paris and a resplendent career in, of all places, the Army! Why the Army? Because Monsieur de Merveilleux, a recent acquaintance, had a nephew, Colonel Godard of the Swiss Guards, and this simple fact was enough to make the not too tall Rousseau see himself in the glorious uniform of the six- and seven-foot Guards. Surely, after such a debut, the dream of eventually rising to the splendor of Maréchal was not beyond reason. After all, was he the blood kin of Uncle Bernard, that architect of fortifications, for nothing? Surely some of the family military genius had passed into him, Jean-Jacques. Meanwhile he was filling his notebook with melancholy verses that had nothing to do with martial glory:

Why, cruel love, in this sweet solitude
You come, and in my heart the gentle habitude
Retrace, of happy moments gone?

What sweet habitude was he lamenting? His interlude with Mademoiselle Galley? With Graffenried? With Mademoiselle Vulson? Or was he sighing for the tender intimacies of Maman? He had all the leisure of a fortnight's tramping for his melancholy speculations before reaching Paris. Alas, by the time he arrived, Maman, on one of her usual missions to extract some consideration or other for her multiple intrigues, had already left the capital. He still had a good part of Monsieur de Bonac's money in his pocket, allegedly, and to make it last as long as possible, found lodgings in the Faubourg Saint-Marceau, in keeping with his modest pocketbook. To the foreigner who had expected marble palaces, noble columns and stately monuments at every turn, his first view of Paris, in one of its shabbier quarters, was disillusioning indeed. So this was beautiful Paris—these narrow streets with all kinds of foulness in the gutters, these dingy houses, these untidy shops sometimes no bigger than a cell, these raucous yells of hucksters crying their wares. Even the Opéra, which his imagination had envisioned as all beauty and enchantment, left him disillusioned. No doubt he had expected too much, or perhaps to salve his ego of twenty, he was playing the sophisticate. At any rate he saw no virtue anywhere—not even at Versailles nor, later, when for the first time he was taken to view the ocean. Jean-Jacques was not impressed. How could it have been otherwise with one who declared with no false modesty: "It is impossible for man and difficult for nature itself to surpass the riches of my imagination." [1]

As for the people themselves, he had expected to be greeted by everyone with open arms and overflowing hearts, judging by his own, always eager and expansive. He found only casual politeness or outright indifference. What of his dream of being the tutor of a young nobleman and its concomitant benefits? Not only was there no nobleman young or old; there was not the least shadow of a sister to fall in love with nor of a brother to swear to eternal friendship. If only he had found Maman, at least! But Maman was cross with him for having left Annecy, gone to Protestant territory and perhaps fallen again into heresy.

Forced by his need, he wrote to Esther Giraud, Maman's pietistic friend, hoping she would plead for him with Madame de Warens. He did not know, or he would not admit, what faults could have made him appear guilty in her eyes, while the dread of making things worse deterred him from writing to her. "If you would now exert yourself to plead for me, Mademoiselle, this is the favorable moment and at your solicitation she will surely grant me permission to write to her, because it is a boldness I would not dare venture on my own account. . . . Could I ever conceal anything from one to whom I owe all? I eat no morsel of bread that does not come from her; without the kindness of this charitable lady I would perhaps already have starved to death, and if I am alive now, it is thanks to the medical care that she obtained for me. Make haste, then, Mademoiselle; intercede for me and try to obtain her permission to clear myself." [2] This letter, however, so persuasively written, was never sent, for there was another, which Madame de Merveilleux had given him. However, when he presented it, he found that the only place that was open would have made a valet of him, and he would have no more of that. There was nothing for him to do but to go back—but where? He decided on Lyon, which had at least the virtue of being less far from Chambéry than Paris. Why Chambéry? Because Maman, on the ascendant once more, thanks to the gracious consideration of King Charles Emmanuel III, had now established herself there after King Victor-Amédée had obligingly abdicated in favor of his son, Maman's new patron.

She was very skillful at ingratiating herself, charming Maman, and like a cat, she always knew which way to jump to land solidly on her pretty feet. The house had none of the charm of Annecy, no brook, no flower garden, no herb plot and, alas, no view, for it was tucked away at the bottom of a closed alley. But to Jean-Jacques, even if he had known these details, it would have been paradise nonetheless. How could he manage to go back to her? Fortunately he was not starving, for the considerate Monsieur de Bonac had sent him another hundred francs for his trip back. Without regret he left Paris and finding lodgings at Lyon, waited for word from Maman—for surely she would not forget Petit. Indeed, she did not. Soon she sent him just the sort of letter to make his heart rejoice, and there they were all together again at Chambéry, Maman and Claude Anet and the rest of the household—all this accompanied by the blessing of Pope Clement XII, who had sent a tangible gift of ten écus to Maman and one écu to Claude Anet, His Holiness thus unconsciously marking the value he set upon the piety of mistress and servant.

Jean-Jacques set out on his way as before, but with a difference. He was now no gawky adolescent but a man approaching twenty and not unattractive, as he could not help being aware. He took his time about returning, wishing to savor to the full the countryside and its enchanting prospects. Almost it was as if he were for the last time indulging the pleasures of youth and freedom before entering manhood. Walking always stimulated his mind and it was this physical activity which seemed to liberate his soul and stir his imagination to daring thoughts. "I then dispose of all nature like a master. My heart, flitting from object to object, merges, identifies itself with what most flatters it, surrounding itself with charming imagery, intoxicating itself with delicious sentiments. . . ." [3]

Full of his fancies, he lost his way on one of these walks, and it was not until after several hours' wandering that, hungry and nearly dying of thirst, he came at last to a small peasant hut. The poor devil who lived in it at once betrayed the dread of one who did not know what evil to expect from the visitor; but soon, reassured that he had only a hungry youth as guest, he fetched bread from a hiding place under the floor and a jug of wine from another cache, looking suspiciously toward the door while he fed his visitor and partook of his own tasty bounty.

Never had Jean-Jacques eaten with such relish, savoring the wheaten loaf and the slices of ham that were later produced from the same secret place. As if these were not enough, his host prepared a fine thick omelette as a special treat. For Jean-Jacques it was a banquet so memorable that he never forgot the smallest detail—least of all the bit of information he acquired from his host at parting when he, Jean-Jacques, tried to give him some token of his gratitude. Fearful, almost rude, his host pushed the money from him saying he would take no payment. There was such terror in his rejection that Jean-Jacques wondered whether he was dealing with a maniac. Finally the man, still glancing fearfully about, explained that he hid his wine because of the imposts and his bread because of the taxes. "I'd be a lost man," he said, "if *they* didn't have the impression that I was starving."

This crude but simple fact came as a shock to the youth, who learned for the first time of abuses and oppression by those who have toward those who have not. How conceive that a man should fear to eat the bread he has earned by the sweat of his brow? That he, having a loaf, should be compelled to pretend he is starving, like a good many of his neighbors? It was this circumstance that suddenly, for the first time, made Jean-Jacques the poet and dreamer begin to nurture "the germ of this unquenchable hatred which later developed in my heart against the vexations of the unhappy people and against their oppressors." [4]

On the road again, the reflections stimulated by his recent experience giving way to those evoked by nature and association, his spirits were restored. The weather was fair, the landscape romantic, of a romanticism linked with the dreams of his boyhood. This was sacred ground rich in association, which he would be treading, if he went a little out of the way to the banks of the Lignon. Ah, the romance of *Astrée,* so dear to his childhood and still capable of giving him a thrill or two. He inquired the road toward Forez only to learn, alas, that it was a good, thriving place, where anyone could easily find work at any of its foundries. If the young man cared to go there he would have no trouble in getting hired.

Jean-Jacques quickened his step in the opposite direction. Alas for the sylvan gods and goddesses. Alas for the Dianas and the Sylvanders. They had been frightened out of a world suddenly become alien through progress.

He made his way toward Lyon, also because at Lyon lived a friend of Maman's, another pietistic lady, Mademoiselle du Châtelet, whose acquaintance he had made the previous year when he had gone to see her with Le Maître. Jean-Jacques had no particular interest in her, but he knew that she would have news of Maman, which indeed she had. Madame de Warens, she said, had passed through Lyon, but she had left almost immediately, whether to go to Piedmont or to Savoy, Mademoiselle du Châtelet did not know. Jean-Jacques was hoping that after such cheerless information the lady would offer him the hospitality of her house, for he had nearly come to the end of what little money he had; but since her concerns were purely spiritual, she did not descend to anything so worldly as offering the obviously needy youth supper and lodging for the night.

For a few days he was able to pay his way at a shabby inn. Then his money gave out and he had no choice but to sleep al fresco, with others in the same confraternity of poverty. One evening he was lying on a bench in the little square when an abbé came by and asked him whether he had no lodging. Jean-Jacques, always ready with his "little story" made such an impression that the abbé invited him to spend the night at his place—just a single room, he said, but big enough to shelter two.

When they arrived there the good host served him cherries in brandy, and after chatting awhile he showed the youth to his bed and then lay down beside him. Before long the abbé was proceeding in the same fashion as the Slav at the hospice in Turin. At first Jean-Jacques was alarmed, not knowing into what hands he had fallen, and fearing for his life, thought it wiser not to make an outcry. While the abbé was endeavoring to achieve his purpose Jean-Jacques, with not wholly assumed naïveté, told him of his earlier experience and in such terms of horror and revulsion that the abbé, feeling no doubt like Potiphar's wife, relinquished this new Joseph to his chastity.

Another night, sleeping in the open, he heard a nightingale singing from the tree arching overhead, and his dreams were enchanted by that rapturous song. Ah, he had heard the nightingale! Ah, nightingales still inhabited the trees! A truly wonderful nightingale it must have been, to sing so many months out of season, even for such a lover of nature, for the month was September.

Nightingale or not, he was convinced that it was its rapturous song he had heard, and for him that conviction was enough. One does not have to be a specialist in ornithology to be thrilled to the soul by the song of a bird in the dusky hush of the woods. Why not a nightingale? Perhaps it was even a phoenix—or was it the swan that sang before it died?

Alas, he had graver concerns than nightingales on his mind, and if Maman did not soon materialize Petit would be in sad straits indeed. Still the streets, the open country, the changing skies seen through the branches, the many delightful discoveries of the flora and fauna along the way, and most of all his freedom, filled with such rapture that, imitating his nightingale, he made the air thrill to his singing. He had a wide and varied repertory, from the sentimental ballads of Tante Theodora to the arias of the Italian composers whose music he had learned to copy with exquisite precision and beauty. Indeed, he could have set up shop as a copyist with his talent, that is, if he could ever settle down anywhere long enough to take root.

But that was the last thing that would have occurred to the nympholept, the searcher after nature's beauties. So on he wandered, singing an aria from one of Battistini's cantatas for the delectation of the wood nymphs, if any were still about. As chance would have it, there was a listener that he was not aware of, an Antonine who was following the same road a little distance behind. Jean-Jacques turned, saw him, and noting the expression of pleasure on his face, wondered whether his singing might not earn him at least a dinner.

The Antonine greeted him pleasantly. "Do you know music?" he inquired.

"A little," replied Jean-Jacques with an inflection that implied the opposite. On the next breath he was recounting his *petite histoire* once again but modifying it to suit the present circumstances. The Antonine, who introduced himself as Monsieur Rolichon, then asked him if he had ever copied music.

"Very often," replied Jean-Jacques, lying a little.

"Well, then, come with me," said the Antonine. "I can give you employment for a few days during which you would lack nothing. That is, provided you stick to your labors."

Concealing his elation, Jean-Jacques followed his new employer, a man of means and a musical dilettante, who sang and played and who delighted in participating in musicales with his friends in his own salon. They were pleasant gatherings though often heated by the arguments of the musical enthusiasts. Jean-Jacques was given a little room filled with music and there put to work—his initial task the copying of the very cantata that he had been singing and which his patron and his friends would be performing in a few days.

In his cozy cubicle Jean-Jacques labored with a will. He finished the Battistini and set to work on other scores. He was in excellent spirits—and why should he not have been? He was comfortably lodged in a room of his own, left quietly to his work and fed four times a day. Fed? That was too limited a word. After his long enforced dieting he stuffed himself with a will. He worked with the same enthusiasm as he ate, which was prodigious, and he was soon at the end of his task. The copies were beautiful, each note of the score exquisitely executed, the ornaments done with artistic aplomb. He had enjoyed the task which, being largely mechanical, gave him leisure to think his own thoughts, build his own castles of music—for, among his ambitions, foremost was that of becoming a musician.

Rousseau's task accomplished, Monsieur Rolichon, pleased with the beauty of the copies, thanked him and gave him his fee, together with his blessing. Jean-Jacques was again on the streets, though this time with money in his pockets. Monsieur Rolichon, delighted with the fine copies, distributed them to his musical friends. Alas, when they came to their rehearsal they found the scores unplayable—so full were they of duplications, transpositions and lacunae. But what a work of art they were! With a sigh Monsieur Rolichon had to set them aside as beautiful but useless. Still, how could he have expected an obviously dreamy youth to keep his thoughts from wandering while making black dots on a page and equipping them with a mast and sails? Several days later, meeting him on the street, he gave Jean-Jacques an écu, which the copyist himself admitted had been badly earned, and the two parted company with the best of feelings.

Rousseau's spirits soared now that he had money in his pocket, and since good things, like bad, never come unaccompanied, he also had the joy of hearing from Maman. She was at Chambéry, where the whole happy family was reunited, she said—and with that welcome news she also sent him money for his journey home. Had he had wings he would have flown to her at once, but there was a long catalogue of commissions which she had sent to Mademoiselle du Châtelet, and Jean-Jacques had perforce to wait—which he would have enjoyed in his present euphoric state had Mademoiselle du Châtelet been younger and prettier. Things were going well with him; he had money and the happiest of prospects before him. There was even a charming Mademoiselle Serre, much younger than

Mademoiselle du Châtelet, who would not have disdained his admiration. But because his world had turned suddenly bright this lover of melancholy was chagrined that there was nothing to give him the pang without which enjoyment was incomplete. How dull not to have to worry about money, now that he could hear the jingle of silver in his pocket. And what delectation was there in walking when he could afford to hire a horse? Even the prospect of joining Maman lost its glamour compared to the shimmering fervor of his anticipation. So he found little pleasure in reading *Gil Blas,* which Mademoiselle du Châtelet lent him. He was in no mood for it, overflowing as he was with melancholy, tears and sentiment. "It is a very singular thing that my imagination never soars so agreeably as when my situation is least agreeable, and that on the contrary it is less gay when everything is smiling about me." [5] He was like the salmon that must swim rough currents, and upstream. He would have languished and died in still waters.

Nevertheless he enjoyed what there was to enjoy along the road, pausing to admire the landscape, standing rapt at Chailles to see the frothing, bubbling little river far below, rushing its way downward through the passage it had carved for itself—in how many millennia? Farther on there was the cascade, arching outward and down from the rocks of the mountain, tempting one to dash through the arch without getting wet. The lure was too strong. The exuberant lover of nature leapt through the misty barrier—and was drenched. But what was that small discomfort against the exhilaration? The sun would soon dry him.

He cut the pathetic figure he desired when he appeared before Maman—and Claude Anet. Though he was a man full grown, he saw that he was still Petit to Maman, which was as he would have it. How touching to have her fussing over him and asking a thousand questions of which she already knew the answers. How reassuring to be made to feel so important and so welcome, for Maman, expansive by nature, did not conceal her joy at his return, nor her admiration of his development.

He had left her a boy; he returned a man—a transformation that would have thrilled any Maman, particularly this one, who had known how to enjoy it in Claude Anet.

There was another guest in the house on Jean-Jacques' arrival, Monsieur l'Intendant Général, Don Antonio Petitti. What was this stranger doing there? He soon knew. Taking him by the hand, Maman led him to her guest, cooing in her most dulcet tones: "Here he is, Monsieur, this poor young man. . . ." (Why was he all of a sudden poor when he felt so rich in the exhilaration of his freedom?) "Be good enough to put him under your protection as long as he shows himself worthy, and I shall not worry about him for the rest of his days." [6]

What an extraordinary introduction! Jean-Jacques had barely got over his wonderment when Maman addressed him. *"Mon enfant,"* she said, "you belong to the King. Go thank Monsieur l'Intendant who is providing you your bread." [7]

Too bewildered to know what to think, Jean-Jacques could only stare at her and at the Intendant, and back again at her. Who was this Intendant, and why should he be providing *his* bread? Was Maman washing her hands of Petit? What had he done to be cast out when he had come to her in such happy anticipation of resuming their life on its early footing? The circumstances were not so grave as he thought, however. It was only Maman's clumsy dramatization that had made them seem so. Perhaps it had been the only way to tell him that he would have to be earning money on his own account under Monsieur l'Intendant who was in charge of the *cadastre,* or census of property and property owners for purposes of taxation.

Soon the aspiring poet and composer found himself at a desk, taking the census among other clerks. At present he had to make the best of the situation. Still, he wished they could live in the country and he painted an idyllic picture of it. "That is all very charming," Maman agreed, "and you know it would be very much to my taste. But this is where we must live. By leaving this prison, I risk losing my bread; and when we wouldn't have any left in the country, we'd have to come back to seek it in the city. So let's not leave it altogether. Let us find some place far enough away from the city to enjoy a peaceful life and yet close enough to return to it whenever necessary." [8] However, that time had not yet come.

Jean-Jacques saw the good sense in what Maman had said, and agreed. But ah, for his apartment at Annecy, he sighed whenever he retired to his sunless room in a cul-de-sac, with no view but a blank wall and crickets and rats for company under the rotting boards. Why had Maman, usually so astute, agreed to such a move? He did not realize until much later that she had outdone even herself in cleverness by establishing her household in such an unattractive place. For years, ever since she had placed herself under the protection of the King, she had been presenting herself regularly at Court for fear of being overlooked or wholly forgotten. She was all the more solicitious to make an appearance because of the active enmity which the Comte de Saint-Laurent showed toward her. Since he was the Intendant-General of Finance and thus the source from whom her blessings flowed, she had somehow to propitiate him. Intriguer that she was, she learned that at Chambéry he had a decrepit, unattractive house which was almost always empty. She rented it from him with such subtle diplomacy that Saint-Laurent, completely ignorant of the ruse, not only renewed her pension, which she had considered already doomed, but also counted her as a friendly ally. Thus, as a homely proverb has it, one hand washed the other and both of them washed the face.

The wanderer, happy to be home again, saw everything through an aureate veil. Maman he found more beautiful than ever. Though her embonpoint had considerably increased, her complexion was still fresh and rosy with a glow of health and, yes, satisfaction that he did not remember having noted before. Claude Anet, on the other hand, with his grave face and long black gown, appeared more somber and distrait than ever. However, he went about his tasks as usual, slow, poised and aloof, and always with deep regard for Maman. He had a poetic melancholy that belied the "peasant from Montreux," as Jean-Jacques alluded to him long afterward with still lively rancor.

What position did the handsome Claude hold in that household? Maman treated him at times as a caretaker, then as botanist and pharmacist and, in unguarded moments, as favorite. Jean-Jacques, more than ever the household darling after his return, found himself being jealous of Claude, even though Maman made so much of him at times that Claude could not conceal his anguish. "And so among the three of us there was established a society without parallel on earth," crowed Jean-Jacques, chief beneficiary in this arrangement.

It was a strange, perverse game that was being played in that mysterious house, with Claude as the chief victim. Was it conscious on the part of Maman and Petit? Or had their tantalizing, affectionate play become so overt that Claude, long since seduced, saw his rival and successor in Jean-Jacques? Who can say what ramifications of sensuality and perversity entangled the passionate yet always unsatisfied woman and her two protégés, the one already initiated and therefore now less tempting, the other still to try and so doubly alluring? Medical science, which was to attribute a good part of Rousseau's character and behavior to a chronic tendency to retention of urine, saw in Madame de Warens one of those women difficult to arouse and always sexually defrauded—the kind who under less favorable circumstances become prostitutes and case histories.

The three continued enacting their outward roles, Maman as the gracious mistress, guide and provider, now concocting drugs from the herbs which Claude gathered, now botanizing with Petit who, supplied with scissors, paste and ink, placed the specimens on the pages, arranging them, pressing them and identifying each with its botanical and its common name—the calligraphy, of course, provided in Petit's most exquisite lettering. In the evening there would be music with Maman at the clavecin; or Jean-Jacques would sing. Or perhaps they might read aloud, an innocent family group, like many another in their milieu.

Was Jean-Jacques aware of the love that Claude had for Madame de Warens, a love which was all the more tormenting for having to be secret? It may well be that Jean-Jacques did not even surmise it or recognize it, what with his self-engrossment and his conception of passion as a spate of romantic mouthings accompanied by soulful attitudes, as in his favorite romances which, of course, were also those of Madame la Baronne.

Little by little, as was inevitable, the still young and voluptuous woman roused feelings in Jean-Jacques that were far from filial. She encouraged them in him, as she had in Claude, as she had in his predecessors. She was sensual, demanding, and still ardent. Since another marriage was out of the question for her in Savoy, where her divorce was not recognized, she had to content herself with illicit affairs, discreetly kept at home. If anyone remarked on her succession of handsome valets, it could be argued that Madame la Baronne had a highly developed aesthetic sense—and what harm was there in that?

Now, however, she was sacrificing her virtue for a cause. Yes, she was offering herself for the sake of Petit, for his welfare— for who knows?—some latent genius within him which she might awaken. Maman, prudent in everything, never yielded herself except for a cause. It happened in the early spring. Snowdrops and jonquils lifting up their heads from the ground were the only witnesses. Jean-Jacques, no doubt, knew how to conduct himself at his initiation, for Maman had considerately given him a week in which to prepare himself.

As the familiarities between Maman and Petit became more overt, Claude Anet grew more depressed and melancholy; but he said not a word, not in the presence of Jean-Jacques and the servants, certainly. But there would be scenes and remonstrances with Maman, recriminations, sobs and tears that eventually ended with mutual forgiveness—and retirement to the boudoir. Whatever the feelings Madame de Warens now had for Claude, they had the predictability of the known as against the still unexplored, and Madame de Warens was nothing if not adventurous. The austere young man was a puzzle to Jean-Jacques, who could not conceive of a *grande passion* without amorous oratory and languishing attitudes. The lover was the victim, the prey of Eros. He must wear melancholy on his face and hold his hand to his transpierced heart, while he filled the air with sighs. It took Maman to awaken him to her true relations with her faithful Intendant; but this awakening seemed to have made no difference; for the self-centered Jean-Jacques, assured of what he had in Maman, could afford to ignore what he had taken away from Claude.

In a house so charged with emotion, so full of secrets that were no secret, of sensuality whetted with piety, it was not long before Maman inducted Petit, as she had earlier initiated Claude. Not that Jean-Jacques had not known what it was to be "treated like a man"; but Madame de Warens, so accustomed to her pietism and good deeds, brought into this act of hers the devotion of a mother and the harlotry of the priestesses of the ancient temples. She did not conduct her rape without its preliminaries of offer and denial, teasing and abandonment, making of the seduction a delightful game in which half as son, half as lover, the bewildered Jean-Jacques participated. There must have been for her, if not for him, the added piquancy of a touch of incest.

Claude Anet grew leaner, paler and more melancholy. His nerves, keyed to the snapping point, made him break out into fury, not against Madame de Warens, but against his young successor. Not a day passed without its scenes, which Maman, now the statue of Justice with the balances, sought to weigh and rectify. Jean-Jacques, the favorite, had nothing to complain about and he lorded it over the roost. Claude, despite his anguish, never forgot his responsibilities. Quietly, as before, he conducted his mistress' affairs as he had done for years when, after his services of the night he had attended to her business of the day, the one following the other as if that were the natural order of creation. But now his sensitive organism began to be undermined. Bravely he went about his duties with the same devotion as before—after all, *he* loved her—but neither his nerves nor his heart could take the blow.

One morning they found him twisted in agony which he tried manfully to repress. In his despair he had swallowed a quantity of tincture of opium which somehow they succeeded in having him reject. In a few days he was again the same somber, faithful servant, and for a while Jean-Jacques regarded him with admiring eyes—almost with envy. How wonderful of Claude to love to the point of wanting to die. Here indeed was a *passion fatale*. Would he, Jean-Jacques, ever feel so deeply for any woman, for any being, for that matter? But then, in love as in friendship, he preferred tenderness to passion, and even with Maman the most rapturous moments for him were still those when she treated him like a child. He was the recipient, the beloved, the caressed, almost the passive one, whose contribution lay in the reflection of his own enjoyment.

Meanwhile he continued going to the office of the *cadastre* like any other employee, sitting at his desk for the specified number of hours and doing more or less what was required of him, though his mind could not be kept from wandering through dreams and ambitions which waited, he knew, in the future. He had taken to reading again, after his ecstatic reveling in the book of nature which, more than the printed word, had been charging his mind and heart. He also set down the strains of music that would occur to him and which Maman would obligingly make audible to him on the clavecin.

There were adventures, however, in which Maman did not participate and which occurred during those compulsive excursions that were so necessary to his untrammeled nature. He would be missing for days or weeks, writing to Maman if he thought of it, or forgetting about her in the exhilaration of his freedom. What he did, what he saw, what went on in his mind and imagination would be stored for later reminiscence. One document, however, a letter with no date, survives, wherein he recounts an idyl which would not have given pleasure to Maman. It was addressed to Mademoiselle La Bussière, whom chance had brought for a moment within his orbit, when he spied upon her as she was bathing in a stream.

"Scarcely can I admit to you, Mademoiselle, the circumstance to which I owe the happiness of having seen you and the torment of having loved you. Chance began and love concluded this event. But what say I? Chance? No, love accomplished all from the moment I heard your enchanting voice. It was love's fault that it penetrated my heart; it was love that pricked me to an indiscreet curiosity. Love it was that spread out to my avid gaze the most dangerous of treasures; love that, since the baths of the twentieth of this month, troubles my reason; it is love that has dictated this letter. But why keep from you the most redoubtable of its snares, that snare without which perhaps I might have escaped all the others? I shall not fear to avow it, Mademoiselle: it should do honor to us both. Yes, it was not so much those eyes whose gentleness equals their vivacity; it was less the freshness of those lilies spread in such profusion over your person; it was less that svelte slim waist which loses nothing by being naked; it was less that elegant form, those graceful contours which it would be as bold for me to describe as it was for me to have beheld them. It was less, I say, the detail and the ensemble of so many charms that seduced me, as much as that endearing blush, daughter of modesty and innocence, which I beheld covering your brow the moment I offered myself to your view after having, too cunningly, betrayed my indiscretion by a couplet that I began to sing. Ye gods! How beautiful you were and how true it is that virtue is the most seductive source of beauty. . . ." [9]

On and on he poured out his eloquence. Would she forgive

him his indiscretion? If only out of pity she must pardon him; for pity, he said, was the privilege of beautiful souls; surely it must have a place in hers. So the young gallant pleaded his cause, though, it would seem, in vain.

7. *First flights*

Already, however, Jean-Jacques had begun to court another mistress, Solitude, with her handmaidens, the Muses. He saw the need for preparation in this courtship also, and he read and studied as never before. Did he, with his extraordinary perceptions, sense that the Chambéry idyl could not last forever and that, in fact, it was showing signs of doom? In the beginning of March, 1733, Claude Anet, who according to Jean-Jacques had gone to gather *génipi* on the mountain heights, caught a severe cold and died. Certainly Jean-Jacques' botany was at fault, for if indeed Claude had gone on that errand at that time, he would have found only snowdrifts. Whatever the cause—could it have been suicide?—Claude did fall ill. He died on the thirteenth of March and was buried with precipitate haste the following day, at Saint Léger.

Some thought the death mysterious and speculated on causes other than the consequences of a cold caught while gathering herbs. Among the skeptics was Saint-Germain who, on writing of his relations with Rousseau in his own *Oeuvres complètes,* published in 1819-1820, queried: "Can one believe that Monsieur Rousseau . . . could have been a poisoner, a scoundrel? True it is nevertheless that in the matter of his search for herbs, he has been taxed with trying to find poisons, and there is mention of a man on whom they say he experimented, for the fellow died in the agony of a nephritic colic, despite the aid Monsieur Rousseau brought him." [1]

Whether Madame de Warens felt the loss of the lover in the sober, handsome, devoted youth, she most assuredly mourned the faithful manager, the trusted friend and counselor. At this same time her protector and patron, Monseigneur de Bernex, who looked after her pension and saw to it that she received it regularly, also died.

Through it all Jean-Jacques followed his own concerns, studying Rameau and seeking to emulate him. With the composer's treatise on harmony before him, he applied the rules and endeavored to ape him. He did the same with Marivaux, in this instance producing an imitation of the master's *Petit maître corrigé* in his own *Narcisse, ou l'amant de lui-même.*

It was a pleasing little farce in the manner of the day, in which Valère, a handsome youth in love with his own good looks, pays scant heed to his fiancée, Angélique. To cure him of his vanity his sister Lucinde, Angélique's bosom friend, has his portrait painted in the semblance of a woman and makes him a present of it. Of course he falls in love with the portrait, and from then on the giddy little farce speeds on its way to a happy dénouement. Though dated, it is still sprightly in the reading, and the situation would evoke a smile or two from an unsophisticated audience. For Jean-Jacques, who was very much of a Narcissus himself, it was a gem—for had he not created it? Indeed, when many years later he was compiling an edition of his collected works, he wrote a preface to *Narcisse* which was longer than the play itself. "I wrote this comedy at the age of eighteen," he began, lopping off two years from the age of the precocious dramatist, "and I guarded against showing it about as long as I placed any stock on my reputation as an author. At last I have summoned up the courage to publish it, but I'll never have the courage to say anything about it. Therefore it is not a question of my play but of myself. . . ." The floodgates were opened and the old man emptied with a rush the torrent of his grievances and persecutions.

Young Jean-Jacques, playing the tyro, did not stop at Marivaux. There was the saturnine Voltaire, then in the full glory of his *Lettres philosophiques*. There were the great of the past—Descartes, Malebranche, Leibnitz, the works of Locke, the *Logique* of Port-Royal. He read them all with equal ardor, noting that one contradicted the other, yet deriving something of value from each. At times, through his own reasoning, he sought to bring accord into the confusion, only to confound himself. The intellectual stimulation, however, was its own reward. Then there were women, the inspiration, the spur, sometimes the destroyers, of men. He must write about women. After all, did he not know them from experience and from his reading? In his creative ferment he scarcely knew what to undertake next, whether drama, prose, music, verse. He felt himself capable of entering any field. One person and one place he must celebrate worthily, Maman and her milieu, but he was not yet ready for that celebration.

Meanwhile, at the height of his literary fervor he convinced himself and tried to convince Maman that he was dying—that polyp of the heart again. He was so persuasive that in great alarm Maman agreed to his leaving the *cadastre* and its office, stinking with breath and sweat, to devote himself to his writing and his music, while still, however, acting as her overseer. In that capacity there was little enough for Petit to do, since the able and devoted Claude had left everything in excellent order.

Not long thereafter his dream was realized when Maman bought the delightful property of Les Charmettes, an estate belonging to Monsieur François Joseph de Conzié. It was near Chambéry but, according to Rousseau, retired and solitary as if it had been a hundred leagues away. The environment held all that he desired: high hills, a little valley extending north and south, and a stream that made its way among the trees and pebbles. There were few houses to disturb his privacy, and it offered the right asylum for one who was fond of unspoiled nature with a touch of urbanity. The house Rousseau found "very habitable." A garden with a terrace lay in front. Above it was a vineyard; below, an orchard. To add to its charm there was also a little forest of chestnut trees and a fountain nearby. In short, he declared, it had everything required for the country house they intended to set up.

Once Jean-Jacques was free to do as he pleased, his polyp considerately disappeared, at least for a time. Maman, too, kept herself industriously employed with her intrigues and holy works and threw her salon open to rich and poor, nobles and bourgeois, in a fine democratic spirit that tangentially brought its rewards, though her situation was not as flourishing as it had been, despite—or perhaps because of—the wild enterprises she would engage in—like the cultivation of flax, which had been a total loss.

Among the frequenters of her salon were a cavalry captain in the service of the King of Sardinia; a Father Caton, of the Order of the Cordeliers; Monsieur de Conzié, whose house dominated the valley of Les Charmettes; and two *savants,* both doctors, Salomon and Grossi. With all these connections Jean-Jacques was able to obtain a few pupils—a demoiselle by the unattractive name of Lard but according to him as beautiful as a Greek statue, and a Madame de Menthon who, on seeing the personable music teacher, decided that she needed to cultivate her voice.

Jean-Jacques was willing to instruct her but Maman, who judged other women by herself, quickly put an end to the lessons, for she was not one to surrender to another's enjoyment what she had so painstakingly helped to create. She was proud of her young genius, who could please her as a woman, who wrote verse and who, besides singing and composing, could pick up the baton and conduct a little orchestra. And he also played the flute. Those were delightful evenings when Jean-Jacques as *chef d'orchestre* led the musicales, while Maman blended her agreeable voice with Monsieur de Gauffecourt's and Père Caton's, and another habitué, Abbé Palai, presided at the harpsichord, surrounded by a group of violins.

What all this varied activity indicated was that Jean-Jacques had not yet found himself among his many selves and, chameleonlike, assumed the hue of the influences that played upon him. One thing he knew from self-observation and he set it down among his other jottings: "The mind cannot be colored differently from the heart."

He was still scattering his energies, reading indiscriminately but with the acquisitive zeal of the self-taught, recording the thoughts of others for his guidance, but also treasuring his own. Ambition stirred in him—but toward what? He saw himself capable of any undertaking. If he read a novel he envisioned himself as a novelist; a tragedy—he would be a tragedian; a poem—nothing would do but that he must prove himself a poet. On the publication of Rollin's famous *Ancient History* he saw his own path marked out, and that he might constantly be reminded of his grand scheme, he set down the title of the stupendous work he intended to write: *A Universal Chronology of General History of the Times, from the Creation of the World to the Present—Composed and arranged by Rousseau for his own use.* How modest that "for his own use."

His literary excursions did not by any means dull his passion for his sudden flights. Without a word he would make up his bundle and set out for whatever destination beckoned his need or his imagination. On one occasion he decided to go incognito to Geneva to visit the Résident de France, Monsieur de la Closure, who had once loved Suzanne Rousseau, and who indeed was still deeply affected on speaking of her. Most of Rousseau's relatives were gone. Abraham, his cousin and childhood playmate, had perished in the service of the King of Prussia. Uncle Bernard, too, had died across the Atlantic Ocean in the Carolinas, in the city of Charleston he had helped to found. As Jean-Jacques was going through his uncle's papers, he came upon his *Plan for the Fortification of Geneva*. Maman immediately saw its value if it were placed in the right hands and she had no difficulty in persuading Jean-Jacques to turn it over to the head of the *cadastre*. Her rewards were not mentioned, but there were rewards, in which Jean-Jacques certainly shared. Now she became truly his Maman, the being closest to him in the whole world. The fires of the earlier seduction had been well-nigh spent, for Maman, in the estimation of her contemporaries, was now well on into middle age. As if to establish the new relationship, Heaven itself seemed to have intervened, or so Maman, and therefore also Jean-Jacques, believed.

For some time he had been ailing of a malaise which he could not define, a weariness that deprived him of incentive, of the least energy. Following the custom of the day, he drank the curative waters and, thorough in that as in everything else, he so overdid the cure that in less than two months he had nearly destroyed his stomach. Maman tended him with all tenderness and solicitude, for whatever the true nature of their relationship, there was by now a solid basis of mutual devotion which was to last as long as they lived, no matter what other influences entered their lives.

She was distressed by Jean-Jacques' morbid state, which was chiefly psychological, but no one seemed able to cope with it. One morning, while he was setting up a small table, he suddenly reeled and fell senseless. "I felt within my whole body a sudden revolution . . . a kind of tempest that rose in my blood and instantly affected all my members. My arteries began to beat with such force that I not only felt their beating, but heard it too, expecially that of the carotids. A tremendous noise in my ears followed and this noise was triple, rather, quadruple: it was a low, deep humming, a clearer murmur

like that of running water, a very shrill whistling, and the beating I have mentioned, whose strokes I could count without
feeling my pulse . . . This internal noise was so great that it
dulled the keen hearing I had always had, and finally made
me not deaf, but hard of hearing . . . This accident, which
should have destroyed my body, only killed my passions: and
I thank Heaven each day for the beneficial effect it had upon
my soul. I can well say that I began to live only when I thought
of myself as a dead man." [2]

Having come so close to death it was inevitable that Jean-
Jacques turn his thoughts to the other world and here Maman
was of great comfort. Easygoing, without hate or rancor, she
saw the hereafter as an ideal region where all terrestrial in-
equities were corrected and all lived like angels. Incapable of
vengeance, she could not subscribe to the Hebraic justice of
an angry God, demanding an eye for an eye. God to her was
goodness and mercy, and so she rationalized to her devoted
listener that there could be no justice in God to be just toward us; for not having given us those qualities which make
for justice and clemency, He could not demand more than He
had given. As for Hell, she absolutely refused to grant that
there was such a place, though she believed in Purgatory.
"That was because she did not know what to do with the souls
of the wicked," Jean-Jacques elucidated, "since she could neither damn them nor give them a place among the good until
they actually became so. One must admit," he conceded, "that
both in this and in the other world, the wicked are always
quite embarrassing." [3]

Thoughts of the other world, which often morbidly occupied him, had made him turn his mind to such practical matters as how to dispose of his goods if he should die. Isaac
Rousseau was still very much alive, but there was an inheritance which would come to him, Jean-Jacques, after his father's
demise and he himself had certain obligations which he was
not only honor-bound to respect, but compelled to fulfill by the
dictates of his heart.

Some time earlier, while occupied with his chemicals in making sympathetic ink with quicklime and sulphur of arsenic, the alembic exploded in his face and for a while he believed himself doomed, for he had also swallowed some of the mixture. Preparing for the worst, he took stock of himself, made a passionate profession of faith as a Catholic, commended himself to the Blessed Virgin and to a half dozen patron saints, among them St. John and St. James after whom he was named. He also drew up his will. Maman, formally named as Madame de Warens, was of course his beneficiary, whom he humbly begged to accept his inheritance as the sole token he could offer of his lively gratitude for all her goodness toward him. Furthermore he declared that he owed the said lady two thousand Savoy livres for the food and keep that the said lady had furnished him during the past ten years, which sum Rousseau promised to pay her within the next six months, if spared.

Good Catholic that he had become, he also remembered with various bequests the Capuchins, the Augustinians and the Ladies of St. Claire at Chambéry. His worldly affairs disposed of, he prepared to face death. But death, happily, did not meet the appointment. His father, however, did go to Geneva from Nyon. Thanks to Monsieur de la Closure, who handled the legal formalities, by the end of his father's visit Jean-Jacques found himself the richer by 6,500 florins, his father keeping the same amount from the inheritance of his deceased wife and Jean-Jacques' mother.

The money had come just in time, for Jean-Jacques had incurred a number of debts from the local merchants. With punctilious zeal he paid them. The rest of the money he laid at the feet of Maman who, in the financial straits in which she now permanently found herself, accepted it with tearful gratitude. She insisted on one condition, however: the money was to be merely a loan, and so it was.

Alas, on his return from Geneva, his elation at being able at last to compensate Maman for all she had done for him was considerably abated by the presence of another young man, as handsome as Claude Anet had been, but with the considerable advantage of being very much alive. He was called Wintzen-ried, Jean-Jacques learned, and he came from the romantic Château de Chillon where his father was the concierge, and where Wintzenried himself had carried on the profession of wigmaker. He was tall—which Jean-Jacques was not—blondish and, according to Jean-Jacques' prejudiced view, insipid, with a face as flat as his mind, and expressing himself with the vanity and insolence of a cock—which under the circumstances of his employment would prove rather advantageous qualities, considering the propensities of the fair chatelaine.

Seeing himself already doomed, Jean-Jacques tried to find comfort in the conviction that he himself was not much longer for this world. He had no fear of death but he was in terror of being forever damned. What was the condition of his soul? Would he be saved? Or was he to be doomed? He tried to find out by pitching stones against a tree trunk. If the stone hit the mark, then he was saved; if it did not, he was damned. Since he was no great marksman, he must have had his moments of anguish.

What, however, afflicted him more than his post-mortem condition was his present situation, for certainly he, who was so keen at finding meaning in all things, could not have been blind to the retributive justice of a Wintzenried serving him as he himself had served Claude Anet. Maman had made him feel that he was a man, capable of giving complete fulfillment to a woman; but now he found that he was being cast aside for another. Retributive justice? Perhaps. Yet deserved or not, it hurt. What was he doing there, where he was daily confronted with loss and humiliation? Besides, that polyp of the heart required attention. Wasn't there a specialist for just such conditions at Montpellier—a certain Monsieur Fizes that Claude Anet had told him about? Making up his little bundle once again, he was on his way on a fine morning in mid-September.

Two days later he wrote to Maman from Grenoble. Every-one had been kind to him, so kind indeed that he felt as if he were in another world. (Was it a reproach to the uncouth denizens of Chambéry for not appreciating the genius in their midst?) He had dined with a Monsieur Micoud in the company of other distinguished gentlemen, and in the evening, after enjoying a performance at the Comédie, he supped with Monsieur Lagère. Unfortunately he had been unable to see either Madame la Présidente or Monsieur le Président de Tencin, for they were in the country. As for Monsieur de l'Orme, Jean-Jacques had been able to deliver into his own hands the letter that Maman had written him. Monsieur de l'Orme had also given him an écu worth six francs, which out of modesty Jean-Jacques had felt compelled to accept; but on leaving the house he had given the money to the porter. He was no lackey; he would not crawl. "I don't know whether I did well," he wrote like Tartuffe, "but my soul would have to change its mold before I could decide to do otherwise." [4] Were there any other commissions that Maman had for him at Montpellier, where he would be going next? And would she take the trouble to write him, so that he would have news of her and not worry? "And please look after your health. Are you not my dear Maman? Have I not the right to take the liveliest interest in it?" [5]

As for his own health, it had been much shaken at the the-ater where they were showing *Alzire*—rather poorly, it is true, but still he was so much affected that he could not catch his breath. Indeed, his palpitations had been so violent that he feared he would be suffering the consequences for some time. "Why is it, Madame," he inquired, "that there are hearts so responsive to the grand, the sublime and the pathetic, while others seem to have been made only to crawl in the baseness of their own sentiments? . . . This accident has compelled me to renounce the tragic, until my health has been reëstab-lished. So here am I, deprived of a pleasure which has cost me many tears. . . ." [6] How sensitive! How divinely poetic!

Surely there was not another soul so sublime in the whole world.

That sublimity, however, was soon to suffer, or rather, enjoy a change as extraordinary as it was unexpected, considering the nature of his love for Maman. His feelings at the time made any adventure propitious, since he and Maman had had some little difference toward the end, so that their leave-taking had not been of the tenderest. This the gauche formality of his letters to her showed. Travel always lifted his spirits, however, so that as he got farther and farther away on the horse that he had engaged, he felt his energies renewed and the world become a place of excitement and adventure. The latter, as it was, had not been lacking since a certain Madame de Larnage and her pretty fifteen-year-old daughter had joined the traveling party of Mr. Dudding, the Englishman, into whom Jean-Jacques had transmogrified himself, thus acquiring the romantic character lacking in the undistinguished Rousseau.

Madame de Larnage, it appeared, was acting as chaperone to a newly married Madame du Colombier, considerably younger than herself, but of no interest whatever to Jean-Jacques, particularly in his role of Mr. Dudding. Perhaps Madame Colombier was too modest, and Jean-Jacques always enjoyed being the wooed, rather than the wooer. More likely Madame Colombier was also too much in love with her husband, to whom she was bringing her virginity, to take any notice of the youth. However it was, Mr. Dudding was well content. He had had the desired effect on Suzanne de Larnage and he knew that the consequences would be such as he devoutly wished and as the lady herself seemed to anticipate. If only her face had not been marred by the rouge she used. But then, what bold, sparkling eyes she had! Did he know then, or did he discover later, that she had borne her husband ten children? Well, what if she did not have the graces of springtime? She was still a desirable creature, ardent and generous, as he could see. Indeed, from the moment she had met his eyes there had been an unequivocal entente between them. If only Mr. Dudding had not been bothered by that bore of a Marquis de Taulignan—Jean-Jacques had understood the name as Taurignan—who insisted on questioning him on King James, on the Pretender, on English affairs, of which he knew exactly nothing. Luckily the Marquis did not think of addressing him in English, but even that worry ceased to trouble Rousseau-Dudding in the state in which Madame de Larnage had put him. Polyps of the heart? Shortness of breath and palpitations? Were these the cause of his agitation, his flushing, his turning hot and cold, and ardent again, as he met Madame de Larnage's all too eloquent looks?

Those looks did not belie her. What sort of young man was this, however, who flushed and looked away instead of seizing at the first opportunity the bounty so generously offered? True, they had not had the occasion as yet, but it would soon come. At a point along the journey they had to change chaises. Could she succeed in melting that English icicle before they reached Bourg-Saint-Andiol where she would have to leave the party? But that was still several days away. Some leagues farther at Saint-Marcellin, she had Jean-Jacques conduct her to Mass. Worse and worse! As she studied him from the corner of her eye and noted his devout mien and concentrated fervor, she knew that his guardian angel had the upper hand in that struggle between virtue and temptation. Madame de Larnage, however, was not one to give up, even against such odds—and, indeed, she had never encountered their like. Subtly, persistently, with a lingering look here, an inadvertent gesture there, she made her meaning as explicit as she could to that phlegmatic Englishman who still stood as firm as the rocks of Dover.

Miles later, at Valence, her desire egged on by pique, she resolved to get rid of Taulignan who had the gout and could not walk, and proposed a promenade to Mr. Dudding. They had become a little more familiar that morning, when they had had breakfast together, in the company of Madame Colombier. "He knows little of the world," he had heard Madame Colombier comment to Madame de Larnage, "but he is very nice." As praise never failed to go to his head, he was more than favorably disposed toward the woman who found some virtue in him. But it was Madame de Larnage who made the overtures.

They took their walk, Mr. Dudding not relaxing for a moment his assumed British reserve. Instead of falling back discouraged, Madame de Larnage, like a general before great odds, only strengthened her attack and from words went on to deeds; but the more she caressed him the more certain he became that she was merely playing. Still his vanity, if not his heart, was finally touched and before long Madame de Larnage had her triumph which, to his amazement, he wholeheartedly shared. For the first time he was enjoying to the full the uninhibited sexual act, simple, generous, uncomplicated. Completely a woman, unselfish and wholehearted, Madame de Larnage had more than passion to offer him—appreciation of his masculine pride, tenderness, gratitude. As for Jean-Jacques, he found himself suddenly very much in love with her. "If this were only real," he sighed, "I would be the happiest of men."

Their idyl lasted five days. Rousseau never forgot it, nor the woman who had fulfilled him as a man. "With Maman my pleasure was always troubled by a feeling of sadness, a secret heartache that I could not overcome. . . . Instead of congratulating myself that I possessed her, I reproached myself for debasing her. With Madame de Larnage, however, proud of being a man, and happy, I yielded to my senses with joy, with confidence. I shared the effect that I had upon hers. I was sufficiently myself to contemplate my triumph with as much vanity as voluptuousness and to derive from it the means of redoubling it. . . . Oh, those three days! (He had shortened the interval in his reminiscence.) I have had occasion to long for them at times. Never again have I had their like." [7]

Madame de Larnage had affected him so powerfully that he could think only of her and of the life they would have together at Saint-Andiol, where she had her handsome property. And there was that adorable fifteen-year-old daughter. How she would love him, her Maman's good friend! His imagination soared to ecstatic heights, transcended only by the sight of the Pont du Gard at Nîmes, the magnificent Roman bridge whose grandeur was all the more impressive in the surrounding solitude. "Ah, why was I not born a Roman!" he sighed as he stood there for hours, unable to tear himself away from that magnificent scene. He rejoined the waiting company in a reverie that was not favorable to Madame de Larnage. She had thought to warn him against the girls of Montpellier, but not against the Pont du Gard and its evocation of grandeur.

By that time, however, his dormant conscience had awakened as passion began to feel surfeited. He had his duty toward Maman, so good, so generous—and alas, so overwhelmed with debts, yet paying the expenses of his "cure" even now, though doubtless from the inheritance he had laid at her feet. No, he could not be so base toward the one being who really loved him. The party was nearing Saint-Andiol. Instead of stopping there with the rest, he went on his way, feeling as heroic as a general after a hard-won battle. He was worthy of his own esteem, he told himself with pride—for had he not preferred duty to pleasure?

8. *The orchard of Madame de Warens*

At Montpellier where he expected his cure to be prolonged
and arduous, Jean-Jacques took lodgings in the rue Basse with
an usher of the Exchange, Monsieur Marceron; but he was not
there long, thinking it wiser in his valetudinarian condition to
be where help was right at hand. He went to lodge, therefore,
with two specialists, Monsieur Fitz-Morris, an Irishman, and
his associate, Monsieur Fizes—of whom Claude Anet had
spoken. There he eloquently described his polyp in grim detail
—after all, had he not been its host for months?—and begged
them to rid him of it and restore him to health. The doctors
tapped him, listened to his heartbeat, his pulse, and lent their
ears to his complaints. His graphic account over, the patient
waited pathetically for the words of doom to issue from the
doctors' lips. What was his dismay when the hearty Irishman
patted him on the shoulder and said, laughing: "Do me a
favor, my friend, and drink a good glass of wine from time to

time." Knowing his patient, however, he also prescribed a number of harmless panaceas, curative waters and a simple diet.

Long-faced and pathetic, Jean-Jacques pursued his regimen, with little improvement, indeed, since there was small occasion for it. Fitz-Morris then suggested that his patient attend his anatomy classes. He would learn a great deal about the human animal and he might perhaps discover some latent genius for medicine. Jean-Jacques was easily persuaded. Already he saw himself another Aesculapius. However, after a session or two he became so sick from the stench of the cadavers for dissection that he gave up all thought of medicine. He enjoyed the company of his fellow students, however, and scattered his few louis for his pleasure and theirs. As for his career, he was accomplishing absolutely nothing.

While he still had some money left, he contemplated his next step. Two roads opened before him, one leading to Chambéry and Maman with, alas, Monsieur de Courtilles (Wintzenried's newly assumed name) permanently installed in his place, and the other to Saint-Andiol, lusty Madame de Larnage and her budding nymph of a daughter. Now Jean-Jacques was a man of conscience, but he was also human; hence his quandary was not without its moral struggle. Pleasure pointed to Saint-Andiol; duty inflexibly to Chambéry.

"Am I, as a reward to the mother for her goodness toward me—am I going to try to corrupt the daughter, to establish the most detestable relationship, bringing dissension, dishonor, scandal and hell into her household?" The prospect filled him with horror; but it was a typical twist in his logic that convinced him. "Why expose myself to this struggle? What wretchedness to live with the mother, of whom I would be surfeited, and to burn for the daughter without daring to reveal my heart to her!" What was the sense of exposing himself to trouble, affronts, remorse, for pleasures whose charm had already vanished? There, on the other hand, was that wonderful Maman, so good, so generous, who, though saddled with debts, had the double charge of his foolish expenses—that dear Maman who was doing everything possible for him, while he deceived her so shamefully. But De Courtilles! He must not forget that *blondin,* who had literally usurped his bed and board. Alas, that there should always be a fly in the ointment— and such a fly! Perhaps there was more than onomatopoeia in the nickname of the blond one—Zizi.

Conscious of his almost empty pockets, his thoughts reverted more and more to Chambéry and that dear Maman who had never failed him. He wrote to her in his most cajoling vein, but he received no answer. He wrote again and yet again, and on the twenty-third of October that year of 1737, tried to reach her once more by three different routes, emphasizing his des- perate need but dwelling even more eloquently on the concern which her silence was causing him. Certainly his situation was none of the pleasantest—"But I protest with the utmost sin- cerity, Madame, that my deepest concern derives from the fear that something might have happened to you. . . ." Even more, it was occasioned by the proximity and the attractions of his rival, who had supplanted him more thoroughly than he knew. "If I don't hear from you," he closed pathetically, "I shall be obliged to leave in the greatest disorder and try to reach Cham- béry as best I can." [1]

Well, let him come back for Saint-John's feast day, Maman answered nonchalantly. Saint-John's! That would be in 1738, eight months away! The thought set wings to his feet. Eight months! "You exhort me, Madame, to remain here until Saint- John's," he went on. "I will not do it, even if I should be cov- ered with gold!" A little later he wrote again. If he could only go on living close to her he would not care, whatever the cir- cumstances. When a man thought as he did, it was not difficult to elude the reasons that she did not mention. "In God's name, manage things so that I shall not die of despair. I approve of everything; I submit to everything. . . . Ah, my dear Maman —are you then no longer my dear Maman? Have I then lived a few months too long?" He had evidence of that in Maman's tepid and infrequent letters. As if he had not justified himself enough he added a postscript. "Whenever I act, I think I am doing the most beautiful things in the world, and then it turns out that they're only so much foolishness. . . ." [2] In December, he added, he thought of going to Provence to drink asses' milk, but he needed two hundred livres to cover expenses.

Maman let him chew his fingernails to the quick before she sent the money—she who had always anticipated his every whim before he uttered it. No doubt about it. The influence of that *blondin* had almost canceled Petit from her mind. Concerned, jealous and hurt in his pride, Jean-Jacques nevertheless did not act impulsively but made the best of the situation. Maman had another reason for not wanting him to be about just then. She was making arrangements to move to a larger and pleasanter house belonging to a Monsieur Noiret and she hoped to be installed in the new domicile by Saint-John's.

Jean-Jacques, who now that he was on his way was impatient to arrive, wrote to Maman from Valence, giving her the exact day and hour when she might expect him back. It was a long-established habit, from his many wanderings. It forewarned Maman and also gave her ample time to plan a suitable welcome and a banquet for the prodigal. Full of anticipation, pricked also by the thought of the *blondin* and the position that by this time he might have usurped, the traveler gave spur to his impatience. The weather was cold and wintry. Leaving the carriage, he scanned the road to the house, his heart beating in anticipation of Maman coming out to meet him. There was no one on the road, no one in the courtyard; no one at the door or at the windows. What had happened? Was there no one at home? Were they all dead?

He was reassured when he came upon a group of laborers eating in the kitchen. For the rest, there seemed to be no preparation whatsoever. Indeed, the servants stared at him in astonishment. He flew up to Maman's room, panting. Was she ill, his *chère Maman?* He burst into her chamber—and there she was, as cool and composed as if he had just come in from the next room. Eagerly he flung himself at her feet. She had him rise, then she kissed him, quite casually. "Ah, there you are, Petit!" she said, as if he had never been away. "Did you have a pleasant journey? How are you?"

"Did you not receive my letter?" he asked in turn, taken aback by her offhand manner.

"Yes," she replied.

"I would have thought you had not," he said, his tone chilling on the appearance of De Courtilles. One glance sufficed Jean-Jacques to know that he had been in every way supplanted. How he hated the fellow's "Leander" looks—and even more the affectation of his speech. Soon he had to swallow the *blondin*'s boasting of the many women he had gone to bed with, many of them *marquises*. "This was the substitute they found during my absence," he commented bitterly to himself. "This is the compaion they're offering me on my return." [3]

He felt hurt and betrayed after his valiant effort to make something of himself to please Maman. In his righteous indignation he chose to forget Mr. Dudding's interlude with Madame de Larnage. After all, it had not been the same thing—it was all passion with no poetry in it. With Maman it had been a glorious rite, an initiation into manhood, an incestuous connection, almost, such as the gods, above good and evil, had enjoyed. But there was De Courtilles, as sleek and replete as a favored tomcat. How could she have supplanted him, Jean-Jacques, so completely and so soon? He had to admit, however, that De Courtilles, for zeal and accomplishment, was worth ten of himself, Jean-Jacques. A Jack-of-all-trades, he stopped at nothing and was everywhere at once; at the planting, at the haying, in the stables, in the woods. The only occupation he did not care for was gardening—and that, said Jean-Jacques with a touch of spleen, was because it did not make very much noise. "Maman thought him a treasure for her affairs," he said. "In the hope of attaching him to herself she employed all the means she thought proper, not forgetting the one on which she counted most." [4]

As for himself, he had long ceased to desire Fanie—as Mr. Dudding, the Englishman, he had anglicized her name of Françoise, pronouncing it Fahnée. "Our being so long accustomed to living together, and innocently, far from enfeebling my sentiments toward her, had strengthened them; but at the same time it had given them another aspect—more affectionate, perhaps more tender, but less sensual." [5] Even earlier, during the incumbency of Claude Anet, Jean-Jacques had learned to share her—but then it had been more difficult since it was his first experience of such sharing. "We lived in a union that gave happiness to all of us and which only death was able to destroy. A proof of the excellent qualities of this lovable woman was that all who loved her loved one another." [6] He had somehow to gloss over the whole unpleasant business. Time and his imagination, mellowed by sentiment, made confession easier for the old Rousseau when he was setting down his reminiscences.

For the youth of 1738 to 1739, sensibility and imagination were the anodyne. Facts were facts, unpleasant actualities which he had to accept; but in accepting, he could also modify them for himself and perhaps even for the world. He had for some time been trying his hand at verse. He would treat in that exalted medium the idyl of his life with Maman by celebrating *Le verger des Charmettes.* Surely no one could find anything amiss in such a poem.

Verger cher à mon coeur, séjour de l'innocence,
Honnoeur des plus beaux jours que le ciel me dispense,
Solitude charmante, asyle de la paix,
Puissé-je, heureux verger, ne vous quitter jamais. . . .

Through two hundred and thirty verses he celebrated that orchard dear to his heart, that charming solitude where peace dwelt, the plaint of Philomela among the branches, the murmur of the running brook. Oh, foolish mankind, with your frivolous taste and your tumultuous days, he pitied from his height. Such a life did not arouse any desire in him to imitate it. *His* were simpler yet loftier pleasures, whether he rose early to watch the sunrise gild the hill, or whether in the heat of noon he shielded himself from its fierce rays beneath the shade of a leafy tree. There, reading his Montaigne or his La Bruyère, he could well afford to smile at the miserable human lot—miserable but for one.

> *And you, Warens most wise, Minerva's pupil fair,*
> *These transports, ah! forgive, for their too reckless air!*
> *Yet had I ever sworn never to venture rhyme,*
> *Still would I dare to sing your virtuous gifts sublime.*
> *Ay, if my heart now joys in this most tranquil state,*
> *If now on pleasant paths I follow Virtue's gait,*
> *If in these realms I savor such sweet and guileless balm,*
> *To you alone I owe so fair and rare a calm.*
> *In vain have hearts most base, and mean minds bent on gain,*
> *Sought in a hundred ways to wrest me from your reign;*
> *What guess they of the joy, the happiness you know*
> *In wiping tears away, in healing human woe?*
> *Of Titus and of Trajan—their gifts and bounties free,*
> *What stir they in such hearts but scornful mockery? . . .*
> *Oh, let them as they will indulge their horrid way;*
> *For me, I shall not go and seek their favor—nay,*
> *I shall not go and crawl, their pleasure to obtain—*
> *My heart at need will face all misery and pain. . . .*[7]

It was years since he had told his father that he would never crawl, but he had crawled again and again. He was crawling even now to maintain himself in the good graces of the mistress (in a double sense) to whom he owed his keep. In his poem he scattered praise with a lavish pen, for it was the only compensation, besides his services as bedfellow and some of the duties he had assumed after Claude Anet's death, that he could give her. Well might he write of her:

> *Oh, you who my young years yourself bound to arouse*
> *To knowledge . . .*

You who shaped my heart to virtue,
You whom I dare call by the tender name of Mother . . .
Virtuous Warens, through you I obtain
A man's true bliss and all its solid gain. . . .

The allusion to Madame de Warens was meant, of course, to silence the tongues that had been wagging in that little village where everyone busied himself with his neighbor's affairs. Indeed, further on in the poem he became more explicit about the risk his protectress might incur if the gossip reached the ears of her protector, the King of Sardinia. But that would never be.

This great king honors you; he knows your loyal zeal
And to his noble word he always has been leal;
But to leave nought unsaid, your heart will whisper true
And make for answer this: He owes them all to you.

He was very proud of the poem "published in London by the house of Jacob Tomson" he told all and sundry, though in truth it had been merely printed. But one must set a value on one's works, for nobody else will—or so he reasoned. Therefore, not content to let the poem speak for itself, like all tyros he had to attach a note in praise of his benefactress and an apologia for himself—"a sick man, two inches from the grave." What ailed him he did not state explicitly, but people in his confidence, which meant everyone with a sympathetic ear, had to listen endlessly to his accounts of the suffering caused him by that nonexistent parasite feeding on his heart.

Employing the full diapason of misery to obtain consideration as well as pity, he had succeeded not long after Anet's death in enjoying more leisure for his own thinking, reading and writing. It was Maman who had been straining for freedom, especially since the advent of Courtilles. It seemed to make little difference to her that he, Jean-Jacques, could compose, write verse and prose, conduct an orchestra, make agreeable conversation, help her in her affairs and be the factotum and chief attraction at her entertainments. De Courtilles obviously possessed some charm that he himself lacked, or no longer provided. He was still invaluable to Maman as her secretary, however, and as her moral guide, for he had always composed her morning prayers, thanking God for all the blessings, including the "union" with him. There were no such prayers for her now, but he did write one for himself, full of contrition, resignation, self-accusation.

"I feel there are no true pleasures save those one experiences in the exercise of virtue. . . . Accept my repentance, O my God. . . . Henceforth all my actions will I refer to Thee. I shall meditate upon Thee and bless Thee and serve Thee and fear Thee. . . . I shall resist temptation and live in purity; I shall be temperate and moderate in all things, and I shall allow myself only those pleasures authorized by virtue. Most of all I shall repress my anger and impatience and I shall endeavor to be gentle toward everyone. . . . From the bottom of my heart I shall always forgive those who may offend me, as I forgive from this moment and unreservedly, all those who could have given me any offense. . . . And I shall prepare myself for death . . . and await it without fear, as that instant which will deliver me from the subjection of the body and join with Thee forever." [8]

Not that Jean-Jacques really feared an early demise; it was simply much more romantic to think of oneself as so talented, so young and so doomed. As a piece of writing it was infinitely better than the poem. The lines had dignity and a fine solemnity tolling through the unconscious measure. Also there was no posturing. The language sprang from emotion, a solemn emotion this time, and that mood ennobled the lines. He had not struck an individual note in his poetry, indeed he never did strike it; but there were intimations of it in his prose.

Meanwhile Maman, getting more deeply involved in her amours, found Petit's presence increasingly embarrassing, much as she enjoyed, more through vanity than literary appreciation, having herself and her orchard celebrated in verse. He was no longer an adolescent, for that June of 1740 he would be twenty-eight years old. His tasks, such as they were, had by this time been delegated elsewhere, for besides De Courtilles there were a number of other servants and lackeys—Bernard Dumoulin who had been reprimanded for stealing several measures of chestnuts, and a certain Claude Cende whose pockets, too, had been found stuffed—this time with nine pieces of bread weighing about a pound, a rosary which he claimed as his own, some beans in another pocket, and a leather purse containing twenty-one sous. The judges at that improvised trial had been Courtilles and Rousseau. Surely the memory of a certain stolen ribbon must have stirred the conscience of one of the judges.

Knowing that henceforth his days with Maman were numbered, Jean-Jacques nevertheless could not tear himself away, despite his ever present humiliation before the favored Courtilles, so favored, indeed, that he, Jean-Jacques, had had on one occasion to apologize to him. "Since you found that I was in the wrong," he wrote to Maman, "I must necessarily have been; so, without any chicanery, I wholeheartedly made my apologies to my brother and I herewith do the same, by offering them to you most humbly. . . . You also sent word that on your birthday you would forgive me . . . but I am certain that when a heart such as yours has loved anyone as much as I remember having been loved by yours, it is impossible to arrive at such bitterness that religious considerations have to be dragged in for a reconciliation. . . ." [9] He smarted also at the inequity in the way Maman dispensed justice, punishing him, Jean-Jacques, often unjustly and forgiving the *blondin* everything, even his betraying her with the chambermaids.

He felt ill. He was so short of breath that his father, learning of his condition, wrote to him from Nyon with unusual concern, attributing Jean-Jacques' ill health, however, to his chemical experiments—rewarding enough in their way, he said, but most assuredly not profitable. Maman, for reasons of her own, shared Isaac's views; but more enterprising than the father, set

to work to remedy the situation. Writing to her many connections, she recommended Jean-Jacques highly, though of course
not in the field she knew best. Her efforts were rewarded.
There was a very promising post for him at Lyon, as preceptor
to the children of Monsieur de Mably, Grand Provost of the
town.

By this time Jean-Jacques was as eager to leave as Maman
was anxious to let him go. He was hurt as a lover and even
more as a man. Somehow, somewhere, he had failed if Maman
could prefer that vapid puppet to himself. Yet he lingered on
in his love of self-torment and humiliation. It was still sweet to
enjoy the morning ritual of their early cup of coffee together in
the new day; still delightful to feed the pigeons; still exciting
to make plans for profitable enterprises, such as the establishment of a diligence service linking France, Switzerland, Germany and then, crossing Mont-Cenis, onward toward Piedmont. Surely the King of Sardinia would encourage the project.
His Majesty could not have cared less, however, and the plan
died almost as soon as it was conceived.

Did Jean-Jacques notice how Maman had changed through
the years they had been together? She was still fresh and rosy,
but alas, there was so much of her that she could scarcely carry
her weight about. She also had financial worries, for nothing
she undertook now seemed to succeed, from the cultivation of
flax to that plan for a diligence service, which was not even
given a chance. Well, at least Petit would have the opportunity
to prove himself. Thanks to that ambitious educational plan
which he, Maman and the Jesuit Fathers had drawn up together, Jean-Jacques could not fail to impress Monsieur de
Mably.

Jean-Jacques, however, felt that he owed his employer a fore-
warning of his unusual nature and he drew up a candid analy-
sis of himself, not omitting an air of constraint and embarrassment, a plain, unornamented manner of speech, a shyness both
idiotic and ridiculous. Furthermore he had an unconquerable
predisposition to melancholy. "I carry within me a source of

sadness whose origin I cannot fathom," he confessed. "I have almost always lived in solitude, for a long time infirm and ailing . . . with a keen sensibility in a soul which has never been exposed to anything but sorrow, and always carrying within my breast my own sufferings and those of all who are dear to me. . . ." [10]

On the delicate subject of his remuneration and his keep he wrote to an intermediary, Monsieur d'Eybens. After all, he was no lackey—still that concern!—and therefore he expected suitable consideration. Money meant very little to him, he wrote, but he was very much alive to the treatment that was owing to an honorable man maltreated by fortune yet devoted to his duties. He would deem himself amply rewarded, he declared, if esteem and consideration supplemented the remuneration. However, he cautioned, it would be folly to imagine that any man whose heart was warped by poverty or harsh treatment could inspire noble or generous feelings in his pupils.

Monsieur de Mably was no doubt impressed by such sentiments, for he engaged him. The acceptance of what he had to offer—of himself, in short—at once touched the spring of tender sentiments always ready to gush for the enchantment of the listening heart. He was leaving a cherished Maman with whom he had passed the happiest years of his life, loved by her, instructed by her in what it meant to be a man and in the duties that he owed to his fellow creatures. Yes, he was leaving a mother, but he would perhaps find a father. Certainly it was this desire that he expressed to Monsieur de Mably, while proposing at the same time to act the part of respectful son toward him. Then he poured out the well-rehearsed litany of his afflictions: taken in infancy from his own country, he had nobody on earth but a benefactress, a mother by adoption. Thus, besides what he owed to her virtues and her benefactions, he would bring to the Mably household the sentiments of zeal and affection which nature and friendship ordinarily enfeeble in other men by dispersing them among too many objects. That, certainly, should impress Monsieur de Mably.

It did, for on the twentieth of April, 1740, while spring was lavishing its blossoms on the orchard and scattering wild-flowers over the grass, Jean-Jacques took his last long lingering look at the beloved scene and, moved by the memory of the nightingales that had filled his last night with their song, departed for Lyon. First he stopped off at Grenoble to thank the d'Eybens, and then he wrote to Maman, bidding her take care of her health and also of the library. Magnanimously he sent his heartiest greeting to his rival, now in full possession of Maman and Les Charmettes. But a new life was opening up before him and he thrived on change. Still he inquired ruefully as of a beloved being: "How is Les Charmettes doing?"

Now that he was leaving it, perhaps forever, he saw it as a place of enchantment where he had spent the happiest years of his life, though with a more realistic vision he could not but see it as a house which, like its owner, had known better days and was slowly sinking toward ruin. Could he have done anything to save it he would have stayed on and lent himself to any scheme that would have served the purpose, so close did he feel to *his* orchard, *his* garden, *his* trees. Most of all it was Maman's presence that haunted him and often, when about to fall asleep at night, he would start at the tender "Petit" whispered in his ear.

He had always thought of himself as an excellent teacher and, indeed, had not done badly whenever he had undertaken to instruct. The two young devils of Monsieur de Mably, however, seemed to have been sent from the infernal regions to disabuse him of any such confidence. The elder, the nine-year-old Sainte-Marie, was a handsome boy, gay, charming and full of fun; but nothing in the world would make him admit that he could learn anything. In vain Jean-Jacques reasoned with him, pleaded, implored or sought to arouse some human emotion in him. At the end of all his efforts it was the master who was in tears, while the pupil looked on with an air of triumph. As for little Condillac, named after his uncle the philosopher, he heard nothing, responded to nothing and showed no emotion until he had driven Monsieur Rousseau into a fury, at which point the child would look up at him with pitying tolerance.

The poor tutor fared no better with Madame de Mably, with whom he had hoped to reach at least a sentimental understanding. Nothing of the kind. She had expected to find in her sons' instructor a sort of major-domo as well, but when she saw how awkward, how shy and inept he was, how lacking in social grace, she would have nothing to do with him—a procedure which, of course, made Jean-Jacques fancy himself ardently in love with her. He relieved his inevitable frustrations by having little feasts of wine and brioche by himself in his room. Not that he did not get enough to eat; but these small treats he found more delectable than any banquet.

Since he could not offend the lady of the house by asking for brioche—as if she did not feed him sufficiently—he would set out in the evening to obtain a small supply, taking care to go to a remote part of town so that nobody he knew would see him. What! A gentleman with a sword at his side, a member of Monsieur de Mably's household, buying brioche for himself? Shocking! Anyway, he often ranged the town to get it, amusing himself by a recondite bit of knowledge he had acquired somewhere, about a great princess who, when told that the peasants had no bread, suggested: "Let them eat brioche!" Hence Marie Antoinette, years later, was not the originator of that advice always attributed to her.

His stay at Monsieur de Mably's was not wholly unproductive for with his customary thoroughness, which made him learn by teaching, Rousseau wrote a long essay, *"Projet pour l'éducation de M. de Sainte-Marie,"* more than a foreshadowing of his later *Emile*. The teacher of young Sainte-Marie had taken his first step toward becoming, in his particular way, the teacher of humanity.

9. *From Les Charmettes to Paris*

One day in August, 1740, Jean-Jacques received a package from Maman at the Mablys'. It was a large silver vase which she wanted him to sell for perhaps five louis. He managed to have Madame de Mably buy it, at a bargain for four-and-a-half. He sent Maman the money, adding somewhat more from his own earnings. But one could never outdo Maman in generosity. She sent him back several dozen fine linen nightshirts. They were so beautiful that he complained of her extravagance. Why had she not had them made of rough homespun, without trimmings? But they would not be wasted. He would wear them in the daytime.

If his emotions and his always susceptible heart suffered in the cold intellectuality of the Mably household, his mind and his manners were the gainers, though he was never free of constraint and a sense of ineptitude before the Abbé Mably and the philosopher and linguist, Condillac. Unconsciously his intellect was absorbing the theories and ideas floating in the philosophical atmosphere of the time, as manifested in Marie Huber's *La religion essentielle,* which assuredly was to color the faith of Rousseau's Savoyard Vicar many years later and help to clarify the theories of *The Social Contract.* It is not unlikely that the seeds of those works may have been planted at this time in a mind which retained forever all that impressed itself upon it.

Valiantly, meanwhile, he struggled to get out of himself, to be with others, to resemble them; to long less for the past and to build himself a future. The tie to Maman, however, was still too strong. Everything carried him back to the only real happiness, the only security he had ever known, and he longed for it like the orphan that he was. No sooner did the first April blossoms begin to open than the enchantment of Les Charmettes came irresistibly before him—the first periwinkle, which would send him and Maman into ecstasies; the showers of petals from the flowering orchards, the choir of hidden singers among the branches, the nest building, the cooing and fluttering in the dovecotes. The memories were too much for him. Impulsively he left everything—his pupils, Madame de Mably, and set out for the one place that for him had been and remained home.

It was as beautiful as ever in the full glory of spring, so very beautiful that even he who saw with the eyes of memory and imagination could not avoid perceiving the contrast between all that fresh loveliness and the ponderous torpidity of Maman. The pity of it made him love her all the more, for his senses no longer obfuscated the heart. There was now a gentleness in her, a peace of the spirit, which gave depth to her thought and meaning to her life. God was no awesome abstraction but a kindly Providence, a tender Father above all dogma, cherishing his creatures and pointing to the wide-open gates of salvation. Before her gentle faith Jean-Jacques felt almost ashamed of his philosophical boasts drawn from Descartes and bolstered by

Locke. For a while, at least, he returned to the simple religion of his boyhood.

Again, possessed with divine fervor, he composed prayers for Maman, as he had done before. They were loftier now and less simple, like life itself, which expanded and grew complex according to the scale of one's experience. Each prayer was an invocation uttered in the near presence of the Almighty, and often it was Jean-Jacques speaking for himself as for mankind. "Eternal Father, my heart is uplifted in Thy presence. . . . My conscience tells me how sinful I am. I am filled with regret that I have made such ill use of the life and the liberty Thou didst grant me that I might have the means to make myself worthy of eternal bliss. Accept my repentance, O my God. . . . I shall bear in mind that Thou art witness to all my actions and I shall endeavor to do nothing unworthy of Thine August Presence. I implore the same grace, O my God, for my dear Maman, my dear benefactress, and for my father. Grant them, Father of Mercy, all the help they need; forgive them the ill they have done, inspire them toward the good they must do, and grant them the strength to fulfill the duties of their condition and those others that Thou dost exact from them. Remember in general all my benefactors. Let fall upon them all the good they have done me. Grant the succor of Thy divine benedictions to all my friends, to my country and to the human race in general; remember, O my God, that I shall be indulgent toward others and severe toward myself. I shall resist temptation and I shall live in purity; I shall be temperate and moderate in all things and I shall allow myself no pleasures except those authorized by virtue. . . . I shall prepare myself for death as for that day when I shall be accountable to Thee for all my actions, and I shall await it without fear as that instant which will deliver me from the subjection of the body, and join me with Thee forever. . . . Remember, O my God, that Thou art the common Father of all mankind and have pity on us in the fullness of Thy mercy." Almost Jean-Jacques was telling the Almighty how to run his universe.

Fiercely proud, with a pride that became exacerbated whenever he felt himself consciously or unconsciously humiliated,
he employed all the resources of his wit and his already remarkable style to heal the hurt and punish the offender. A
neighbor of Maman's, a Madame de Sourgel, had thought to
help the young man whom she mistook for a lackey, by sending
him a castoff *justaucorps,* a coat that fit the body and came
down to the knees. Feeling that the recipient had not been
sufficiently grateful, Madame de Sourgel made some remark
about it which precipitated an avalanche of words on the part
of Rousseau, who, stung as he was by the gift he had not
sought, was doubly humiliated by its having been made the
subject of gossip. First of all he gave the lady to understand
that her advances had never been sought or desired either by
Madame de Warens or by himself, so that the "crawling" of
both Madame de Sourgel and her daughter had had quite the
opposite effect upon individuals who despised such a procedure.

"Now for that famous *justaucorps,* which together with myself holds so honorable a place in your letter; I have the honor
to tell you, Madame, with all the respect due you, that I never
dreamed of accepting your present, no matter in what state of
abasement fortune had chosen to place me. I am more circum-
spect than that in the choice of my benefactors. Indeed, I
would have fine matter for mockery in describing this superb
garment, already turned inside out and remade, full of grease
spots and in such a condition that, in short, all my modesty
would have been at great pains to make me wear such a thing.
I am in a position to prove what I say and to exhibit this
trophy of your generosity; it is still there, in the same ward-
robe that contains these precious effects of which you make so
pompous a display. . . . As for myself, Madame, though you
presume to speak of me in an equivocal tone, I have, if you
please, the honor of informing you that, while I have not that
of being known to you, I am nevertheless known to a great
number of persons of merit and distinction who know that I

have the honor of being the adopted son of Madame la Baronne de Warens, who has had the goodness to raise me and inspire me with a sense of right and a probity worthy of her. . . ." [1] *That* for Madame de Sourgel and her sister gossips.

Meanwhile his curious genius, refusing to be confined to any one art, ranged through Parnassus. He had always flirted with music but being largely self-taught he had had no guide through the stumbling blocks along his way except for Rameau's *Treatise on Harmony*. What labor to follow the complexities of composition, with only those little black notes! How much more simple to use numbers instead. Accordingly he devised his system, *Projet concernant de nouveaux signes pour la musique,* hoping to revolutionize the musical world. The new signs for the notes of the scale would simply be numerals: 1, 2, 3, 4, 5, 6, 7 for *ut, re, mi, fa, sol, la, si,* and on that basis he built his new method. The *Projet,* however, was merely an introduction explaining his use of the substitute symbols. Later would follow a *Dissertation on Modern Music,* preceded by its own preface—for Jean-Jacques was nothing if not thorough. Meanwhile he collected as illustrations well-known pieces, such as the *"Menuet de Dardanus"* and a Trio arrangement of the Milanese Carillon, whose Italian text—strange forerunner of Poe's "The Bells"—"rang for mourning, *din don don don,* rang for joy, *dan di, ra, din.* . . ." [2]

His work completed, he proposed to submit it to the Académie des Sciences. For that, it was imperative of course to go to the capital. Again the prospect of fame and fortune shimmered before him, dazzling not only himself but Maman. This time, however, he had something tangible upon which to base his hopes. Disappointment had taught him humility; hence when he prepared to leave Les Charmettes, it was not as a conqueror of fortune but as a suppliant to the Supreme Power of the Universe. "Being of Beings," he invoked. "Be propitious to me. Cast upon me the eye of commiseration. Look into my heart. It is pure, without crime. I place all my faith in Thy sublime Beauty, all my cares in absorbing Thine immensity, Thy Grandeur, Thine Eternity. Without fear I await that mandate which will part me from mankind. Speak: end my life and I am ready to appear on the Steps of Thy throne, there to receive the destiny Thou didst promise on granting me life. . . ."

He was in a creative mood and everything inspired him to write or compose, from an opera, *The Discovery of the New World,* in which he exercised both talents, to verses which he copied in a notebook, oddly entitled *The Works of Tom Thumb.* One long poem, "To Fanie," was his grateful offering to Maman, who, greater than Aesculapius, had delivered him from the horrors of Tartarus and restored him to life, astonishing even the God of the Underworld. Another poem, a *virelai* also addressed to Maman, celebrated, of all things, the capture of four rats. But then, that was no small achievement in a day when plagues of rodents were not unknown. Therefore well could he sing:

> *Madame, pray you, hear me tell*
> *How four rats were trapped and taken,*
> *Four rats, no mere bagatelle . . .*

and so on, mock-heroically for a score of lines. It was as if his whole being, charged with more creativeness than it could contain, released itself in minor explosions before the major outburst, although each, as it occurred, convinced its creator that it was true Jovian thunder.

Pricked by ambition, nothing in his life now pleased him. Nature itself lost its magic. He felt strangely isolated, even with Maman, who for so long had been the center of his life. He longed for new places, other worlds, where he could give expression to the thoughts teeming within him. He was poor, and the prizes of the world were for the rich, his observation told him. He resented the injustice—but what could he do to remedy it? Others had tried, but always, as he wrote in an epistle in verse to a friend of his, Bordes:

Oppressed by hunger, low must merit lie,
And in its saddened heart will let all virtue die.

Nonetheless, boldly he determined to assail the capital of French culture, Paris, which had fostered so many noble minds. With fifteen gold louis in his pocket, his comedy of *Narcisse,* and his ambitious project of publicizing his new system of notation, he set out, confident of fame and fortune. He had a number of recommendations in his favor, he told himself, among them an agreeable appearance and talents to reënforce it. However, he counted more on a sheaf of letters of introduction which he had obtained at Lyon, thanks to the influence of the Abbé de Mably's brother: letters from Fontenelle himself, from Père Castel and one even from Monsieur de Boze, who as Secretary of the Academy of Inscriptions had contact with the Maréchal de Richelieu himself. Humbler and equally generous friends were not lacking, like that kindly Monsieur Perrichon, a friend of Maman's who paid for his place in the diligence. While at Lyon he called on Madame de Mably, who invited him to dine on several occasions.

Before leaving that city he sold his geometry books which he had brought with him and then called on the famous surgeon, Parisot and his wife, "the gentle Godefroi," as Jean-Jacques called her. "Nothing is more revealing of the true leanings of a man than the nature of his attachments. When one had seen the gentle Godefroi, one knew the good Parisot." [3]

Perhaps to fathom his own true nature he went to call once again on his boyhood love, Suzanne Serre, whom he saw with more pleasure than ever and who left him with the tenderest memories. "My heart was smitten, and very keenly, and I had some reason to think that hers was not averse; but she let me into a secret which overcame my temptation to take any advantage of it. She had nothing; neither had I. Our situations were too similar for us to bind ourselves. Besides, with the views I then held, I was far removed from any thought of marriage." [4]

Not long afterward Mademoiselle Serre introduced him to a Monsieur Genève. Magnanimously Jean-Jacques, after studying him the few times they were together, admitted that he was a good man and, assured that Mademoiselle Serre would be happy with him, urged him to marry her, which the gentleman obligingly did. Jean-Jacques in the role of Hymen congratulated himself on his noble self-sacrifice. Not wishing to trouble their innocent love, he unselfishly hastened his departure. Alas, it was an unnecessary sacrifice, for death, less considerate than the young lover, snatched the bride from her husband's arms after a brief interval of happiness. "However costly the sacrifices one makes to duty," the rejected lover philosophized, "one is well repaid by the sweet memories they leave within one's heart." [5]

They were memories, however, colored by hurt pride and the still smarting vanity of the rejected lover, who soon after that visit sent a letter to Mademoiselle Serre—a letter which she kept and which was later published. Far from welcoming his visit with tender emotion, as he maintained, she had not only received him coldly but repulsed him "with incredible harshness," he complained, despite his assurances that he had left Les Charmettes solely to see her again. He had also committed the unforgivable breach of telling her point-blank that he knew perfectly well she had rejected him because of other liaisons, particularly with "that lucky mortal" whom she was overwhelming with her favors. Certainly anyone even far less virtuous than this chaste Suzanne would have sent such an outspoken gallant packing.

Though wounded, Jean-Jacques' heart was not broken, and even that lesion, more to his vanity than to his self-esteem, eventually healed, especially when he succeeded in convincing himself that he had nobly relinquished his own happiness for the sake of Mademoiselle Serre's. But he would soon be once more in the French capital, that Mecca of the ambitious.

"I arrived in Paris in the Autumn of 1741," he noted in his remimiscences, mistaking the time by a year; for until July

1742, except for brief absences, he was still at Les Charmettes. In his earlier visit he had really seen little of the metropolis, and then only through eyes still dazzled by the beauty of Turin, which his memory had exalted all the more as he meandered through the narrow stinking alleys of the Faubourg Saint-Marceau. Then, too, he had come as a stranger, whereas now, armed with letters of introduction from persons of note, he could count on being received as a notable himself.

The entrance was effectively accomplished with his introduction to the salon of Monsieur and Madame de Boze, which the Abbé Mably himself undertook. Jean-Jacques refrained from gaping at such luxury and splendor, comparable only to something out of the novels of his boyhood. Never had he seen such exquisite taste nor such impeccable deportment, which immediately deprived him of all self-assurance and converted him into an awkward mute. Both Monsieur and Madame de Boze had the humanity to overlook his clumsiness and the generosity to introduce him to Monsieur de Réaumur, who had connections at the Académie and promised to bring Rousseau's musical notation to its attention if there was as much merit in it as its inventor maintained. Jean-Jacques' head was turned by the prospect, though not as much as by the exquisite Madame de Boze, so lovely and so young that she might have been the daughter of her elderly husband, who, the bold critic noticed, was a pedant as well. Monsieur de Boze was generous, however, and often invited Rousseau to dinner where, playing the exquisite to impress his hostess, he would reach out for the smallest morsel whenever the platter was presented to him. Thus he would return home hungry but with self-esteem intact.

One day Monsieur de Réaumur, to the delight and astonishment of Rousseau, informed him that the Académie des Sciences had agreed to listen to his exposition of his new musical notation. On the day established, August 22, 1742, Jean-Jacques, clasping the sheets of the lecture he had conscientiously revised and improved, appeared before the august body of Academicians with, he noted, less timidity than when he had been introduced to Madame de Boze. He was put even more at his ease by an obviously cordial reception. As he proceeded in his reading, he was certain of triumph. How could they fail to see the merit, the clarity, of the new notation? His lecture over, many hastened to compliment him, others to ask questions which he answered with uncommon readiness. All in all, it had been a success. Meanwhile he had to await the decision of the three Commissioners, the Messieurs Hellot, De Mairan and De Fouchy—all worthy gentlemen, Jean-Jacques admitted. But what did they know about music?

He had occasion to ask himself the question again and again during his conference with them, when they plied him with queries and specious objections that had nothing to do with the case. He replied to their dissent and did his best to clarify their doubts, but he was as unsuccessful in making them understand him as they were to bring their objections home. Jean-Jacques, convinced that he had revolutionized musical history, turned deaf to any contradiction. The Academicians, for their part, swathed in the togas of their authority, refused to be convinced. Then one of them unearthed, Heaven only knew from where, a monk, a certain Father Souhaitti, who long ago had devised that same method of noting the scale by using numbers. That had been enough to make the rest agree that Monsieur Rousseau had really nothing new to offer.

In spite of the fact that Jean-Jacques had never heard of Father Souhaitti, they intimated the method was identical. In vain he argued that the mere manner of writing the seven notes of the plain chant without taking the octaves into consideration could not possibly be compared with his, Rousseau's "simple and convenient invention to set down in numbers every imaginable kind of music, clefs, rests, octaves, measures, time and the values of the notes, things that Father Souhaitti had never even dreamed of." [6] Still, Jean-Jacques had finally to admit that so far as the elementary expression of the seven musical notes went, Father Souhaitti—whoever he had been—was the original inventor. He was aggrieved, however, that the examining body failed to see that the advantage in his own method lay in eliminating transpositions and clefs; for the same piece could be transposed at will, into whatever key one wished, merely by the change of a single initial letter at the beginning of the composition.

After endless discussion and deliberation the august body passed judgment, deciding that Jean-Jacques Rousseau's method was good for vocal, but bad for instrumental, music—with which opinion the inventor disagreed, saying that on the contrary it was good for the vocal and even better for the instrumental. The Académie, however, did present him with a token of their appreciation: a fine document full of flattering compliments which, when rightly interpreted, merely stated that Rousseau's musical system was neither new nor useful.

However, he found a critic he could respect in Rameau, to whom he subsequently submitted his method. The composer approved of the signs Rousseau used, since they simply and clearly determined the value of the notes. "But they are bad," he added, "for the reason that they require an effort of the mind which cannot always keep up with the speed of the execution. The position of our notes reaches the eye without the help of this operation. If two notes, one very high, the other very low, are joined by a series of intermediate notes, I see at once the progress from one to the other by joint degrees. But in order to be sure of this series according to your method, it will be necessary for me to spell your ciphers, one by one. . . ." [7]

The voice of authority convinced and, for once, humbled Rousseau. He found Rameau's objection unanswerable. Only the greatest knowledge of his art could have suggested it to the composer. It was therefore not remarkable that such an objection should have eluded every single Academician. But then, Jean-Jacques dismissed them, they knew so much that they had mastered nothing beyond their specialty.

10. *Widening circles*

As in Turin, Jean-Jacques wandered about Paris, endeavoring to soothe his crestfallen hopes. But they were lifted when his *Dissertation sur la musique moderne* was brought out by his optimistic publisher, who, like himself, expected music-loving buyers to come flocking. The *Dissertation* merely suffered dessication on the shelves. That, to Jean-Jacques, was the hardest blow of all. He had done something original, something helpful for the untutored lover of music. Wasted effort, all of it. Yes, here was another Hieron's fountain, and broken at that. What was the good of trying to help mankind? How foolish of him to waste himself in that labor of Sisyphus! Mankind was not worth it. Shrouding himself in his misanthropy, he brooded on his failure, on the indifference of all the high and mighty to whom he had presented letters. With few exceptions they had greeted him charmingly, promised much and done nothing. The Abbé de Mably, Fontenelle and Marivaux were exceptions

—particularly Marivaux, who, nobly unselfish, found enough merit in Rousseau's *Narcisse* to retouch it. It was remarkable generosity on the part of a rival playwright, who must have found in the refined sentiments of *Narcisse* more than a touch of his own alembicated sentimentalities, which had added the word *marivaudage* to the French language. But then, was not imitation a tribute to one's genius?

Through the Abbé de Mably Jean-Jacques met Père Castel, a Jesuit who edited a small newspaper and who, like himself, had published a small music book. It was called *Le clavecin oculaire,* a title implying instruction for sight reading. The two found a basis for friendship in their common interest, but their conversation ranged through the wider fields of their intellectual curiosity. A practical man, Père Castel appreciated the high thinking of his friend; but he also noted that wealth was not one of his assets; also that in some respects he suffered from an appalling naïveté.

"You must frequent the company of women," Père Castel advised him one day. "One does not get anywhere except through women. Don't limit yourself to one by being her lover, but try to get acquainted with as many of them as possible. Women," he added, geometrically, "are the curves of which sensible men are the asymptotes. They never touch, though they constantly approach them."

Jean-Jacques listened to Père Castel's worldly wisdom but did nothing, much as he yearned to find another young and lovely Madame de Warens. Then one day the Jesuit said: "I've talked about you to Madame de Beuzenval. Go pay her a visit for me. She's a good woman, who would be happy to see a compatriot of her husband's. There you will also meet Madame de Broglie, her daughter, a very witty lady. Madame Dupin is another to whom I've spoken of you. Take along your book. She is eager to meet you and would make you quite welcome."

In his misanthropic state Jean-Jacques was in no mood to play the courtier; but there was great sense in what Père Castel advised. After all, had not Maman shaped and civilized the bear cub who had come to her door—how many years ago! Certainly his reading poetry at the Luxembourg all by himself, and even his games of chess with the Prince de Conti, would not lead anywhere, even though he himself won. It was in another, more complicated chess game, with living kings, queens and pawns, that one had to prove oneself.

One day, accordingly, the awkward bear made his appearance before Madame de Beuzenval, who greeted him with simple grace as if they had been old friends. Put at his ease by her, he did not lapse into stammering confusion when her daughter, Madame de Broglie, came in. "My child," she said, "this is Monsieur Rousseau whom Père Castel told us about." She also complimented him on his work and to show that she was not merely playing the gracious hostess, she gave him proof of her admiration by exhibiting his music right there on the clavecin. Since he noticed by the clock that it was nearing dinner time he made as if to leave, but Madame de Beuzenval detained him. "You're quite a distance from your quarters," she said. "Stay and dine with us."

Jean-Jacques was delighted and promptly accepted. Then suddenly it occurred to him that what she meant was that he should dine in the servants' quarters. After all, Madame de Beuzenval had all the prejudices of her class and never let anyone forget her illustrious Polish antecedents. He stiffened and turned somber, and suddenly recalling a previous engagement, was about to make his excuses when Madame de Broglie said something to her mother in an undertone. The lady then turned sweetly to her guest. "I was hoping you would dine *with us,*" she said. "You will—won't you?"

Jean-Jacques gallantly forgot his previous engagement and accepted with a sudden burst of *sympathie* toward Madame de Broglie. She would not regret her gesture, he vowed silently to himself in gratitude. He had no pleasure from that dinner, however. The other guest was Monsieur le Président de Lamoignon, younger than himself but already how exalted! Despite the prestige of his position, perhaps because of it, he could afford to dispense the lively gossip of Paris, keeping the ladies amused and adoring and delightfully shocked, all with the natural grace of a bird in flight; but there was no soaring in his conversation, which was more like the release of so many bright squibs. All those little jokes, all those clever allusions— while there he was, Jean-Jacques, as stiff and mute as a block. That sort of easy brilliance was not his, he told himself, and had the good sense to refrain from playing the witty gentleman.

However, he *happened* to have in his pocket his letter in verse to his friend, the surgeon Parisot, in which he, Jean-Jacques, poured out all his noble sentiments, his aspirations, his view of the human condition. He was asked to read it, a request which he instantly satisfied. Some of the verses must have sounded like the clarion of revolution in that aristocratic and wealthy household, and like the cry of wounded, unrecognized genius. "What matters after all what others choose to think?" he asked in rolling numbers. "Do their tributes, does their scorn make us what we are? And cannot one aspire to happiness without the art of winning admiration? The pleasures of the heart are the wise man's bliss," he concluded.

These were the pleasures for which at the time he was starved, and they were the heart's most essential nourishment. It is strange that even in boyhood, except for his cousin Abraham, he had had no close friend, no comrade with whom in the manner of adolescents he had sworn eternal friendship. He had dreamed of it, this loyal manly devotion, but it had never been his. It was only with women that he had had that *épanchement,* that outflowing of the heart which is the great privilege of intimacy. However, he was soon to acquire a congenial friend through Madame Dupin.

She had a fascinating history, Madame Marie-Aurore Dupin, who in her middle years was still considered one of the most beautiful women in Paris. According to Rousseau's information, she was the daughter of Samuel Bernard and Madame Fontaine. Her descent, however, was far more romantic and

distinguished as revealed by the act recorded, years later, in
the *Collection de décisions nouvelles . . . relatives à la jurisprudence actuelle,* where it was solemnly stated that Marie-
Aurore was "the natural daughter of MAURICE, COMTE DE SAXE,
Marshal General of the Armies of France, and of Marie Rinteau." The Act itself, in Volume III, page 704, in the Paris
record office makes its eloquent commentary in the capitals of
the noble father's name, and in the ordinary print of Marie
Rinteau's.

At fifteen Marie-Aurore, whose education had been super-
vised by the Dauphine, found herself released from the walls
of Saint-Cyr only to be thrown into the marriage bed of the
Comte de Horn, one of the bastards of Louis XV. The marriage, purely one of convenience, was never consummated,
thanks to the husband's indifference and the bride's innocence.
There was only one memory she cherished of that wedding—a
dispensation she had obtained from the King for the release of
a number of political prisoners. When they all came to thank
her later she burst into tears of joy.

Another memory stood out vividly. They were holding a
great ball one night. In the midst of it Comte de Horn disappeared, but Marie-Aurore thought nothing of it and went on
dancing. Toward morning a servant came to her saying the
count wished to see her. She followed him and from the thresh-
old she saw that there were others in the room. When they
made way, her eyes fell upon the Comte de Horn, half reclin-
ing on the bed and supported by one his valets. A doctor was
at his side. As she approached, the valet cried: "Take her
away! Take Madame away!" She noticed a large white hand
hanging over the side of the bed. She saw the doctor lift it and
lay it across the other on the dead man's breast. He had just
been killed in a duel.

Aurore, now a young widow, retired again to a convent.
There she meditated, read and formed the habit of copying out
in a careful hand the passages that struck her for eloquence or

spiritual comfort, which, with reflections of her own, comprised a sort of commonplace book for her moral guidance. She was too young and too beautiful to remain immured from the world, however, and the Dauphine granting her a modest pension, she returned to her former life but on a less ambitious scale, for the creditors, after the count's death, had seized everything.

She did not marry again until she was thirty, when she chose Dupin de Francueil, son of the Farmer-General, Monsieur Dupin. The Dupin de Francueils were not of noble descent, but their family was of ancient origin and had its impressive armorial bearings. Years later, when Madame Dupin was talking of love and marriage to her young granddaughter, who had asked her why she had married a man twice her age, she said: "An old man loves one more than a young one, and it is impossible not to reciprocate such perfect love. . . . Your grandfather, my child, was handsome, elegant, well groomed, perfumed, gay, amiable and affectionate. . . . Younger, he would have been too attractive to have had such a peaceful life and perhaps I would not have been as happy with him, for other women would have tried to snatch him away from me." The young girl to whom Madame Dupin gave this advice was later to become an authority on love, both in life and in her art. She is known to the world as George Sand.

Dupin de Francueil, Rousseau's friend and a stepson of Madame Dupin's, was a man of many talents. He composed, he painted, he made locks and he embroidered better than any woman. In the evening the Dupins would gather together a group of friends. Then the salon would echo to music, singing and conversation, while Madame Dupin kept her hands occupied unraveling old bits of tapestry for the gold thread in them, while dropping golden sentiments into the conversation. Jean-Jacques was often of the company since he had become the secretary of the husband and the literary adviser of the wife. Inevitably he fell in love with her. How could he help it? He was now living in the Dupin mansion, the handsome Hôtel Lambert, and his duties were not so absorbing as to deprive him of leisure to dream of the beautiful Aurore.

As it was, his first meeting with her had turned his always unsteady head. She was at her toilette, as public as any monarch's, for beauty like royalty has its privileges. Her arms were bare, her morning gown was open at the breast, and her hair flowed down her shoulders. That intoxicating vision had been enough. He found, however, that she was no Madame de Warens, for Madame Dupin's virtue was equal to her beauty.

He presented her with his work on music. To his astonishment she discussed the book with authority and, sitting down at the clavecin, paid him the compliment of singing from it, accompanying herself the while. At dinner, unlike Madame de Beuzenval, Madame Dupin always had him sit beside her, with no coquetry, no ulterior motive, but only out of regard for one whose genius, though still latent, she recognized.

"Come and see us whenever you wish," she told him.

He took her at her word, called on her daily and dined at her table two or three times a week. He was dying to show her what a wise, what a brilliant man he was and how worthy of her consideration; but in her presence he became so overwhelmed that a fish could not have been more mute. He had reasons for his reticence. His entrée into so distinguished and opulent a household as the Dupins' was a passport into the great world, even to fortune. For once he was prudent in his behavior, so that the door would not be closed upon him. The watchmaker's son in him, awed by the dukes, the ambassadors, the *cordons-bleus,* cringed and was ill at ease among all those titles. Almost breathlessly, in reliving those soirées in his old age, he crowded De Fourmont, De Bernis, Buffon and Voltaire in a paragraph, not forgetting Madame la Princesse de Rohan, la Comtesse de Forcalquier, Madame de Mirepoix, Madame de Brignolé and Milady Hervey, as if he were reliving the inebriating excitement of so much wealth, fame, aristocracy and beauty.

After a period of prudent behavior something must have turned his head—perhaps Madame Dupin's kindness, or some *gentilesse* which he may have overinterpreted. Whatever it was that incited him, he wrote her an impassioned letter. For two days she kept it, holding him in suspense. On the third, she sent it back to him with a few very candid words that instantly chilled his ardor. He did not hold it against Francueil who had been chosen as the unwilling emissary. The lover of Madame de Warens, of Mademoiselle Serre was so taken aback that for once he was struck dumb. But not for long, since he could not afford to lose such a patron. "Madame, I perceive with the keenest distress that I have deserved your displeasure," he wrote. "I feel its effect even while experiencing your goodness and I know beyond a doubt that it was only a feeling of generosity on your part that spared me the treatment I deserved. Your indulgence, Madame, has brought me to my senses. . . ." Since he had no answer from her, he wrote to Monsieur Dupin, full of contrition and apology and almost abject in his plea for forgiveness. "I had flattered myself that I would be attached to you for the rest of my days and therefore I sacrificed all other prospects. . . ." What prospects did he allude to? "If Madame Dupin and you, Monsieur, are merely just, my fate is sealed and I must submit. . . . Just a word in answer," he begged. That word came and it was favorable for he soon resumed his visits. As for his friendship with Francueil, it remained as cordial as ever. Finally he succeeded in ingratiating himself completely with Madame Dupin by acting as her son's *gouverneur* while she was looking about for another tutor to replace his present master.

With his tendency toward dependence on others stronger than himself, Jean-Jacques, who was taking a course in chemistry at Rouelle's with Francueil, left the Saint-Quentin where he had been staying and found lodgings near the rue Plâtrière, where his friend lived. Their tastes were congenial and they often went to the theater together. One day Francueil suggested a performance at the Théâtre Français.[1]

"By all means," said Rousseau. "It will be good for a couple of hours' yawning."

They set out together. Francueil then bought two tickets, gave Jean-Jacques one and walked in with his own. Jean-Jacques followed, but there was a crowd at the entrance so that he could not go in. One might easily get lost in such a crowd, he reflected. He peered in again. Everyone was standing. What if he should, not altogether accidentally, vanish? No sooner did the thought occur to him than he acted upon it. Hence, instead of pushing his way in to follow his friend, he pressed in the opposite direction. At the exit he gave back his ticket and collected the money. When his conscience bothered him later, he rationalized his act. He had not really stolen the money for the ticket. He had only stolen its employment. Still, said his inveterate conscience, the lesser the theft, the greater the infamy. Madame Dupin, when she learned of this "borrowing" of Jean-Jacques' years later, wrote among her notes: "It always seemed to us that there was something of affectation in his boasting of this fraud. Francueil did not recall it at all and went so far as to think that Rousseau had invented the whole thing to demonstrate the honesty of his conscience and to keep people from thinking of the faults which he did not confess. Even if that were so, good Jean-Jacques, you would have to crack your whip much louder to make us prick up our ears." [2]

In the midst of his troubles Jean-Jacques fell ill with a bronchitis which forced him to keep to his bed. While incapacitated in body, he was not idle, for the fever quickened his imagination and delirium heightened the spiritually amorous drama unfolding in his brain. He was no longer in France but in Italy. He was not Jean-Jacques Rousseau but Tasso, in an ecstasy of love for the Princess of Ferrara, who, less cruel-hearted than Madame Dupin, gave him all the pleasure of a Mohammedan houri. The clear-eyed sun the following morning revealed, alas, the deception of dreams and the flaws in the masterpiece.

Reality was no kinder. His employment with Madame Dupin

was leading him nowhere, for she did not provide the warm, half-mistress, half-motherly relationship that he came to expect from women. The other ladies, however, Madame de Beuzenval and the charming De Broglie, made up for Madame Dupin's indifference by putting to work all their charm and influence in his favor. Père Castel, Jean-Jacques admitted, had indeed given him good advice.

Among their friends the ladies counted a brother of the Comte de Montaigu, a *gentilhomme de la Manche* in the Dauphin's court who had just been appointed Ambassador to Venice. The Abbé de Mably was also intimate with Montaigu. Therefore, what with the cajoleries of the ladies and the persuasiveness of De Mably, the newly appointed Ambassador was convinced that he could not possibly do justice to his office without the assistance of an able secretary like Jean-Jacques Rousseau, who had the advantage of knowing Italian. Jean-Jacques was flattered. Though he painted himself as the most modest and least ambitious of men, he had a passion to dominate—whether in prose, poetry, musical composition or in the game of chess—it did not matter. Often when he had played with Diderot, whom he always beat unmercifully, he could have given the games more parity and made them more interesting by allowing some advantage to his adversary, but he would not yield an inch.

"Does it pain you to lose?" he would ask Diderot.

"No," Diderot replied. "But I could make a better defense and you would gain more pleasure out of it, if I did not always lose."

"That may be," agreed Rousseau. "But let's leave things as they are."

The two youths were almost the same age. Like Rousseau, Diderot, the son of a master cutler, loved music, had studied theory, wrote, planned and had a passion for doing something for mankind. He had not the good looks of Rousseau, but his high broad forehead and his keen large eyes, arched by dark brows, gave his face a shrewd and at the same time a benevolent look as if, while seeing through mankind, he still loved it. Born in the little town of Langres, he was only fifteen when he proved that it was too small for him by running away. His father caught him before he had gone very far.

"Where are you going?" he asked the lad.

"To join the Jesuits, in Paris."

"Ah, good! I'll escort you there myself in the morning."

Shaking his head the elder Diderot wondered at this strange boy, so impatient to run away to school instead of from it. He kept his word, however, knowing how important it was to set such an example to a trusting young mind. Denis seemed to learn everything without the least effort, whether it was Latin, English, literature, mathematics. With his gay, trusting nature and his generosity in doing the homework of his less gifted fellow students he was understandably popular. He had one close friend, François-Joachim Bernis, whose fantastically ascending career of Ambassador, Minister of Foreign Affairs, Archbishop of Albi and Cardinal no one would then have guessed.

Diderot, *père,* was anxious for his son to follow the profession of doctor or lawyer. He had no taste for murder, he said to the first suggestion. He was equally uncomplimentary of the second. But there were three mouths to feed at home, his mother, his sister and younger brother. He left them to the charge of his father, who had performed that task competently for many years, and himself set out for Paris, not knowing exactly what he intended to do, yet feeling that he belonged there.

At first, like Rousseau, he tutored, but his pupils' inanity compelled him to give up. "Perhaps I am succeeding in making men of your sons," he said one day to his employer, "but they are quickly making a child of me, so I must leave." He then sought what hack work he could. He translated, he compiled catalogues, he composed sermons for untalented preachers— till he found nothing at all to do that would bring him any money. He changed his lodgings for a dingy little hole in the wall. One day his landlady found him unconscious. He had eaten nothing for days. She fed him and took care of him and in no time he was his same, free, careless self, translating, writing, doing anything to earn him enough for a few days.

At about the time he met Jean-Jacques, Diderot had fallen in love with the daughter of a seamstress, at whose house he was lodging. Antoinette Champion—Nanette, as Diderot called her—was a fresh, simple, pretty child of the people, with no pretensions and utterly devoted, though in the eyes of the fastidious Rousseau, *"pie-grièche et harengère"*—a magpie and a herring woman. But then, only *ladies* would do for him. Therefore, whenever he and Jean-Jacques were together they did not talk of Nanette but rather of Diderot's great ambitions, which so far had materialized only in hack work and translations.

Did Jean-Jacques go to the wedding when the pretty seamstress and Diderot were married? As it was, the games of chess at the Regency Café were not interrupted by the marriage, nor did Jean-Jacques fail to see his friend at the houses to which literary men, without their wives, were invited. Did he wonder at the union of a man of extraordinary intellect with a simple, unlettered girl? Certainly Diderot had nothing to complain of in the arrangement. He was well cared for in every way and he also had the freedom to go wherever he chose, whenever he pleased, while his wife waited devotedly at home. Indeed he, Jean-Jacques, would have considered himself fortunate in such a comfortable situation.

Meanwhile the ladies, Mesdames Dupin, De Beuzenval and De Broglie had not forgotten their protégé, particularly the last, who liked to think of herself as a *dea ex machina*. Somehow her plan had gone awry and the Comte de Montaigu had departed for Venice not with Rousseau whom she had recommended, but with a certain Follau, who turned out to be quite mad. Before long the Ambassador and his secretary quarreled, parted company, and Jean-Jacques was sent for, on his own terms which were modest enough, since he received a thousand livres for doing the work of Monsieur de Montaigu, who merely lent the post the prestige of his name.

To Jean-Jacques, proud of what he considered a diplomatic office, the post was not merely a step forward but a soaring flight. For once he was placed in a position for which Heaven itself had endowed him, for which he had been prepared by the best of women and—justice where justice is due—for which he had striven to make himself worthy. To read his reminiscences one would have thought he was ascending the highest throne of Europe.

He started out for Venice on the tenth of July when the plague, which had broken out in Messina, that year of 1743, was beginning to reach epidemic proportions. Everyone was taking the usual precautions, carrying herbs, vinaigrettes, charms and blessed images. He himself was thinking of the woman he had once adored and whom he still loved. Therefore, taking the Châlons and Lyon route, he paid a fleeting visit to Maman and her retinue of priests and monks, which he noted had become larger than ever. He had reason to adopt a little the pose of the conquering hero before his reverend "uncles" and Maman's household. Was he not Secretary of the Venice Embassy?

Returning to Lyon he went on to Avignon and then to Marseilles where he boarded a felucca that anchored at Toulon and went on to Genoa. The vessel was slow, overcrowded, verminous and unprovided with even the most elementary conveniences. No sooner did it cast anchor than the English fleet placed it at once in quarantine, giving the passengers the choice of remaining aboard or of going to the lazaret. All chose to remain aboard, but the heat and the filth, the massing of all that humanity on the bare decks sent Jean-Jacques scurrying to the lazaret, which was nothing but a two-storey structure, windowless, bare of furniture and without even a pile of straw to lie on.

Since he faced the prospect of three weeks' confinement, Rousseau improvised himself a bed by spreading his shirts and waistcoats on the floor, after having carefully depopulated them of the fleas that had settled on them. He then arranged his books in a row, set one of his trunks flat for a chair, and the other on its side for a writing table; and there he had a room nearly as comfortable as his lodging in Paris.

It was not a disagreeable life, but after two weeks of it he wrote to the French Envoy, Monsieur de Joinville, being careful to disinfect and perfume the letter. Probably this courtesy touched the gentleman, for he had Rousseau stay at his house till he was ready to leave for his post.

The traveler journeyed unhurriedly through Lombardy, making the most of his remaining leisure, pausing at Milan, Verona, Brescia and Padua. "At last I arrived in Venice, impatiently awaited by the Ambassador," he noted with self-satisfaction. It was the fifth of September when his gondola had deposited him at St. Mark's Square, at the foot of the columns. Certainly the patron lions perched atop of them must have made some sign.

He had taken some of his writings with him, work in progress, essays, published and unpublished articles. Among these was a manuscript entitled *Le nouveau Dédale,* dated 1742. Did he fancy himself another Dedalus? At any rate, the article was concerned with the possibility of man's conquest of the air. Long before him Leonardo da Vinci had dealt earnestly with the subject and had even designed flying machines. After all, what was to prevent man, who had conquered the ocean waters, from also conquering the air? Besides, had anyone proved that it was impossible? Humanity is always inclined to be skeptical of the new. Had anyone believed Harvey when he first discovered the circulation of the blood? But now no one would dream of doubting it. "Yet if all chimeras were destroyed," Rousseau declared in his essay, "we would lose with them an infinity of real pleasures." [8]

Part Three

11. *Venice*

He was still sailing on the flying machine of his imaginative anticipation when he settled in Venice. The City in the Sea spread before him all her magical splendor, but alas, he could not spare the time to enjoy it, for a desk loaded with letters and dispatches awaited him at the Embassy, since the Ambassador had neither the inclination nor the knowledge to read, and even less to decipher, the communications in code which seemed to have accumulated since his incumbency in July, 1743. Not that Rousseau knew the code, but as self-acknowledged genius, within a week he had penetrated its arcana and translated the mass of material. He did that thankless work gladly, for now he was nobody's lackey but an important functionary with a high-sounding title: Monsieur the Secretary of the Embassy of France in Venice. He had observed the prerogatives of the title from the outset when, to Monsieur de Montaigu's mute astonishment, Monsieur Rousseau had grandly squandered six livres to get from Padua to Venice, when he could have saved at least four if he had come by the ordinary vehicle used by less exalted mortals. But Jean-Jacques felt that he was somebody at last and he had to demonstrate it in a language that all could understand—for money always talked, even to the comprehension of the illiterate.

This lavishness only aroused the mistrust and dismay of His Excellency, who had such an exaggerated sense of economy that he would invariably have three shoes made instead of a single pair, arguing with rather eccentric logic that three shoes were the equivalent of two pairs. As one shoe invariably wore out earlier than the other, the third shoe offered a solution pleasing to common sense and satisfying to the pocket. To Jean-Jacques, now a diplomatic functionary, such economy was little short of meanness. His Excellency, however, deemed it a virtue and exercised it liberally—his only instance of liberality.

The two temperaments inevitably clashed. His Excellency, accustomed to dictate, full of his own importance and prerogatives, had established what he considered an equitable order among the gentlemen in his employ. A few days after Jean-Jacques' arrival, Montaigu invited his staff to a concert and had them go with him in his gondola. Jean-Jacques immediately took umbrage that His Excellency had not given him precedence over the rest in the seating, arguing that he, Rousseau, was after all his chief of staff. "Of course I decided against him," said the democratic Montaigu. Thereupon Rousseau, the future author of a famous discourse on inequality, penned him an epistle, unfortunately lost to posterity, in which he defended the rights of precedence.

Except for such occasional conflicts the post afforded Jean-Jacques many satisfactions. First, it gave strength and assurance to his self-esteem, for besides the dignity of the title he enjoyed the privileges of his authority, which he did not fail to exercise, as much for equity as for altruistic reasons. The very thought that he played a part in affairs of state intoxicated him, though his fundamental good sense kept him in balance.

Indeed, he had need of such ballast in the beautiful, melancholy, corrupt, Most Serene Republic of Venice, all golden domes and lofty steeples, clangorous of bells and fluttering with flights of doves. Together with the bird beloved of Venus, the city had also a considerable share of Venus's votaries who, more than her doves, attracted the male visitors. Jean-Jacques at that time was too much occupied in clearing His Excellency's desk to think of paying his tribute to the goddess, so that the intoxication of ambition—after all, did he not sign in his own name all dispatches to the highest courts of Europe, from Venice to Constantinople?—won over the desires of the flesh. Moreover, his health at the time was none of the best, what with the fatigue and inconvenience of the journey and a latent disease of the kidneys which now manifested itself and was to give him hours of misery throughout his life.

On the whole, however, it was a time of triumph which he must communicate to that dear Maman whom he had, alas, rather neglected. But then he had had no letters from her either and he must have them, he wrote, else he would die altogether. The Warensian idiom then followed. "I am well and I love you more than ever. Allow me to send a thousand good wishes to all your friends, not forgetting Zizi and Taleralatalera, and all my uncles . . . A thousand times, dear Maman, it has seemed to me that I haven't seen you in an age. Indeed, I cannot live away from you," he closed on a pathetic strain.[1] He was living extremely well, however, so well that like any prince or ambassador he allowed himself all the luxuries of the city. A devotee of music and the theater, he went often to concerts and plays, and he never ceased to pride himself, years later, on the fact that it was to him France owed the two actresses, Coralline and her sister Camille, whom he had discovered in Venice.

The whole proceeding had had the air and the trappings of an *opera buffa*. The actor-impresario, Veronese, the girls' father, had engaged himself and his company to go to France; but after pocketing the two thousand francs he had received for the journey, he complacently and profitably settled down at the Theatre of St. Luke. In vain the Duc de Gesvres, First Gentleman of the Chamber—how Jean-Jacques loved those titles—wrote to the Ambassador, demanding Veronese and his daughters. Veronese would not be budged. A number of intermediaries were then brought into the case, all persons of high rank; but the actor chose to play the part of a deaf-mute, when he was not altogether invisible.

It was Carnival time. Jean-Jacques had a moment of illumination and instantly acted upon it. Borrowing the Ambassador's gondola, he went to the Palazzo Zustiniani disguised as a woman, and there had himself announced to its owner as a masked lady. When the senator entered, Jean-Jacques, removing his mask, revealed himself and his errand in Venetian. The startled senator listened to the curt harangue from the woman who was really a man, and no doubt thinking himself in the presence of a maniac, assented to the demand that Veronese be sent at once to France.

Jean-Jacques included Her Excellency, the Ambassadress, soon to arrive in Venice, in his epistolary blandishments. He had no idea of what she looked like or how she would take his letter; but he plunged boldly into a chatty familiarity about his roaming all over town, to plays, to parties. He wished, he said, to make Venice appear as alluring as possible so that she would hasten her voyage and so fulfill the desire of her Venetian household of which he considered himself a member, more for his zeal than for his rank. It was still an obsession, that rank, as if he feared that unless he stressed it no one would notice it or, worse, take it seriously.

His diplomatic post was satisfying to the ambitious, the worldly Rousseau. Therefore he resented it when His Excellency took away the gondola which as secretary he had for his own use. He protested even more the ascendancy taken over Montaigu by Vitali, a ruffian, a pimp and a notorious *maque-*

reau, who soon brought another of his kind to the Ambassador's palace where they carried on their homosexual orgies, almost making a place of assignation of their lodgings, like the brothel which the *maquereau* ran at the Maltese Cross. Except for the Ambassador's private quarters, which were none too respectable as it was, Jean-Jacques complained that there was scarcely a corner of the palace fit for an honest man. Almost as much as the general immorality he disapproved the Ambassador's covering with pine panels the exquisite mosaics of the palace—because *this* was the latest fashion in Paris.

Despite his many grievances the secretary managed to do his duty, and did it well. The artist, however, wished to be recognized by his works. As humility was not his chief virtue, he chanted loud and long the praises of his poetry, his music, his cantatas, his ballets, his dramatic pieces, which, of course, his friends were eager to hear and see. He did not allow himself to be coaxed for long. One day he paid out an écu for the rental of a clavecin and gathering together some of the musicians of the Saint Chrysostom orchestra, he had them give a concert for his guests. Then a group of professional ballerinas performed two ballets of his own invention. Music, other composers' as well as his own, gave him the deepest pleasure. The great paintings of the Venetians—and they counted such artists as Titian, Tintoretto, Veronese—affected him little, if at all. As for architecture, he had seen grander creations from Nature's hand.

Still, there were occasional moments of delight, as when along the lagoons he heard the gondoliers exchanging verses from *Jerusalem Delivered*. He also enjoyed the opera for which he had to have a box to himself—for a good reason, since in Italy as in England and to a certain extent in France, it was the social life, the chitchat and gossip that counted, while the singers swelled their throats, often in vain, against the conversation and the laughter.

Enchanted by the music Jean-Jacques would sit, rapt and emulous. Oh, to sustain that glorious melodic line of the *bel canto,* or to blend voices and notes in celestial harmony—as in the Scuole, the charity schools for young girls to which Monsieur Le Blond, the French Consul, would take him for the vesper service. He could barely distinguish the singers behind their grilles, in their white garments with pomegranate blossoms behind their ears; but their singing was like the choiring of angels. Angelically beautiful they must be to have such voices.

One day he insisted on seeing the faces of those sublime choristers. Monsieur Le Blond granted his wish. Alas, for poor mortality. Those angels' voices lodged in misshapen bodies, in rachitic frames.

"Come, Sophia," said Monsieur Le Blond.

Jean-Jacques found her hideous.

"Come, Cattina."

Cattina was blind in one eye.

The girls who did not have minor imperfections had major defects. Jean-Jacques was sobered. The children of poverty, the unwanted offspring of illicit unions, reared by charity which is quite different from love, nevertheless offered their gratitude with the gift which, while they gave it, made them beautiful.

From the sublimity of that singing he, being merely human, would descend to more worldly levels to satisfy other, exacting needs. It was not Rousseau the poet or musician now, but Rousseau-Tartuffe, who was about to indulge in something that he keenly desired but which made him flush with shame: he was on his way to the house of the beautiful courtesan, Zulietta.

He had met her one day when he had been the guest of Captain Olivet, who in gratitude for Monsieur Rousseau's services had sought to reciprocate with a banquet on board his vessel. With him went the Secretary of the Spanish Embassy, Carrio, who lent his own kind of prestige. Altuna, his young Biscayan assistant, a high-minded and virtuous young man whom Jean-Jacques admired without emulating, was not of the party.

As they approached the vessel Jean-Jacques expected a few salvos of greeting, if not for himself, at least for Carrio, and he was piqued when not the least firecracker went off in their honor. Their reception, however, and the company which Jean-Jacques noted, put him and His Excellency the Secretary in a pleasant mood. The dinner, the wines left nothing to be desired. Nothing? Well, something—but the considerate Captain Olivet had thought of that, too, for midway through dinner he said, pointing to an approaching gondola: "Watch out! Here comes the enemy!" Jean-Jacques, whose sense of humor was not of the quickest, looked about and asked: "What do you mean?"

The answer came with the arrival of a radiant young woman, coquettishly dressed to set off her figure, which indeed spoke for itself. Before Jean-Jacques was aware, another place had been set, and there was that voluptuous siren sitting beside him. Suddenly her eyes opened wide as if she had discovered a long lost friend, and she flung her arms about his neck crying: "Good Heavens! Ah, my dear Brémond! How long since I saw you last!" With that convenient ruse, her lips clung to his in an interminable kiss. Too bewildered to know what to do or say Rousseau stared at her, his blood tingling and passion stirring at the look she gave him from the depths of her dark, languorous, oriental eyes. Somehow the dinner proceeded; Captain Olivet and his guests were too much accustomed to the ways of Venetian courtesans to do more than teasingly compliment Brémond-Rousseau for his conquest of the gorgeous Zulietta.

Within a few days Zanetto, as she renamed the helpless Rousseau, was her slave. Indeed, Zulietta would not let him out of her sight day or night and had him escort her everywhere like the most dedicated of cavaliers. Jean-Jacques had no cause to complain. After all, he had held other ladies' gloves and fans; he had been ordered about to do this or that; he had lost sleep and despised himself without enjoying a fraction of the pleasure Zulietta gave him. She wished him to understand from the beginning, however, what their relation would be; for though he might look like Brémond, he was not that flower of chivalry.

"Listen, Zanetto," she said to him one day. "I don't wish to be loved *à la française*. Anyway, it wouldn't do. So the instant you feel the least bit bored, go away. Don't do things halfway —I warn you."

One evening after Jean-Jacques and Carrio had taken Zulietta to the glassworks at Murano, where they bought her a number of bibelots, they returned to her apartment. Jean-Jacques, while they were conversing, caught sight of two extraordinary objects, at least as ornaments on a lady's dressing table— a pair of pistols. "Ah, ah!" he cried, picking one up. "Here's a novel box in which to keep your beauty patches. May one know what it is really for? I, for one, know that you have other kinds of arms, far more efficient than these, to set a man afire."

After listening to his banter, in which Carrio joined, she said with simple dignity: "Whenever I have to be gracious to persons I don't care for, I make them pay for the ennui they inflict upon me. It is only fair. But though I must suffer their caresses, I will not endure their insults."

She was light-hearted, proud, generous to the point of folly, with an almost contemptuous disregard for money, her own as well as other people's. In only one respect she was exacting— the price men paid for her favors. The higher it was, the greater her pride, for after all there was art in her métier as in everything else, and she was one of its best exponents.

Jean-Jacques accepted the relationship on her terms and refused to permit his conscience to ruin the pleasures he anticipated by admitting that it was wrong to visit a courtesan, though society accepted it and even encouraged it to protect what it called the sanctity of the hearth. Anyway, there he was now at Zulietta's door, about to enter, he persuaded himself, the sanctuary of love and beauty. Beauty there was, since even for a Venetian Zulietta was remarkably endowed. Jean-Jacques saw a goddess, humanly accessible. Subtly, delicately, she began to caress him, stirring up what was already afire, when all of a sudden this strange guest tottered, sank into a chair and burst into tears.

The girl stood there, mute and perplexed by his unexpected reaction. What was wrong? Did she not please him? Had she been too bold? She drew away, confounded and shamed. Did he reveal to her the scruples that had passed through his mind and which he was much later to record? There she was, a masterpiece of creation, an instrument of love, so perfect, so beautiful that she should have had princes for slaves, while kings laid the tribute of their scepters at her feet. Instead, she was merely an object that any man might purchase. Did she carry a dagger concealed in her bosom, he wondered—like the rest of the girls of her trade? He had heard that this was the Venetian custom so that the women could defend themselves against dangers that might come their way among the nondescript customers disgorged by the vessels from many lands.

Zulietta undressed. Now the aesthete, overwhelmed by such beauty, must seek perversely to discover some flaw in her that would bring her down to the level of common humanity. What if she were tainted? It was a terrible thought which he dispelled at the freshness of her body and the delicate pearliness of her skin. Nervous and puzzled by this strange behavior, Zulietta paced about the room, pausing before the mirror— was she not beautiful enough for him?—and now and then giving him a quizzical look. Finally she understood his trouble. It was not revulsion but shyness, and she set about curing him of it. Never had he experienced such pleasure as she gave him, not from Madame de Larnage, nor from the corrupt, precocious little Goton. He lay back, contemplating that unmarred beauty and, stirred again with desire, leaned over to kiss her breasts. Suddenly he stopped and stared. *There* was the flaw.

She was human, after all, and no goddess. "Your nipples are not the same," he remarked, unconscious of his cruelty at that moment. "One of them is flawed."

In her hurt she pretended to make a jest of the matter and, pathetically, to distract him and herself, said and did foolish, delirious, outrageous things, seeking by inflaming his senses to deaden the terrible perceptiveness of this strange monster. At his obvious contrition she grew even more embarrassed. Flushed, she rose from the bed and pulling her wrap about her, walked to the window and stared out. He followed and stood by her, but she left him and sat down on the divan. Not for long. Agitation, shame, hurt, kept her pacing restlessly about, trying to cool her face with her fan. Suddenly she flung at him scornfully across her shoulder the words that she was unable any longer to repress. "Zanetto, let women be and go study mathematics."

"Will you see me tomorrow?" he inquired in propitiation.

"No, the day after tomorrow," she said. Then smiling, she added with a touch of irony, "You'll need to rest, you know."

On the appointed day he was burning with impatience to be with her, eager not only for the anticipated pleasures but even more to prove to her how well he could atone for his previous deficiencies. The gondolier who had proceeded upstairs to announce him returned with the information that the lady had left for Florence the night before.

Now that he had lost her, for he knew that he would never see Zulietta again, he was in despair, and full of self-recrimination. What most distressed him was that in his awkwardness and stupidity he had left with her unworthy memories of himself—and it was now impossible to dispel them. Seeking to quiet his conscience about her, he entered into a brief liaison with the dancer, Bettina, who had entertained his friends not long since in several ballets from his *Muses galantes*. But she was no Zulietta. Moreover, she had a protector in a certain Fagoaga, and the youth who had submitted to a *ménage à trois* with Maman would not tolerate it now. Was it to Zulietta that he wrote a set of very indifferent verses, found long afterward among his papers, wherein he called her Aspasia and gave her the dominion not only of himself but of France, Spain, Switzerland and Italy—all eager to bear her shackles?

Of them all I alone sought to keep myself free
But alas, well I know you have also bound me. . . .

Mistresses, however, for an hour, a month or a season could be had at the wink of an eye in Venice, but out of fear for his health he was wary of them. Only once, piqued by the teasing of his associates who had decided to make the rounds of the bordellos, he joined them—"So as not to seem too great a cullion."

La Padoana, to whose establishment they went, was a handsome woman, but hers was not the sort of beauty that appealed to the exacting young man. She cooled him with sherbets, she wooed him with singing, she petted and flattered him, but she would have had better success with a graven image. Finally he got up to go, thanked her, and placed a ducat on her table. La Padoana had her own code of ethics, however: she refused to touch what she had not earned. For his part Jean-Jacques had too much regard for money to want to throw it away. The two, therefore, reached the inevitable conclusion and retired to the alcove.

On his way home Jean-Jacques was suddenly seized by the conviction that he had become *poivré*, and begged his physician in a panic to prescribe the proper specifics. For three weeks he drank every kind of potion—he was still the amateur pharmacist—but not all the reassurances of the doctor could rid him of his dread that he had been contaminated, though he could see for himself that beyond his chronic bladder weakness he was as well as ever. "Moreover," said the doctor, "your conformation is so unusual that it would be difficult for you ever to become infected." It was *carte blanche* for further dissipation, but Rousseau's moments of panic had taught him prudence. Still, temptations in that corrupt and beautiful city persisted and Carrio, with whom he often explored the darker, more sinister sections, infected him with his taste for novel experiences. One night Carrio suggest that they add a touch of spice to their adventure by sharing a girl. Jean-Jacques, always avid for novelty, agreed.

"We've got to make sure that she's safe, though," said Carrio.

After searching about, Carrio came upon a girl of eleven or twelve whose mother was willing to "sell" her to him for his purposes. Jean-Jacques went with him to see the child, an innocent, flaxen-haired Venetian angel, as gentle as a lamb and as pure, and he revolted in horror at the crime to which he was lending himself. Carrio was shamed into abandoning the project, especially after the girl sang for them in a sweet, true voice. Perhaps she might have talent, said Rousseau. The two bought her a spinet and engaged a singing master for whose services each patron paid two sequins a month, "and we had a far more agreeable time," said Rousseau, "than if we had possessed her. So true it is that what binds us most to women is not so much debauchery as a peculiar pleasure in living close to them. Imperceptibly my heart was drawn to little Anzoletta, but in a fatherly way in which the senses played so small a part that . . . I would have felt as much horror at the very thought as if I were committing an abominable incest." [2]

Jean-Jacques was not granted the pleasure of indulging his paternal sentiments very long, for the tension and antagonism which had been building up between himself and Montaigu were nearing the breaking point. In the office they were like two enemies, yoked, each on the offensive and defensive against the other. His Excellency, daily made to feel his incompetence by his arrogant secretary, would be on the verge of dismissing him every hour. Rousseau, feeling nothing but contempt for the fool who was nevertheless his superior, insulted him by his own intellectual prowess, which never failed to assert itself. The dictating sessions were the most exasperating for Montaigu, who, neither quick-witted nor ready of speech, would stammer and grope for words, while the bored scribe, taking up a book, would employ the master's lacunae by reading, now and then casting a pitying look in his direction.

Then there was always the matter of proper regard, for Jean-Jacques insisted upon it more than ever. On one occasion when His Excellency, then in Padua, urgently sent for him, the secretary refused to go because he would have had to make the voyage on the *barchello* which, he said, was only fit for riffraff. Whether in the office or at public functions, his position had to be respected. Woe to Montaigu if, when planning the seating arrangement for a dinner of state, it was even remotely suggested that his secretary sit with His Excellency's gentlemen— which indeed happened during the visit of the Duke of Modena. Angry words flew back and forth, hard as bullets, but on that occasion no harm was done. However, since not a day passed without its unpleasantness, each adversary being constantly on the alert for some pretext to affront the other, a culminating incident was bound to occur. It did. One day, after His Excellency had dictated a memoir to Rousseau for the Senate, he brought it back in the handwriting of the Under Secretary. "Why didn't *you* write the memoir?" His Excellency inquired. "Are you incapacitated?"

"No," said Rousseau, grinning. "His handwriting is more beautiful than mine."

That remark brought His Excellency to the end of his patience, but he controlled it sufficiently to ask him mildly to rewrite it and bring it back to him in the afternoon. When Jean-Jacques reappeared, His Excellency informed him that he was no longer in his employ. "Your insolence from the moment you came here, and your abuse of your functions, give me no choice but to regard you as the worst rogue one could possibly engage." When His Excellency added that he was going to settle his accounts, Jean-Jacques commented: 'It would be unjust to do so according to your will, and only fair according to mine."

At that, the infuriated Montaigu reminded him that time

was when such an insolent rogue as he would have been thrown out of the window. Did he, Rousseau, not remember the beggarly situation from which he, Montaigu, had delivered him in Paris? After reproaches of the same kind, he added what to Rousseau was worse than a whiplash across the face: "You have all the bad traits of a very bad valet and I'll deal with you accordingly."

Always the hated word. Always insult and humiliation from the powerful rich. It appears from Montaigu's account that Jean-Jacques was roused to such insolence that His Excellency threatened, if he did not alter his behavior and leave Venice, he would make the culprit feel how far his authority extended. "Leave my house at once," cried he in the traditional tone of melodrama. "Go quickly or I'll not be accountable for what I may do!"

Rousseau did not leave, nor did Montaigu really intend to relinquish him, for the secretary, despite his vexing pride, was invaluable in his office. The frictions, however, persisted. A grave one arose, not long afterward, when the Duke of Modena and his family, visiting Venice, were given a dinner by His Excellency. The secretary was instantly on the alert. Of course he would be at the official table, where he had his place daily. But no, His Excellency would not hear of it. "What!" he cried. "My secretary, who is not even a gentleman, has the pretension to dine with a sovereign, when my own gentlemen are not invited!"

"Yes, Monsieur," the secretary coolly replied. "The post with which Your Excellency honored me ennobles me so well while I still fill it, that I even have precedence over your gentlemen, and I am often admitted where they cannot be. Surely you are aware that the day you make your public entry, etiquette demands, from immemorial custom, that I follow you in my ceremonial robes to dine with you at the Palace of Saint Mark? Besides, I don't see why a man who has the privilege of dining in public with the Doge and the Senate of Venice cannot dine with the Duke of Modena."

As it happened, all the arguments and the acrimony were wasted, for the Duke of Modena did not come to dine with His Excellency. Jean-Jacques, however, had made up his mind to leave his post. Of course he told his tale to the friends he had made in Venice. One of them, Monsieur Le Blond, the French Consul, gave him a splendid dinner and, because His Excellency had discharged his secretary without a sou, the Consul made an impromptu collection for him which, together with the few louis that Rousseau had on his person, gave him enough to contemplate his departure—and his freedom.

He did not go back to Montaigu's but lodged instead with the Chancellor of the French Consulate, a matter which gave Rousseau the satisfaction of showing the world that France, at any rate, was not an accomplice of the perfidious Ambassador.

12. *Thérèse le Vasseur*

Jean-Jacques was now free, but the prospect was none too pleasing. Where to go? What to do? Once more in his restless life he found himself thrown out upon the world without a rudder to help steer him in the right direction. Should he return to Madame de Warens? He did not harbor the thought for long. True, Maman still loved him and showed him her affection by sending him cakes of soap, the latest product of Warensian enterprise, together with a quantity of chocolate. But that was as far as her generosity could go, in the down hill road which her affairs had taken. "I am more grieved than astonished at your continual suffering," he wrote her comfortingly. "God's wisdom does not like to make useless presents, and by grace of the virtues with which you have been endowed, you are doomed to exercise them continually. When you are ill, it is patience; when you serve those who are unwell, it is humanity." Carried away by his rhetoric he went on: "Since your troubles all turn to your glory or to the comfort of others, they enter the general good and so we must not complain." [1] How could one complain of virtues so close to sainthood? "You ask me what I am doing," he went on. "Alas, Maman, I love you, I think of you, and I complain about my donkey of an Ambassador; people sympathize with me, they esteem me but they render me no other kind of justice. Not that I do not hope someday to avenge myself by making him see that not only am I better than he is, but that I am also more highly esteemed. For the rest, many projects, few hopes, but always for my aim the happiness of ending my days with you. [2]

As he approached Nyon he kept thinking of his father, yet he hesitated about going to see him, not for lack of filial affection but from dread of the clattering tongue of Isaac's second wife, who would be certain to pass harsh judgment on his situation without troubling to hear his side of the story. Duvillard, the bookseller, who showed him many kindnesses when he had last visited Geneva, reproached him for his resolve and arranged to have father and son meet, without Madame Rousseau. Hiring a chaise they went to Nyon and stopped off at a *cabaret*. There Jean-Jacques waited while Duvillard went to fetch Isaac, who hastened with brimming eyes to see his son. They supped together and after an evening which Jean-Jacques found "very sweet to my heart" father and son parted.

Jean-Jacques then set out for Lyon, though not by the shortest route, to look into another piece of mischief of which he suspected His Excellency. He was not disappointed if, certainly, dismayed by what met him there. On his departure and at the Ambassador's request he had sent his modest piece of luggage along with His Excellency's, declaring its weight at forty-five pounds. Montaigu, however, had given the load as of five quintals, and it was on this estimate that the poor ex-secretary had to pay the charges.

His vexations were mitigated, if not altogether forgotten, in the generous welcome given him in Paris by his friends, all, it seems, except for Madame de Beuzenval and her daughter,

Madame de Broglie, through whom Rousseau had obtained his post with Montaigu. Madame de Beuzenval had received him with the coldness of an iceberg and, what was worse, she had taken Montaigu's part in the quarrel. Père Castel, though he did not disapprove of Jean-Jacques' action, did not approve of it either and so, together with the rest, he was also erased from Rousseau's category of friends. Henceforth whoever was not for him was against him, and the rigidity of the line he drew between the ranks was unwavering. Moreover, his pride, which dictated his actions, convinced him that he was in the right, and with that word on his banner he confronted the world and its institutions of discrimination, snobbery and injustice—"that apparent order," as he called it, which was far from either that true order, or that true justice, of which he was already dreaming.

It was his good fortune at this crisis of pessimism to meet again that noble young Biscayan, Ignatio Emmanuel de Altuna, at whom Jean-Jacques had often secretly smiled for his noble ideals in a shabby world. Altuna, however, was neither petty nor vengeful, his thoughts being raised too high for more than cursory notice of human frailties. He welcomed the homeless Jean-Jacques to his lodgings, as well ordered as a monk's cell and radiant with the pure mystical vision of its occupant. Here Altuna worked without respite in the blissful serenity of a monk in his cubicle, while outside the great metropolis shouted and rumbled. Concentrated and self-sufficient, he sought no patrons and needed none, conscious that work well done never failed to speak for itself. A man of talent must count upon himself alone. This lesson Altuna taught without the need of words to Jean-Jacques, who was to remember it as long as he lived.

Another trait astonished him in the handsome youth. Women were not to him the temptation and torment that they constituted for the rest of mankind. Altuna was gracious to them, gallant and charming, but he treated them as adorable children. Jean-Jacques could not believe that so alluring a man, a Spaniard, did not have some secret liaison, but he discovered none and concluded, with more than a touch of awe, that the flames of virtue devouring Altuna's heart did not permit those of the senses to flare up. More than Altuna's virtue, he admired his tolerance, which was that of an angel. It mattered little to him whether his friends were Turks, Jews, bigots or atheists. He sought in them only goodness and honesty. He would never discuss religion. "I am responsible for myself alone," he would say.

By the time Altuna was ready to return to his own country there was so close a bond between the two men that they determined to spend the rest of their days together in his Spanish lands. Life, however, disposed of their plan, for Altuna married and later died. "One might say that only the black plots of the wicked succeed," sighed Jean-Jacques ruefully. "The innocent projects of the good are very seldom achieved." [3]

With little money and no immediate prospects Jean-Jacques, determined never to attach himself to another Montaigu for his livelihood, went back to his old quarters at the Hôtel Saint-Quentin for the comparative quiet it afforded as against the noisy rue St. Honoré. He had much work in progress to keep him busy, his *Muses galantes* as well as innumerable ideas floating in his brain.

He found a new hostess at the Saint-Quentin, a native of Orléans, who had engaged a young woman from the same city to take care of the linens and help with the housekeeping. This girl, Thérèse le Vasseur, came of a good family. Her father had been an official of the mint in that city, but since he had a large family and the mint failed, he found himself and his brood on the streets, especially after his wife's small merchandising business also went into bankruptcy.

"The first time I saw this girl appear at table I was struck by her modest demeanor and even more by her bright and gentle look which for me has never had its equal." [4] He could not say the same for her mother, who, he declared, using eloquent vernacular, *"avait rôti le balai"*—roasted the broom—in other words, had led a disordered life. For some reason which he never found out, Le Vasseur had nicknamed his wife *le lieu-tenant criminel.*

As Thérèse was shy and of an astonishing simplicity, not to say ignorance, Jean-Jacques became her defender against the sometimes rough jests which inevitably redounded to him, her champion. The poor girl, in her gratitude, attached herself to him like a masterless dog that had at last found a protector against the kicks and blows of the human species. Although she was twenty-two or twenty-three years old, she had the naïveté, as well as the mentality, of a child of twelve. The charm of such unspoiled innocence captivated Rousseau more than the blandishments of the most subtle hostess in that fashionable society which he had so far courted to his hurt and humiliation. Here was someone with whom he could be himself, simple if he chose, unpretentious like the son of a watchmaker that he was, without airs, just a man with a man's needs and, alas, a man's disabilities; for that ailment of the bladder had been growing worse with the years. He saw the girl as a healthy, attractive, devoted mate, part servant, part nurse, and always a companion to share the good and ill in the life he had to offer. However, his imagination was so dominant that he often did not see people as they were but rather as he would have them. Thus Thérèse, for all her faults and her want of education, satisfied him, for she gave him all that he then sought—physical satisfaction for the sensualist, an excellent cuisine for the gourmet, and rest for the weary brain of the creative artist. Indeed, for a man who thought himself so little a materialist he had provided well for all his creature comforts. When his mature years gave him the prerogative of telling all, he said: "What will the reader think when I tell him with all the truthfulness of which by now he knows me capable, that from the first moment I saw her and until this very day, I have never felt the least spark of love for her . . . and that the needs of the senses which I satisfied through her have been for me solely those of sex?" [5]

Madame le Vasseur saw what was going on and belabored

the girl with blows, not from outraged morals but from fear of losing an unpaid servant in her own house, who did the work of three. Such persecution only drew Thérèse closer to her protector, who did not remain unmoved. In his deliberate, sensible study of the relationship, Rousseau took the long view. He saw in Thérèse a naïve girl, unspoiled and with no trace of coquetry. In him she saw an honest man—"In which she was not mistaken," affirmed Rousseau. Marriage ordinarily would have been the outcome, but Rousseau did not wish it and told the girl in advance: "I shall never leave you, but I shall never marry you." Thérèse agreed and would have agreed to anything in her devotion. "Love, esteem and naïve faith were the ministers of my triumph," the emancipated Rousseau declared, and for him, as for Thérèse no others were required.

The poor girl, however, went through a crisis of tears and self-recrimination before she yielded. It was the age-old story, but in the naïve Thérèse, worthy of credence. She had not come to her husband intact. In her early puberty, scarcely understanding what was required of her, she had yielded to an unscrupulous seducer—once and once only. Since then, no nun in a cloister could have been more virtuous. Jean-Jacques believed her. She was too simple, too honest to have concocted even such a shopworn story. "Pucelage!" he exclaimed with light-hearted laughter. "As if one expected to find it in a girl of twenty! Ah, my Thérèse! I am too happy to possess you as you are, healthy and good, to be concerned with finding what I did not seek!" [6]

He could not help rejoicing in his good fortune, though at first he had thought of the affair as a little adventure that would give pleasure to both and then be quickly forgotten. However, he was no longer the vigorous youth who had given such joy and satisfaction to Maman. He needed someone to love and care for him. In Thérèse he found the responses of the heart which he sought above everything else: innocence, devotion, gentleness, simplicity. He also found restful companionship and a mother, wife and nurse, though often also a child, in her. Her naïve talk and her astonishing figures of speech delighted him and he would set them down for the amusement of Madame de Luxembourg and other great ladies till they became part of the coterie speech of Paris society. But woe to anyone so rash as to mock. Yet despite Thérèse's denseness in learning—he had been unable after a month's effort to teach her to tell time from the clock opposite their window—she had astonishing common sense that often found solutions which had defeated Rousseau's wisdom. The only thorn in their relationship was the meddling of Madame le Vasseur, who, because as a girl she had been trained in the household of the Marquise de Monpipeau, tried to sophisticate Thérèse with her airs and pretensions, which to the Geneva republican were anathema.

He was not so overprincipled, however, as not to keep informed of the doings at Court, though not with the assiduity of that Jack-of-all-Philosophies, Voltaire, whom he had first noticed at Madame Dupin's. There seemed to be no milieu of importance in which Voltaire had not at least a toehold, though most often it was both feet that he planted securely and to his advantage.

What was Rousseau's amazement, the winter of 1745, to receive a letter from the Duc de Richelieu, Maréchal de France, with an unexpected and flattering request. Since mid-May of that year, when Maréchal de Saxe in the presence of Louis XV had routed the English and the Austrians at the great battle of Fontenoy, all Paris, and particularly Versailles, had been in a whirl of celebration of that signal victory and the rejoicing had not yet reached its height. Pageants, plays, operas were daily performed, but the festivities were expected to culminate with the celebration of the Dauphin's imminent marriage. At the request of the Duc de Richelieu Voltaire had written a ballet-comedy in three acts with various divertissements for which Rameau composed the music. The work was too long, however, whereupon Voltaire obligingly shortened it and changed its title to *Les fêtes de Ramire*. Since there was still a task remaining, to make the words of the libretto fit the music, Richelieu called on Rousseau, for by that time Voltaire had left Paris.

Seized by sudden scruples, Jean-Jacques hesitated to touch Voltaire's text without his consent and therefore wrote to him —not without expectation of a reply from the already famous man. "For fifteen years," Rousseau began, "I have been laboring to make myself worthy of your regard and of the interest with which you favor young talents. Now, for having written the music for an opera, I find myself, I know not how, metamorphosed into a musician. It is, Sir, in this capacity that M. le Duc de Richelieu has assigned to me the scenes of the divertissements. . . . He has even demanded that I make the necessary changes. . . . I offered my respectful objections. Monsieur le Duc insisted. I obeyed. It was the only choice, considering the state of my fortunes. . . ." [7]

Voltaire's answer of the fifteenth of December, 1745 was balm to his spirit, even though there might have been more flattery than sincerity in the compliments. "Sir, you combine two talents which until now have always been separate. Here are already two good reasons for me to esteem and to seek to love you. I am distressed for your sake that you should employ these two talents on a work which is not too worthy of them. Some months ago, M. le Duc de Richelieu commanded me to write, in a very great hurry, a poor little sketch. . . . I did so, very quickly and very poorly. . . ." He did not mention the perquisites that fell to him through royal favor.

Jean-Jacques did his best with the hack work that fell to him, for he was in such reduced circumstances that he had even offered to send back to the tailor, through his friend Roguin, the fancy vest and other elegant garments which he had ordered when playing the man of fashion in Venice. Roguin replied with a magnanimous offer to share whatever he had with Jean-Jacques. True, Fortune was taking her time in doing Rousseau justice, but he must not be distressed. As for himself, Roguin, he marveled at her being so blind to his friend's manifest talents—an attitude in which Jean-Jacques heartily concurred.

Les fêtes de Ramire, as rewrought by Rousseau both in music and text, cost him much labor, especially in the new recitatives that he supplied, as well as the overture, which was entirely his own. The challenge of being the associate of two recognized geniuses inspired him to reach their height, and in that achievement he felt he had succeeded. Alas, when the piece was finally presented at the Opéra, neither Rameau nor Voltaire came to hear it. Well might the grieved and disappointed Rousseau have exclaimed with the singer of the first monologue:

O mort! viens terminer les malheurs de ma vie!

Death, fortunately, did not end his days, though Madame de la Poplinière did her best to embitter them. "You have written music fit for a funeral," she said, and repeated her complaint to Monsieur de Richelieu.

"Who wrote the words?" Richelieu asked Rousseau.

"Monsieur de Voltaire."

"In that case it is Monsieur de Voltaire who is at fault."

Richelieu's outspoken vindication gave little comfort to the heartsick author-composer, who took to his bed and was not seen abroad for six weeks. Neither did it cheer him to learn that Monsieur de la Valmette, the King's maître d'hôtel, had been delighted with the opera. What rankled most was the fact that the libretto had not even borne his name—only Voltaire's. Rameau's had not appeared either, and in his lugubrious mood Rousseau had assumed that the great man had not wished to diminish its éclat by linking it with that of a comparative nonentity. At least he had one solace in his misery, the devoted care of Thérèse, who was wife, nurse, servant and guardian. His friend Gauffecourt also cheered him with his frequent visits, offering what comfort he could to his wounded spirit.

"Why should Madame de la Poplinière hate me so?" Rousseau asked.

"First of all, since she is the titular patroness of Rameau, she cannot suffer any competition," said Gauffecourt. "Besides, you're guilty of an original sin which she'll never forgive you." Rousseau's look invited clarification. "You are a Genevan and therefore you have her enduring hate," continued Gauffecourt. "Oh, it's all very simple. When Abbé Hubert, your compatriot, heard that she was about to marry la Poplinière, he did his best for his friend's sake to prevent it. She never forgave him and since then she has turned her hate against all the Swiss. She is mean. She is clever. You'll never gain anything in that household."

So! That was the way the *beau monde* went! What was genius, what was accomplishment against the dictatorial power of a Madame de la Poplinière! A thousand times better and more honorable to live with his good, simple Thérèse, to whom he was the lord of the world, her husband, brother and friend. He soon discovered, however, that all the virtues did not reside in the humbler world, either, and that there, as elsewhere, selfishness and greed were not unknown.

At this time Isaac Rousseau died. Jean-Jacques was naturally grieved, though, he admitted, not as much as he would have been under less trying and less impecunious circumstances. There was the matter of the inheritance which fell to him, but there was also the fact of his missing brother who, if alive, would be entitled to share it. Here again Gauffecourt's help proved invaluable, though the slow workings of the law gave Jean-Jacques many moments of exasperation and impatience, of which he was ashamed.

"What!" he addressed himself, when after receiving the letter announcing the outcome, he laid it by, to punish his covetousness. "What! Will Jean-Jacques let himself be mastered to this point by greed and curiosity?" Certainly not. Leaving the letter where it was, he undressed and went to bed. On awaking in the morning, he had forgotten all about it, and it was only when he caught sight of it that he took it, opened it and found that it contained a letter of exchange for the respectable sum of one thousand five hundred florins. The money could not have come more propitiously. But alas, his relationship with Thérèse had also given him a horde of kinsfolk who insisted on profiting by the new alliance on the principle that what was Rousseau's was also Thérèse's and therefore theirs as well.

One misappropriation Jean-Jacques found it hard to forgive. Thérèse had washed his fine linen shirts one day, and had hung them up to dry in the attic. They had been Maman's gift, and their fineness and skilled tailoring were the only elegance that Rousseau affected. What was his dismay when he discovered that they had all been stolen by one of Thérèse's scoundrelly brothers. Jean-Jacques took the loss stoically, but he felt it deeply, for they were precious to him because they represented another of Maman's many tokens of her love for Petit.

Before these rapacious parasites had the chance to despoil him completely, he sent part of his money to "poor Maman," who at the time was badly in need of help, what with the wild schemes that had impoverished her and the knot of leeches, frocked and unfrocked, who depended on her for their sustenance. So the inheritance diminished. "There were two of us, four really," Jean-Jacques wryly jested, "or more accurately we were seven or eight. For though Thérèse was of an incomparable selflessness, her mother was not like her. . . . Sisters, sons, daughters, granddaughters, all of them gathered round. . . . Everything I did for Thérèse, her mother turned to the benefit of this crowd of starvelings. . . ." [8] Not at all flattered that they called him Uncle because Thérèse had always been Aunt, he tried to deliver her from their rapacity. In vain. They were like the Hydra. When he lopped off one parasite, ten others made their appearance.

Badly in need of money now that his inheritance was exhausted, Jean-Jacques looked about for remunerative work. The Duc de Richelieu seemed to have quickly forgotten him, and there was little to expect from the Court. He managed to interest Les Italiens in his little comedy, *Narcisse,* but though he waited patiently, they never produced it. He had no choice but to go into harness in the service of some rich patron. He thought of his friend Francueil as the medium for his re-entering the household of his wealthy relatives, the Dupins, hopeful that by this time Madame Dupin had forgiven or perhaps forgotten the bold advances which had cost him her patronage. The Dupins and their circle were more than ever engrossed in their various interests, however. Francueil was still pursuing his studies in chemistry and hoped to write a book, with an eye to attracting the attention of the Académie des Sciences. Madame Dupin, on her own account, aspired more than ever to authorship and so looked on Jean-Jacques as a competent guide to her rather dull Parnassus.

Rousseau's hopes quickly rose, especially when Francueil succeeded through his connections in having the *Muses galantes* rehearsed a number of times at the Opéra, with Rebel conducting—very badly, thought Rousseau, though the piece was repeatedly applauded. He waited in vain, however, for the finished production. Complaining to Francueil, he was reminded by the latter that he had promised a rehearsal, but had not guaranteed an acceptance. Rousseau wished in vain that his friend had been less true to his word, and began to brood again on the injustices he had to suffer through human vanity —for of course the treatment his opera received had not been altogether accidental. Definitely Francueil and Madame Dupin had plotted it all. Both were mere amateurs and therefore they feared that if he, Rousseau, gained a reputation in the world, everyone would know when their books appeared that they had obviously grafted their petty talents on his genius.

Nevertheless he continued serving them to provide for Thérèse. Farewell, for the present, to his dreams of glory and renown. After all, eight or nine hundred francs of certain income a year would take care of Thérèse's needs—or should he say the Le Vasseurs'? Therefore he helped Francueil in his experiments and patiently set down and rewrought the results of Madame Dupin's research and cerebration. He could not help comparing his situation with poor Maman's. She was the prey of her black-frocked *croquants,* as Rousseau called the monks, and he of the Le Vasseur tribe through the weakness of his "poor Thérèse."

Because he was attached by his responsibility to the Dupins, he had perforce to follow them during the autumn, when they set out for their vacation in Touraine, where they owned the beautiful Château de Chenonceaux, once the gift of Henry II to his mistress, Diane de Poitiers. Did Jean-Jacques ponder on the whims of Destiny which made it possible for a Farmer-General to buy the love token that a king had once given to the woman he adored? At any rate, while he enjoyed the autumn scenery, meandering along the banks of the river in the comfortable after-dinner pace of a plump, well-satisfied monk, Jean-Jacques thought of his Thérèse, who, he learned, was also gaining weight, though from a different cause.

A few weeks later he joined her and found her farther advanced in her pregnancy than he had expected. The prospect troubled but did not much dismay him. Children died or were born every day and somehow Providence or society took care of them. Certainly in their situation, without a hearth of their own, he knew that neither he nor Thérèse could take care of them nor give them even the minimum opportunity toward a modest future. Then, too, the responsibilities of founding and rearing a family, legitimate or not, terrified him. It was difficult enough seeking to make something of himself in the world, with little money and only the expectation of what his talents would bring in a competitive field.

As Thérèse's time approached, his thoughts turned more and more to the conversations at the table d'hôte of Madame la

Selle where he and the noble Altuna used to take their meals, together with an assorted group that included an old debauchee, Commander de Granville and his circle of young officers and musketeers, who consorted with the girls of the Opéra and boasted of their gallant adventures and their outcome. Indeed, people of all walks of life except men of the cloth met there, discussing their lives, adventures and problems with the utmost freedom, the Commander encouraging their élan but forbidding any license. From such uninhibited conversation Jean-Jacques, without paying tuition, had had a course in the everyday life of the ordinary citizen of Paris and, for that matter, of any large city. He collected amusing anecdotes, edifying maxims, true stories of illicit affairs, of husbands and wives betrayed, or of clandestine births whose innocent little victims were spirited away and deposited on the steps of the foundling hospitals, Les Enfants-Trouvés.

The infants were not always taken to the foundling hospices. They could be found of a morning on the steps of a convent, in the porticos of churches, at the foot of some public monument. Indeed, one winter's day in 1717, a newborn baby boy had been discovered on the steps of Saint-Jean-le-Rond and baptized Jean le Rond until he changed his name and made it famous as D'Alembert.

As it was, this practice of disposing of unwanted children was general throughout the Continent, and indeed, it presented a problem which, despite the best intentions of society, was often resolved by the death of the innocent victims. The statistics were appalling, particularly in the large cities like London and Paris where, of the infants admitted to the hospices, three-quarters of them died within the year. The number of the exposures nevertheless increased from year to year, as also did the death rate.

Nevertheless, when Thérèse's time drew nearer, Jean-Jacques stressed their miserable circumstances. They had no place that they could call a home; they had no certain income, no means of bringing up a child. Perfectly respectable people whom he knew, he told her, had chosen the expedient of giving their infants a chance by leaving them at the Enfants-Trouvés. In their present circumstances they had no choice but to follow their example. Thérèse wept and at first would not hear of it; but Jean-Jacques was a persuasive reasoner, made even more so by the love she bore him and by his reiterated assurance that he would never leave her. She consented.

Madame le Vasseur lent her aid to the scheme by taking Thérèse to the midwife La Gouin, expert in clandestine deliveries. At La Gouin's Thérèse bore her child, a boy. Jean-Jacques went to see her, bringing with him an identification card for the child in duplicate. One card he kept. The other he slipped into the swaddling clothes of the infant who was taken by La Gouin and placed on the steps of the foundling asylum.

Térèse wept, but there was nothing she would have refused Jean-Jacques, as much from moral weakness as from the gratitude as well as love that she bore him—like the devotion of a dog delivered from kicks. It was this first infant whose sacrifice was to implant the seed of *Emile* in the brain of his father, for in 1761, when Rousseau could bear to speak of his deed, he wrote to Madame de Luxembourg: "The ideas with which my fault crowded my mind contributed in large part toward my pondering the *Treatise on Education,* and you will find in Book One a passage which may demonstrate this—'He who cannot fulfill the duties of a father has no right to become one.' " [9]

The following year, the same inconvenience recurred and again the same expedient was adopted, except that the identification was neglected. "There was no more consideration on my part, no more approbation on the mother's," he confessed. Indeed, what could the poor girl, so ignorant and so pliable, have done? Only what she did: she moaned and obeyed. For her, it was an additional sacrifice she was making to the man who had "married" her despite her girlhood fault; the man who, she knew, would hold to his promise never to leave her. To all others she had been no more than a servant, a pretty girl to be teased and taken advantage of, had she not profited by her first hard lesson.

According to Rousseau himself, they had four more sons, each of whom went the way of the first. Did he tell the truth? Or did he fabricate the whole story to build up the figure of himself as a man of Stoic principles, who followed his head rather than his heart for the good of society as for the advantage of his children? Did he honestly feel that the institution of the Enfants-Trouvés could do more for them than the love of their mother and the teaching of their father who, though not yet recognized, knew that he had within himself genius and capacities that could change the thinking of mankind? Of course anyone to whom he would have suggested such a thing, even his friend Diderot, would have laughed. But the time would come when he would reveal the true Jean-Jacques to the world. For the complete expansion of the genius he felt within him such sacrifices might perhaps be justified.

His admirers in future years found it hard to accept his admission of such unnatural, if well-rationalized behavior and one apologist, Mrs. Frederika Macdonald, in 1906, went so far as to concoct a theory which made the weak-willed and ingenuous Thérèse a Machiavelli in the cleverness of her ruses. According to Mrs. Macdonald, Thérèse never had any children. She merely feigned pregnancy, to hold Rousseau by responsibility as well as by passion; and the fact that he was never shown any of his offspring proved to Mrs. Macdonald that they never could have been. How much farther could sentimentality go in distorting the truth?

Jean-Jacques in his confessional zeal, many years after the fact, told even more than he need have told, though when time had been able to bring about the objectivity on which he prided himself. "My third child," he wrote, "was therefore deposited at the Enfants-Trouvés like the first two; and it was the same with the two that followed; for I had five, altogether. This arrangement seemed so good, so sensible, so legitimate, that if I did not boast of it openly, it was solely out of regard

for the mother; but I told it to everyone to whom I had confessed our liaison . . . and freely and candidly . . . though
I could easily have concealed it from the whole world; for La
Gouin was an honest woman, very discreet. . . . The only
one of my friends in whom I felt any need to confide was Dr.
Thierry, who nursed my poor Tante (his pet name for
Thérèse) in one of her confinements, which had proved very
difficult. In a word, I made no mystery of my conduct, not
only because I have never been able to conceal anything
from my friends, but because, indeed, I saw nothing evil in it.
After weighing everything carefully I chose the best, or what I
thought the best, for my children. I could have wished, I still
wish, that I could have been raised and nurtured as they have
been." [10] One might perhaps believe him if he did not protest so
much, or if he had troubled to look into the lot of many of
these foundlings. Did any of his boys reach manhood? Or were
they hastened to a better world by the mercies of the Enfants-
Trouvés?

Whatever their fate, he had been offered the opportunity
both by Madame d'Epinay and Madame de Luxembourg of
having his children raised under their care. Always suspicious,
he questioned their motives. Was it through friendship, through
generosity that they made their offer, or for some dark purpose?
"I do not know," he answered his own questions. "I am certain, however, that they would have succeeded in making them
hate, perhaps even betray, their parents. It is a hundred times
better that they should never have known them." [11]

13. *The contest*

In his rationalization of the disposal of his children to the care
of the state, did Rousseau consider the effect such an unnatural
act would have on the psyche and character of Thérèse? True,
she was by nature submissive, and by love completely under his
domination. She was also one of those closed individuals that
like dumb animals keep their suffering to themselves. Unlike
dumb animals, however, they are capable of rationalization,
of bitterness and resentment; and when the hurt is not openly
expressed it rankles within, altering the whole nature. In
Thérèse the change came slowly, but it made itself felt. Jean-
Jacques was not too much concerned. Through Francueil and
Madame Dupin he had become a familiar of the salons, rub-
bing shoulders with the intellectuals of the day and, at least
once, with Voltaire himself at a gathering at the fashionable
Madame de Graffigny's.

He was more at home, however, at the salon of Madame

d'Epinay, Francueil's mistress, whom Rousseau had first met at Chenonceaux. He acquired immediately the manners and ethics of that facile society and felt not the least dismay at being not only the confidant of Francueil, but also of his wife and his mistress. Indeed, he took pleasure in the intrigue wherein he had in a sense the dominant role of the manipulator of this high society puppet show. However, the salon of Madame d'Epinay, like others in Paris, was not merely a place of amusement, but also an informal stage for the exchange of ideas that were at the time agitating not only Paris but Europe. Writers did not take up their quills merely to pen light compliments to the ladies. An intellectual awakening was taking place, which drew the roused curiosity of creative minds to course through realms hitherto explored by the philosophers. A Buffon produced a *Natural History,* while Montesquieu examined the *Spirit of the Laws,* and Voltaire, turning from the bagatelles he penned for the Court, pondered an *Essay on Morals.*

The thoughts of Jean-Jacques, too, began to turn to graver themes than the pastimes of gallant muses. With young Abbé Condillac he discussed the intellectual ferment of the day, which was also agitating his mind. His desire to assert himself through some significant writing gained impetus when he learned that Condillac was even then at work on an ambitious *Essay on the Origin of Human Knowledge.* Diderot, too, during their weekly dinners together at the Panier Fleuri, discussed with infectious enthusiasm their starting a weekly magazine, *Le Persifleur.* Each would take turns in writing and preparing the issue. Always impulsive, Jean-Jacques immediately drew up the first copy, which Diderot showed to his friend D'Alembert with whom he, Diderot, had just undertaken the translation into French of Chambers' *Encyclopaedia.* As their work progressed, however, and as it gained in scope, they began to see it as a vaster undertaking, an encyclopaedia comprehending all human knowledge and endeavor; thus the *Dictionnaire encyclopédique* was born. For it Jean-Jacques was assigned to write the article on music, which gave umbrage to Rameau. He had, like the other collaborators, three months in which to do it. His was the only work delivered on time, in a fine legible hand for which he had given Francueil's lackey, Dupont, ten écus out of his own pocket. Since Diderot had promised that he would be paid by the booksellers, and since those gentlemen did nothing, Jean-Jacques found himself a contributor to the *Encyclopaedia* in more ways than one, and at a time when he could ill afford such generosity.

Diderot, however, found himself in an even worse state. His *Pensées philosophiques* had already brought him to the unpleasant attention of the authorities. His *Lettre sur les aveugles*—or *Letter on the Blind* sent him to the Vincennes prison. Jean-Jacques, partly from sympathy with Diderot, partly no doubt in envy of his friend's noble martyrdom, did everything possible to have himself locked up, going so far as to make the request to Madame de Pompadour. The lady vouchsafed no answer; but Jean-Jacques flattered himself that it had been his letter which procured Diderot certain leniencies, shortly afterward, in his confinement.

He himself still had his troubles, some of them deriving from the propensity of Thérèse's mother to meddle in his relationships, to insinuate herself among his friends by doing some service or other, and to make herself agreeable with her gossip. Through Rousseau's friendship with Francueil, Madame le Vasseur had managed to become familiar with Madame Dupin and Madame de Chenonceaux. The usual feminine chitchat ensued, with the inevitable shocked comments on the subject of Rousseau's children sent to the Enfants-Trouvés.

"Yes, Madame, I did place my children at the Enfants-Trouvés," he wrote to Madame de Chenonceaux on April 20, 1751, evidently as an answer to some comment which Thérèse's mother had reported. "I have charged with their upbringing the establishment set up for that purpose. If my poverty and my ills prevent my undertaking so dear a care, it is a misfortune for which I should be pitied, and not a crime for which I should be blamed. I owe them their subsistence; I have obtained it for them, better, or at least more dependable, than I could have managed. This is the first consideration. Then comes concern for their mother, who must not be dishonored. You know my situation. I earn my bread with enough difficulty from day to day. How could I possibly support a family? Moreover, if I were obliged to adopt the profession of an author, what peace would I have in my garret and what tranquillity of mind, amid domestic cares and the rumpus of children? . . . Writing dictated by hunger brings in little. . . . One would have to resort to protectors, to intrigues. . . . Finally I would have to subject myself to infamies toward which I have a justifiable horror. What! Nurture myself, my children and their mother on the blood of poor wretches! No, Madame! Far better that they be orphans than that they should have a scoundrel for a father! . . ." [1]

Meanwhile his peripatetic habits and his familiarity in some of the most brilliant houses of Paris, the Dupin, the Chenonceaux, finally the salon of Madame d'Epinay, procured him connections which he would not otherwise have had. With no little vanity he let such names as the Prince de Saxe-Gotha's and Baron de Thun's trip off his tongue. He also met the witty German, Klupffell, and his brilliant compatriot, Melchior Grimm, a young man with great charm of manner, who served as reader to the Prince while waiting for opportunity to present him with something better. Jean-Jacques immediately struck up a friendship with Klupffell, but had to wait a while before the reserved Grimm melted. A conversation about music, on which Grimm spoke with authority, and his dexterity at the clavecin, conquered Rousseau, especially after the shy youth spent a whole day with him, making music.

At dinner one day the Prince de Saxe-Gotha brought up the subject of Diderot's imprisonment and seemed to condone it as the price for his imprudent opinions. Rousseau at once spoke up in Diderot's defense, certain that Saxe-Gotha had sought to put his own loyalty to the test. Well, the Prince and his guests got more than they had been waiting for. When Jean-Jacques returned to Paris he heard that Diderot had been removed from his dungeon and confined, on his honor, in the chateau of the Parc de Vincennes, where his friends were allowed to see him. Rousseau seized the opportunity—but let the man of sentiment describe the scene. "He was not alone. D'Alembert and the Treasurer of the Sainte-Chapelle were with him. On entering I saw only him. I made but one bound, and with a cry, I pressed my face to his, holding him close, speaking to him only with my sobs. . . . His first reaction was to turn to the churchman, saying, 'You see, Monsieur, how my friends love me.' "

Rousseau at first gave the words no special significance but on the way home he pondered them and took umbrage. What a way to take advantage of his, Rousseau's, sentiments! Certainly had he found himself in Diderot's place, *that* would not have been his own reaction.

In his recollection the magnanimity of his faithful visits, sometimes with Diderot's wife but most often alone, grew to a noble sacrifice. Most assuredly he, of all Diderot's friends, showed the most devotion. In the extreme heat of that summer of 1749 it was he, Rousseau, who uncomplainingly trudged the two leagues from Paris to Vincennes to bring the martyr comfort and encouragement. Sometimes, almost fainting in the hot sun, Rousseau would lie in the exiguous shadow of the polled trees along the road. Then one day it suddenly struck him that he would feel less exhausted if he took something to read along the way; and so, holding a book or a periodical, he would peruse it as he walked or rested. On one occasion he chose a copy of the *Mercure de France,* and while turning the pages he came across the announcement of the theme which the Dijon Academy had chosen for the prize contest of the following year: *Does the progress of the sciences and the arts contribute toward the corruption or the purification of morals?* "The instant I read those words I beheld another universe and I became a different person," he declared.[2]

Certainly the subject could not have been better chosen to suit the spirit of the times, fermenting with new ideas on society, on man and his destiny, which he, Jean-Jacques had often discussed with Diderot and Grimm over their dinner at the Panier Fleuri. They were not merely indulging in fanciful theory, they were not making literature, but in a sense preparing the mine that would explode the old evils in the social institutions and prepare the foundations for a new, more equitable society. As it was, all had reasons of their own for desiring a change, and none more than Rousseau who, in the social ranks of the existing system held, despite his talents and his intellect, the place between a literary flunky and an adventurer of the spirit.

Therefore, whenever he philosophized with Condillac, he unlearned much that he had acquired from the Jesuits. However, his essential love of God, which used to make him fall upon his knees at the sight of the first spring flower, remained intact under the young philosopher's potent arguments. On one occasion, somewhat later, while his friends Saint-Lambert and Duclos were hotly inveighing against God and religion with all the armaments of their reasoning, Jean-Jacques broke out: "If it is cowardice to allow people to speak ill of one's absent friend, it is a crime to suffer evil to be spoken of one's God, Who is present—and I, gentlemen, believe in God." [3]

The day he read the announcement of the contest, he arrived at Vincennes in almost a state of delirium, so stimulated had his mind become as it agitated the ideas that came pouring into it. Scarcely catching his breath, he told Diderot of the contest and read to him a long piece, the prosopopoeia of Fabricius which he had written in pencil, in the shade of a tree, on his way to Vincennes. Diderot, always generous, praised it and urged his friend to give full scope to his theme and to enter the competition.

In the élan of creative euphoria, further stimulated by hope and ambition, Rousseau began to write his essay, heading it with the caution: *Decipimur specie recti*—We are deceived by a kind of truth.

"Has the revival of the arts and sciences contributed toward purifying or corrupting morals? . . . What side should I take in this question? The side, gentlemen, that becomes an honest man who knows nothing and does not esteem himself the less for it." With this masterly beginning, defiant yet ingratiating, he could not but succeed in capturing the shocked attention of the Academicians. "How blame the sciences," he went on, "before one of the most learned societies of Europe? How praise ignorance in a celebrated Academy?" Still, honesty was dearer to the virtuous than all the learning of the scholars. What had he then to fear? Certainly, after supporting the side of truth, what did it matter whether or not he won the prize? For one prize there was which would be his in any case—and he would find that in his inmost heart.

Thereupon, with a clarity that he had never till then achieved in his writing, he set out upon a survey of the human condition, from the earliest glimmering of consciousness through Egypt, Greece, Rome, the Empire of the Orient, to the Europe of his day with its materialism and social inequalities, its subverted standards and mean ideals. He wrote during the day. At night, unable to sleep for the thoughts crowding his mind, he would dictate to Madame le Vasseur.

"The soul has its needs, as well as the body," he declared, "for these are the foundations of society; the rest but its pleasures. While government and laws provide for the security and well-being of the social group, the sciences, arts and letters, less despotic and perhaps more powerful, twine their garlands of flowers about the chains that weigh them down, stifling in them the feeling of that original liberty for which it would seem they were born; they make them love their enslavement and make of them what one calls a policed people. It was necessity that elevated thrones. The arts and the sciences have strengthened them. O mighty of the earth, love these talents and protect those who cultivate them. . . . How pleasant life would be here amongst us if our external countenance were always the reflection of the qualities of our hearts; if decency were virtue; if our maxims served us as rules of living, and if true philosophy were inseparable from the title of philosopher! But so many qualities are seldom found together, and virtue never walks in such great pomp. Sumptuousness of garb may announce a man of wealth and its elegance a man of taste. The strong, healthy man is to be known by other traits. It is beneath the rustic frock of a laborer, not under the tinsel of a courtier, that one will find vigor and strength of body. . . . A good man is an athlete who delights in fighting naked; he scorns all those common ornaments that would hinder the use of his powers, and most of which were invented only to conceal some deformity.

"Before art had fashioned our manners and taught our passions to speak a specious language, our customs were rustic and natural. . . . Fundamentally human nature was no better; but men found their security in the ease of their mutual understanding; this advantage whose value we no longer appreciate, saved them from many vices.

"Today when the subtlest researches and a finer taste have reduced to a principle the art of pleasing, a low and treacherous uniformity subsists in our customs, so that all minds seem to have been cast in the same mold; always courtesy exacts and seemliness demands. Always one follows custom, never one's own genius. One no longer dares appear what he is; and in this perpetual constraint, those who form the group known as society, if placed in identical circumstances, would all do the same things if more powerful motives did not deter them. One would never really know with whom one is dealing. . . .

"What a procession of vices would follow this uncertainty! True friendship would no longer exist, nor true esteem, nor solid trust. Suspicion, umbrage, fears, coldness, reserve, hatred, treachery—all would hide ceaselessly behind this uniform and perfidious veil of politeness, behind this boasted urbanity that we owe to the enlightenment of our century. One will no longer profane by oaths the name of the Lord of the universe; but one will insult Him by blasphemy without offending our scrupulous ears. One will not praise his own worth, but he will diminish the merits of his fellow." [4]

It was a forceful indictment of the time and its leaders; but Rousseau had not yet had his say. Invoking that paragon of civic virtue, the Roman Fabricius, he employs him as his mouthpiece. "Ye Gods!" he would have said. "What has become of those thatched cottages, those rustic hearths once inhabited by virtue and moderation? What fateful splendor has supplanted our Roman simplicity? What is this strange language? What are these effeminate morals? What mean these statues, these paintings, these buildings? Madmen, what have you done? You, the masters of the nations—you have become the slaves of the frivolous men you have conquered. It is now rhetoricians who govern you. It is to enrich architects and painters, sculptors and actors that you have shed your blood in Greece and Asia! The spoils of Carthage are the spoils of a flute player. Romans! Tear down these amphitheaters, break these marbles, burn these paintings! Cast out these slaves who subjugate you, whose fateful arts corrupt you . . . The only talent worthy of Rome is to conquer the world and let virtue reign. . . ." [5]

From the ancient world Rousseau returned to his era, lauding man's progress in the arts and sciences but deploring the use he had made of them and of the leisure they had given him. "It is a great evil, the abuse of time. But still other evils follow the arts and sciences. One such is luxury, born like them from the idleness and vanity of man. Luxury is rarely found without the sciences and the arts, and never do they progress without it. . . . The ancient politicians were always talking of morals and virtue; ours speak only of commerce and money. . . . They evaluate men as if they were herds of beasts. . . . Yet Cyrus' monarchy was overthrown by thirty thousand men, by a prince as poor as the least Persian satrap. . . . The Franks conquered the Gauls, the Saxons, England, with no treasures other than their courage and their poverty. . . ." [6]

Subtly Rousseau turned to the decadence of his own day, brought about by false moral values. "Every artist wishes to be applauded," he wrote. "The praises of his contemporaries are the most precious part of the reward." But alas, what happens when the arbiters are unfit to judge? When the artist finds himself at the mercy of frivolous youth, dominated in turn by the tyranny of women? "What then will the artist do?" Rousseau inquired, at once giving the answer. "He will abase his genius to the level of his times, and prefer to create ordinary works which will be praised in his day, rather than marvels which would be admired long after his death." "Tell us, O famous Arouet," he apostrophized Voltaire, "tell us how many male, powerful beauties you have sacrificed to our false delicacy! And how much the spirit of gallantry, so fertile in trifles, has cost you in great things!" [7]

There was no sphere he did not touch upon, nor any social activity that he did not consider. One of his most eloquent passages was an attack on the current educational system for children. "I see everywhere huge establishments where, at great expense, they raise the young, teaching them everything except their duties. Your children are ignorant of their own tongue, but they will speak others that are nowhere current. They will learn how to make verses, though barely knowing what they mean. Without the ability of distinguishing error from truth, they will possess the art of making them incomprehensible to others by specious arguments. However, the words magnanimity, equity, temperance, humanity and courage will have no meaning for them. . . . O Virtue, sublime science of simple souls," he invoked at the close, "does it require so much trouble, so many devices, to know you? Are not your principles engraved on all hearts? To know your laws it is not enough to enter within oneself, to listen to the voice of conscience, in the silence of the passions? That is the true philosophy." [8]

Unlike his expansive self he mentioned the essay only to Diderot and to Grimm, to whom in his usual manner he had become attached and with whom he still spent hours at the clavecin, singing Italian airs, so neglecting Thérèse that she complained of his infrequent visits. They had amusements other than music, however, of which she knew nothing, though she suspected much with the keen perceptions that often go with simplicity.

Grimm's friend Klupffell was keeping a young girl for his pleasure and did not hesitate to make her available to his friends, the better to support her. One evening, after they had all dined together with the girl and drunk plentifully, they took turns joining her in the private room though, Jean-Jacques noted, the poor child did not know whether to laugh or cry. This did not deter him from doing what the others had done. When he returned to Thérèse, she instantly perceived either by his confusion or some other token that something—and she knew by uncanny instinct exactly what—was amiss. Jean-Jacques decided to make a complete confession, for which he congratulated himself the following day, when his good friend Grimm entertained Thérèse with the whole sordid adventure.

Jean-Jacques and Thérèse had often talked of a common ménage, which Madame le Vasseur encouraged, but lack of means, as well as the thought of Thérèse's numerous family, made Rousseau hesitate. The question of money, however, was unexpectedly resolved when Madame Dupin and Francueil raised his annual salary. Moreover, on learning that Rousseau was about to "put himself within his furnishings," as the French idiom quaintly has it, Madame Dupin contributed some pieces which, with those that Rousseau had, enabled them to furnish their small apartment at the Hôtel de Languedoc, on the rue de Grenelle-Saint-Honoré. The rest of 1749 Rousseau spent working with Madame Dupin and Francueil and with his acquaintances, cherishing the while a glimmer of hope that the Dijon Committee might see some merit in his *Discours*.

As the year progressed, with still no word from the Academy, he resigned himself to his failure. He had even forgotten the *Discours* when, the following year, he learned that his essay had carried off the prize and its accompanying gold medal bearing a figure of Minerva and the inscription, *Tergeminis certat.* It was of interest to his household that the value of the gold in the medal was three hundred livres. Noble as the spirit that had animated his essay, its success, he said, "set working in my heart that primal leaven of heroism and virtue that my father, my country and Plutarch had placed there in my childhood. From then on I found nothing greater nor more beautiful than to be free and virtuous, to rise above fortune and public opinion, and to be sufficient unto myself. . . ." [9]

That same year, forgetting his ardent republicanism in favor of the binding sympathies of humanity, he also wrote an inspiring funeral oration for young Louis, Duc d'Orléans, who had been all that a noble prince should be, charitable, righteous and scholarly enough to translate the Psalms and also the Epistles of Saint Paul.

Thérèse, now again pregnant, made Rousseau seriously reconsider his responsibility toward his children. He decided as before. "Too sincere with myself, with too much inner pride to wish to belie my principles by my works, I set about examining the destiny of my children and my relations with their mother by the laws of nature, justice and reason, and by those of this pure, holy religion, as eternal as its Author. . . . If I was mistaken in the results, nothing is more astonishing than the trustfulness of soul with which I yielded. Were I one of those baseborn men, deaf to the gentle voice of nature, and within whom no genuine sentiment of justice or humanity ever sprang, such hardness would be very simple; but this warmth of heart, this very keen sensibility, this readiness to form attachments, this strength with which they enslave me, these cruel wrenchings when they must be broken, this innate well-wishing for my fellows; this ardent love for the great, the true, the beautiful, the just; this horror of evil of all kinds; this impossibility to hate, to injure, or even its very wish; this tenderness, this keen and sweet emotion which I experience before all that is virtuous, generous and worthy of love—can all this ever find accord in the same soul with the depravity which unscrupulously treads underfoot the sweetest of duties? No! I feel it and I cry it aloud: it is not possible! Not for one instant of his life could Jean-Jacques have been a man without sentiment, without entrails, an unnatural father! I could have deceived, but never so hardened, myself. . . ."

Then, in the Tartuffe accent that betrayed a hint of insincerity in the basically honest man, he added: "If I told my reasons, I would tell too much. Since they were able to seduce me, they might seduce many others. I do not wish to expose young people who might read me, to being abused by the same error." [10] It was an edifying homily but not altogether convincing in the light of his own life. He recognized his errors yet he had no choice but to act as he did, confident that a just God would understand the necessity which had driven him to his decision. In the end he was even to place the divine power on his side, when on February 26, 1770 he was to write to Saint-Germain: "Providence has watched over my children for the very sin of their father."

On the publication of the *Discours* with its grandiloquent dedicatory essay to the Republic of Geneva, Rousseau had sent a copy to Voltaire. A comment from the great man, if favorable, would carry weight if rightly handled. Voltaire read it very carefully, to judge by the notes he made in his copy of the book which eventually found its way to the library of Catherine the Great of Russia. "Chimerical . . . false . . . ridiculous . . . abominable! . . . Fool that you are! . . ." were some of his marginal comments. On an admission of Jean-Jacques', blaming himself for his eagerness to be talked about, Voltaire exploded: "How you do condemn yourself, you Ape of Diogenes!"

His letter, however, though candid and unsparing, respected the amenities. "I have received, Monsieur, your new book against the human race and I thank you for it . . . Never has anyone exercised such wit to turn us into beasts . . ." (The French is a delightful pun, *bêtes* meaning both beasts and fools.) "One almost feels like walking on all fours on reading your work. However, since for more than sixty years I have lost the habit, I feel, unfortunately, that it would be impossible to reacquire it; and so I leave this natural posture to such as are worthier of it than you and myself. . . . Letters nourish the soul," he went on. "They correct it and console it, and they work toward your glory even when you write against them. You are like Achilles, who inveighs against glory, and like Father Malebranche, whose brilliant imagination wrote against the imagination. Monsieur Chapuis informs me that your health is very bad," he continued more intimately. "You should come to restore it in your natal air, delighting in liberty, drinking with me the milk of our cows and nibbling our grass. . . ." Rousseau, despite the temptation, remained in Paris.

14. Le Devin *and the social lion*

It was now, to obtain the independence he sought for his creative work, that Rousseau took up seriously the employment of music copyist. He enjoyed it, it kept him in good spirits during the mornings he devoted to it, and it brought him enough to provide for the essential needs of Thérèse and himself. He had tried other means of earning a living, the latest, through Francueil, as bookkeeper, succeeding his cashier, Dudoyer, who being old and rich, had decided to retire. Rousseau worked conscientiously and scrupulously, if also trepidantly, at his desk keeping the books, giving out and receiving money under the guidance of Francueil. Unfortunately Francueil had to absent himself on business, leaving Rousseau in full charge of the accounts. Worry over the responsibility and dread that somehow or other the money would disappear kept him in such emotional turmoil that on Francueil's return he promptly took to his bed and blamed the recurrence of the irritation of the bladder to his constant preoccupation, just as he had attributed an earlier attack of nephritis to his walks in the hot sun when he had gone to comfort Diderot at Vincennes. Always there had to be some aura of martyrdom to his suffering. The present illness, however, was genuine and kept him confined for more than five weeks, suffering agonies each time Dr. Morand, the specialist provided by Madame Dupin, tried to tap the bladder with little success, because of its peculiar conformation.

The weeks spent in bed confirmed Rousseau in the resolution he had made in his delirium: to live out in complete independence whatever life was still left him. Farewell to vain hopes and ambitions. He renounced them all. Being Jean-Jacques Rousseau, such abnegation and stoicism had to set an example to the world and he accordingly applied all the powers of his spirit to burst the shackles of opinion and to accomplish courageously what seemed good to him, unmindful of what the world might think. "The obstacles I had to combat and the efforts I had to make to overcome them are unbelievable." [1] He did not succeed, however, at least not wholly, for many of the people he knew inconsiderately insisted on remaining his friends. "Had I managed as well in shaking off the yoke of friendship as of opinion, I would have succeeded in my design, the greatest perhaps, or at least the most useful to virtue, ever conceived by a mortal. Yet while I was trampling underfoot the senseless judgments of the vulgar crowd, of the self-styled great and the self-styled wise, I allowed myself to be subjugated and led like a child by my so-called friends, who, jealous at seeing me tread the new path alone, did all in their power to make me look ridiculous, while appearing to be much concerned about my happiness. . . . It was not so much my literary fame as my personal reformation . . . that roused their jealousy. They might perhaps have forgiven me for shining in the art of writing; but they could not forgive me for setting them an example through my conduct which seemed to make them uncomfortable." [2]

Yet at the time he adopted the métier of copyist he was at the height of his fame for the *Discours* on the Arts and Sciences, for which Diderot had undertaken to find a printer. "It carries everything before it," he wrote to Rousseau, then sick in bed. "There has never been an example of such a success!" Now for the first time assured of his talent, which he had always doubted, Jean-Jacques determined on his career. He had other gifts, however, which clamored to be exercised—his music, his poetry. He vowed to reform his life, the better to serve the talents that nature had bestowed upon him.

He began by giving up wearing white stockings, and also the *dorure* or gilding for his hair, adopting a round wig instead. As for his fine shirts, his brother-in-law had relieved him of such foppery. Since he never did things by halves, Rousseau also ceased wearing his little sword and sold his watch, sighing: "Thank God, I'll never need to know what time it is!" Now it was his task to eradicate from heart and mind everything that still bound him to the notions of his fellows and, even more, all that could turn him from what was worthwhile within himself, merely out of fear of what the world might say.

As it happened, the world was saying a great deal about his *Discours,* especially the literary gadflies, rival authors who, in the elevation of a fellow scribe, saw a diminution of themselves. Letters and pamphlets rained upon him wherein he was taken to task by critics who revealed that they had not the least conception of what his *Discours* signified. A man from Nancy, a certain Gautier, had a taste of Rousseau's sarcasm that he must have found hard to dissipate; but such a nonentity had been too highly honored as it was by even being noticed.

King Stanislas of Poland, however, who deigned to enter the lists, was another matter, as the Citizen of Geneva realized. He could not be dealt with as high-handedly as a mere man from Nancy, particularly since he, Rousseau, caught the fine Jesuitical accent of a certain Père Menou in the criticism. He retorted with an essay which he, Rousseau, was always to consider unique of its kind, not only for its matter, but for the fact that it dared to show the public how an ordinary individual could defend the cause of truth even against a powerful monarch. His friends, shocked by his boldness, were certain that he would be sent to the Bastille, which doubtless Jean-Jacques would have enjoyed for a little while for the aura of martyrdom it would have given him; but nothing of the sort happened. On the contrary, his essay circulated throughout Europe and he acquired a friend in King Stanislas, who was to show him many favors. But if he won a friend in the King of Poland, he inevitably made enemies in the frustrated and envious who saw in his success a slight to their own genius.

Vexation, worry and overwork affected his health, aggravating the discomfort of his chronic disease. At Passy he had found a refuge in the hospitality of "Strangler" Mussard, the jeweler, fellow Genevan and distant relative, who after making a modest fortune had decided to spend his years of retirement in the enjoyment of nature. One day, while digging in his garden, Mussard had uncovered a bed of fossil shells. From then on he thought, talked and lived conchology, delighting and then boring his surfeited friends. He held pleasant gatherings at his house, however, where Rousseau exchanged wisdom with doctors and philosophers and talked literature with the Abbé Prévost, whom he found simple and amiable—a man whose heart vivified his writings. The company of the ladies he thought rather mediocre: a Madame Denis, Voltaire's niece, who was not yet playing the society wit, and two women whose physical attributes he found wanting, but who sang charmingly.

At first he had come chiefly to drink the waters at Passy, but he soon found himself spending the mornings playing Italian music with Mussard, an adept at the violoncello, and the evenings discussing the *opera buffa,* for which both had a passion. Strange that the French should have nothing in the genre. This woeful lack preyed on Rousseau's mind and he set about remedying it at once; for the following morning, while wandering about, cup in hand, drinking the Passy waters, he found his cranium echoing to the words and music of a pastoral operetta that was gradually taking shape. Retiring to a sort of vaulted summerhouse, he set down three lyrics with their music, and also a monologue and other snatches of dialogue and accompaniments as they came to him.

Soon a pastoral drama in one act had evolved, whose extreme simplicity was not the least of its charms. It had only three characters: Colin, Colette and the village soothsayer. Perhaps the setting of Les Charmettes, more than that of Passy, came to the forefront of his creative imagination. Perhaps unconsciously a certain ribbon given to him by a fair chatelaine, Madame de Warens herself, suggested the one for Colin's hat. To probe deeper still into the workings of the creative imagination, *Le devin du village—The Village Soothsayer*—may have been Rousseau's adieu to the ambitions of the romantic adolescent for the love of the beautiful damozel of the castle, and his settling for the adoration of a plain girl of the people, his own Thérèse.

At the moment Rousseau was chiefly aware of the urge to give shape and voice to the creatures of his imagination.

> *Lost is all my peace of mind*
> *Since my Colin proves unkind,*
>   *Alas! He's gone forever.*

So mourns and sings Colette, as she comes upon the stage sighing and wiping her eyes with her apron.[3]

As she walks toward the soothsayer she counts her coins, wraps them in a bit of paper and then hesitantly hands them to him. She sings:

> *Will Colin ne'er be mine again?*
> *Tell me if death must end my pain!*

"Assuage your grief," counsels the soothsayer, adding what certainly could have brought no comfort to the girl: "Colin to you is false of late."

Ah, me! I die—Go on!
And yet he always loves you. More artful but less fair
The Lady who dwells hard by—
To her he roves?
But you, said I, he always loves—
And always flies! . . .
His heart I'll soon restore—
Beware you never lose it more;
But first his passion to increase,
Feign, feign, fair maid, to love him less.
If uneasy love increases;
If contented, sound he sleeps.

She who with coquetry teases
Fast in chains her shepherd keeps . . .

Following the soothsayer's advice, Colette lures back her roving Colin, and while the villagers dance, she sings the closing air:

Though noise and splendor they boast of in town,
More heartfelt enjoyments our festivals crown:
 While dance and song

 Our bliss prolong
 And beauty warms
 With artless charms
What music e'er with our pipes can compare? . . .

That afternoon at tea with Mussard and his young *gouvernante*, Mademoiselle Duvernois, Rousseau diffidently showed them the arias and the monologue he had written. He would have thrown those scraps into the fire, he said, had both not demonstrated such delighted enthusiasm. Always easily swayed by the reactions of others, he decided to complete the miniature opera, which he called *Le devin du village*. Back in Paris he polished it, added some recitatives and worked on the orchestration. What to do with it, now that it was finished? He longed to hear it—but how could that be managed? He finally thought of Monsieur Duclos, with whom he had become acquainted several years earlier at La Chevrette, through Madame d'Epinay. At that time Rousseau had interested him in *Les muses galantes,* but nothing had come of the interview for Duclos had left town the same day. Now, since everything seemed propitious, Rousseau gave him *Le devin du village,* on condition that if he produced it he was to withhold the name of the author. He had his reasons for such modesty. The first was his fear of secret enemies, who would do their utmost to destroy his work. Another was the value in such secrecy, for everyone would be curious to pierce through the mask of anonymity.

Accordingly *Le devin* was presented respecting Rousseau's wishes and the secret was so well kept that not even the "Petits Violons," Rebel and Francœur, who used to furnish music and gossip to the great houses, succeeded in ferreting it out. *Le devin* triumphed and the following day it was the topic of conversation everywhere. The acclaim did not fail to reach the Court, particularly since Monsieur de Cury, in charge of the *menus plaisirs,* or light amusements, had attended one of the rehearsals and manifested his delight. Immediately the Court requested that *Le devin* be given at Fontainebleau. Duclos, the manager, refused. Monsieur de Cury insisted in the King's name. Soon the Duc d'Aumont himself joined the King's party, pleading for a performance, whereupon Duclos surrendered.

Rousseau, Citizen of Geneva, was pleased at this humbling of royal authority, so pleased indeed that after much pleading he condescended to attend one of the rehearsals. He went to Fontainebleau in the company of the actress, Mademoiselle Fel, who was to play Colette, and with Grimm and the Abbé Raynal, in the comfort and majesty of a royal coach. Poor Thérèse had no part whatever in all this splendor.

The following day Rousseau went as usual to dine at the Grand-Commun Café, where everyone was talking of the rehearsal of the night before and of the impossibility of finding even standing room. At this an officer, dining at a table nearby, said that he had had no difficulty whatsoever in entering. He then proceeded to give a detailed account of the performance, the actors and even the author, whom he now nevertheless failed to recognize though they were sitting face to face. Rousseau listened as fascinated as the rest. There the fellow was, a man old enough to have acquired good sense, if not wisdom, and with the cross of Saint-Louis on his coat, boldly telling his lies that he might have a ray of the aura of that great event. This indeed was fame. Embarrassed though flattered, Rousseau left as inconspicuously as he could, fearful that someone might recognize him and expose the officer.

Later that day, October 18, 1752, he was entering the theater at Fontainebleau when Monsieur de Cury leapt forward to greet him and lead him to his own box, directly opposite that of His Majesty, Louis XV. Rousseau was wearing his usual careless costume. His wig needed combing and his cheeks had the shadow of several days' beard—a carelessness carefully planned for whatever it was that Jean-Jacques wished to prove. His independent spirit? His republicanism? His scorn of inherited greatness as against honor and fame achieved through the exercise of one's genius? If any in the audience noticed his anomalous dress, good breeding forbade either look or word. When the lights flickered on, he was the only one who felt ill at ease, in the forefront of the loge, surrounded by beautiful women exquisitely accoutered and opposite the royal box, slightly elevated above the rest, where the King was sitting with Madame la Marquise de Pompadour, lately a child of the people with the unromantic name of Jeanne Antoinette Poisson. Instead of pondering on the extraordinary chess game played by life and destiny, Rousseau held an internal soliloquy which he later set down.

"I am in my proper place because I see my piece being played, because I am invited, because I wrote it for just this purpose and because, after all, no one has a better right than

I have to enjoy the fruit of my labor and my talents. I am dressed in my usual garb, neither better nor worse. If I begin again to subject myself to public opinion in even one instance, there I shall be, once more enslaved by everything. . . . My appearance is simple and careless, neither crass nor dirty. Nor is the beard in itself unclean, since nature gave it to us. Moreover, according to times and fashions, it has sometimes been an ornament. They'll think me ridiculous, impertinent! Well! What does it matter? I must know how to endure ridicule and blame, provided they are not deserved." [4]

Far from receiving ridicule and blame, he found himself the darling of the most formidable salons, the hostesses clamoring for the privilege of showing off the celebrated bear. How could it have been otherwise with the man whose *Devin* had caused bucketsful of sentimental tears to flow, including a good stream of his own? What exquisite music to his ears had been the comments of the ladies.

"How charming!"

"How ravishing!"

"There is not a note in it that does not speak to the heart!"

He began to enjoy his fame, but not for long, as his chronically apprehensive spirit never ceased to whisper in his ear that one does not remain on a peak forever. His memory obligingly supplied chastening examples. "Still, I am certain that at this time *volupté du sexe* played a far greater part than my author's vanity. Surely, if only men had been present, I would not have been devoured, as I was, by the desire to gather with my lips the delicious tears that I had caused to flow. . . ." [5]

The day following the performance of *Le devin du village* Monsieur de Cury had arranged for the formal presentation of Rousseau to His Majesty, a proceeding which was usually followed by the granting of a pension. All night long Rousseau could not sleep, fears and apprehensions crowding upon him, the most humiliating of them all the dread that his infirmity, in his state of agitation, might cause him to disgrace himself before His Majesty and the assembled Court. His natural timidity on meeting strangers also played its part. Between the two fears he helplessly yielded, failed to meet the appointment with Monsieur de Cury—and lost the royal patronage as well as a possible pension. What of it? he soliloquized. By losing the pension he also lost the yoke of dependence that such a gift would have entailed. Then good-bye to truth, to freedom and courage. Besides, his principles were more precious to him than all the pensions in the world. He had gone as far as he had through his own genius and accomplishment. He would continue along the same path, companioned by the same lofty aims.

The very day of the royal appointment he left Paris, giving his poor health as an excuse and thus starting the tongues of his enemies wagging. Arrogance and pride had made him reject the King's bounty, they said, blaming him for his conduct. Perhaps of all the people in Paris, His Majesty was the least concerned over Rousseau's departure. "All day long," Jelyotte wrote him the following day, "His Majesty has not stopped singing in the most off-key voice in the world:

J'ai perdu mon serviteur,
J'ai perdu tout mon bonheur. . . .

If Rousseau felt spiritual elation at having been sufficiently stoical to refuse the King's bounty, it was not so with Thérèse and particularly with Madame le Vasseur. There must have been much weeping and clasping of hands on learning of that foolish man's determination, for they immediately sent for his wise, practical friend, Diderot, to act as emissary for their pleas. There never had been plenty in the house. Why should Jean-Jacques reject the security of a regular little stream of gold to supply the avidity of the Le Vasseur clan? Several evenings later, as Rousseau was about to step down from the carriage at Madame d'Epinay's door, he saw Diderot descending from a fiacre and coming toward him, his face very earnest. Before

Rousseau could greet him Diderot began declaiming a plea on behalf of the Le Vasseurs. Jean-Jacques gave his reasons for his decision, whereupon Diderot employed his forensic skill to turn his friend from his proud purpose to the consideration of the many needs of the Le Vasseurs. If Rousseau wished to appear magnanimous, he said, he should not do so at the expense of poor Thérèse and her family. After all, it was Rousseau's responsibility to provide for them; therefore he could not afford the luxury of putting up a magnanimous front at their expense. Besides, it was not yet generally known that he had refused the pension, and perhaps the Court had done nothing about it as yet. Why, instead of rejecting such a gift, Rousseau should exert all his efforts to solicit it, no matter what the cost to his pride.

Rousseau listened to him patiently, appreciating his zeal, but giving his reasons for not taking the pension. Still spurred by his purpose Diderot persevered, going so far as to dictate his duty to Rousseau. An altercation ensued, and for the first time the two parted a little less than amicably. From then on, it seemed to the suspicious Rousseau that his erstwhile friend, together with Grimm, aligned himself with the Le Vasseurs and did his best to alienate them from him, promising Madame le Vasseur all sorts of lures, like a salt concession or a tobacco shop. He even suspected the two men of trying to enlist Holbach and Duclos in their league.

Certainly both Holbach and Duclos were not as cordial as they had once been and on certain occasions it seemed as if they wished to injure his reputation, laying all kinds of traps to put him in a bad light. What purpose, other than that of doing him harm, had impelled Holbach to insist on his using a little aria from what he swore was a private collection, for the revised and amplified version of the *Devin,* only to have Rousseau find the same aria conspicuously exhibited on Grimm's piano during a more than usually well attended soirée? However, neither envy nor malevolence could keep the *Devin* from going its way, not even the competition of the Italian troupe in such favorite plays as Goldoni's *La serva padrona*. It was for these later performances that Rousseau composed the incidental music for the *Devin*.

At this juncture all Paris chose to divide itself into musical parties, one aligning itself with the Italian school, the other with the French. The usual pamphlets, the stormy petrels of debate, began flying about, but only two survived: *Le petit prophète* by Grimm and *Lettre sur la musique française* by Rousseau. Grimm's essay received a certain amount of notice, but it was Rousseau's eloquently caustic *Lettre* that raised a storm, all of France's musical cohorts considering themselves affronted in their musical prestige.

Suddenly the long-raging quarrel between the clergy and the French parliament was forgotten as all took up the cudgels in defense of *La musique française*. Whether or not they knew a note of music, they all cried out for the hide of the infidel who had had the effrontery not to place it at the peak of the musical pyramid. Even at Court, it seemed, the choice of punishment for the culprit lay between exile and the Bastille —though one must allow for Rousseau's always fanciful imagination. At any rate he suffered neither the one nor the other and found himself—to the chagrin of the would-be martyr—the recipient of both cash and royal favor for his delightful operetta. Moreover he obtained an additional five hundred francs from Pissot for an engraving to illustrate his *Devin*. "Thus this interlude, which altogether cost me no more than five or six weeks of work," he wrote subsequently, "brought me almost as much money . . . as did *Emile*, later, which cost me twenty years of meditation and three years of labor. . . ." [6]

Matters were quite the reverse with Diderot at that time. Diderot wrote boldly, forcefully, but the police were constantly on his trail, ready to seize his work the moment it left the presses. He had to exercise caution and adroitness not only in his style but in the distribution of his explosive ideas, all the more dangerous from the point of view of the government for their sweet reasonableness and their charm of style. His whole nature, forthright and courageous, rebelled against the necessity imposed upon him of having his works appear almost surreptitiously. Some, like his *Promenade du sceptique,* which he wrote in 1747, did not see the light until 1830, thanks to the vigilance of the authorities who succeeded in seizing it.

On the surface it seemed innocent enough, this thoughtful promenade of Diderot's sceptic, Théobule, a poet in his responses, a philosopher in his reflections. But an explosive force lay hidden under that field dotted with flowers. Writes Diderot: "I soon noted that the topics he seized upon were always analogous to the things he had within his view. In a kind of labyrinth . . . he never failed to talk to me about the fallibility of the human mind, on the uncertainty of our knowledge. . . . When he sat on the brink of a fountain and a leaf happened to leave a neighboring tree and, wafted by the breeze, floated on the surface of the water, troubling its limpidity, he would speak of the frailty of our virtues and the strength of our passions. . . . When we stood on a hilltop dominating the fields and woods round about, he infused in me a mistrust of all that raises a man without making him a better individual. He would point to the thousandfold vaster space above my head than the space beneath my feet, and he would humble me by the relationship between the vanishing point beneath and the vast space above, opening to my view. When we had come down to the valley again, he reflected on the wretchedness of the human situation and exhorted me to expect it without qualms and bear it without flinching." [7]

It was such conversations as Diderot assigned to Théobule that Rousseau himself heard whenever he was with his friend at their casual little dinners. His spongelike mind absorbed it all, releasing the ideas after they had in turn passed through his kindled imagination. Humanly vain, alas, he never gave credit to his friend's creative influence. Diderot, however, knew his own greatness and scattered his largesse freely upon the world.

Part Four

15. *Discourse on inequality*

The following year, 1753, on the first day of March the *Devin du village* was given at the Opéra with even greater success than before, for Rousseau, acceding to the taste of the day, had added a divertissement which increased its popularity. The name of Rousseau, rather of Jean-Jacques as he was generally called, became both a household word and a popular chant, as the balladeers intoned:

> *Les Lullis et les Rameaux*
> *Sont des esprits opaques,*
> *Des ignorants et des sots.*
> *Ainsi l'a dit en deux mots*
> *Jean-Jacques. . . .*

> *The Lullis and the Rameaux*
> *Are but minds opaque,*
> *Ignoramuses and fools,*

So at least says one who knows—
John-Jack. . . .

Again Louis XV requested a performance of the *Devin,* this time at the Trianon and with Madame de Pompadour in the role of Colin. She sent the author fifty louis, which he was reluctant to accept, but the sensible Gauffecourt, who happened to be with him, convinced him that it would be folly to refuse. Jean-Jacques finally surrendered, even penning a stilted little note of thanks which cost him more pains in afterthoughts and erasures than a discourse for the Academy. "In accepting the present which has been transmitted to me on your part, I hope to have vouchsafed my regard for the hand of the donor, and I dare add, for the honor you have done my work. . . ." [1] So much for the bounty of Antoinette Poisson.

Public curiosity, meanwhile, was being aroused by the man Rousseau, and the salons, too, were becoming aware of the carelessly dressed celebrity of the moment, with his large shining dark eyes, his strange asymmetrical face, half-sad half-gay, and his reputation as a defiant, independent spirit. He enjoyed the fluster he created, the flattery of the ladies and the growing regard of the men, but always there was the other Rousseau, suspicious of, yet in a sense eager for, the stinging whips of Mademoiselle Lambercier. Never could he accept unadulterated satisfaction; but even here the gods acceded to his desires, for the Holbach crew and the lesser wits at the Panier Fleuri did their utmost to tear the laurels from his brow. They criticized his *Discours,* trying to find holes in the logic, pitting their intellects against his and ending by betraying the envy that prompted their barbs. Rousseau made himself inaccessible, however. Where another would have docilely performed for his hostesses in their salons, he retired to the country to assert his independence and prove the strength of his personality, out of reach of praise and of flattery.

The *gouverneuses,* as Gauffecourt had nicknamed mother and daughter, had of course to follow him in his retirement, albeit much against their will since Madame le Vasseur and through her influence Thérèse as well, had something to gain in gifts and favors from their unsuspecting lion's friends and enemies. Indeed, ever since the fame of his *Discours,* Rousseau had had to write to his would-be benefactors, begging them not to embarrass him with their unneeded and unwanted bounty. The Le Vasseurs, however, never failed to reach out their eager hands. Nor did malicious tongues cease to wag at the spectacle of the proud, independent man enjoying these gifts, despite his protestations. Still, had the Le Vasseurs not accepted them, Rousseau would have been taxed with pride unbecoming a philosopher, since he was even then being blamed for letting Madame le Vasseur place her eighty-year-old husband in an old people's home, where he promptly gave up the ghost.

During the first week of June the three, Jean-Jacques with Thérèse and her mother, went to Lake Leman so dear to Rousseau's memory; but the excursion was marred by Thérèse, who had begun to acquire the airs of the Paris ladies, as well as their whims and vapors. At Lake Leman the pretext for her sulks was the blameless Gauffecourt for paying too little attention to her and too much to Rousseau, with whom he never tired of discussing topics far above her head. She complained of being left alone, of not being included in their walks, which indeed they took for the blissful privacy they enjoyed along the lake and through the woods. In short, Thérèse behaved like any spoiled, capricious mistress and not his wife, as he considered her. The sulks now had another cause. Gauffecourt was paying too much attention to her, especially when they were out riding in the carriage when, according to Thérèse, he would try to inflame her by reading to her, and showing her pictures, from a lascivious book.

At Lyons Rousseau's thoughts turned to Madame de Warens of whom in his gratitude and honesty he had told Thérèse. He could not be so near and not call on her. Leaving Gauffecourt and Thérèse behind, he set out on his pilgrimage, his heart and thoughts reliving that day, years ago, when the homeless boy had been charmed by the youth and beauty of the chatelaine. Nature was still the same—but Maman, how she had changed! What squalor in her surroundings. His heart sank. How had she come to this? Why did she not leave everything and make a new life for herself elsewhere? She could not, however. There was her pension, irregularly paid, it is true, but still money which she badly needed. All her ambitious plans, her grandiose schemes, had failed. With them had gone her money and the parasites she had fed and housed.

Time and again in his letters Rousseau had urged her to come and live with him and Thérèse. Always the pension weighed more than his pleas, for though small, it was a raft in her sea of troubles. Before parting Rousseau pressed upon her some of the money he had with him, though he knew it would go the way of the rest. Later, while he was at Geneva, she went to see him. Despite her gallant reticence he discovered that she had not sufficient money for her return. Since he had little on his person he sent Thérèse to her with the amount she required. Maman had only one small ring left of all her jewels. This she slipped on Thérèse's finger, "who kissed that noble hand which she watered with her tears," noted Rousseau, overwhelmed with tenderness. "Ah, that was the moment to acquit myself of my debt," he reflected. "I should have left everything to go with her, to bind myself to her till her final hour, to share her fate, whatever it might be. . . . I sighed over her, but did not follow her. Of all the pangs of remorse I have felt in my life, that was the keenest and the most enduring." [2] Madame de Warens had by then found surer comfort than Jean-Jacques could have given her. "You see verified in me," she wrote him, "the chapter that I have just finished reading in the *Imitation of Christ,* where it is written that there, where we place our surest hopes we shall be left most totally wanting. It is not the blow you gave me that afflicts me, but rather the hand that dealt it. . . . Despite it all I am and shall always be your true mother. Adieu." [3]

However, for Rousseau there was Thérèse to consider—Thérèse whose first and second sons had been consigned to the Enfants-Trouvés and who was again pregnant. But Rousseau had another child to think about, a child of his brain, the *Discours sur l'origine et les fondements de l'inégalité parmi les hommes,* for which he had still to pen a dedication worthy of his natal Geneva, the recipient of his homage. He was nothing if not thorough, and thus the dedicatory address to "The magnificent, highly honored and Sovereign Lords" took all of twenty printed pages, followed by a preface of somewhat greater length. The subject had been chosen by the Académie of Dijon for its current contest.

In his essay Rousseau recognized two kinds of inequality: the natural, or physical, inequality established by nature; and the moral, or political, inequality established, or at least authorized, by man. He had read his Aristotle and also his Hobbes very thoroughly, together with the satirical Mandeville, the learned Cumberland and Pufendorf, François Corréal, who had studied the Caribbeans of Venezuela, and whatever else Rousseau could find on the subject. The result of his researches, passing through the alembic of his always original mind, made a challenging and fascinating treatise, although he accepted Mandeville's fantasies as uncritically as Hobbes' logic. He was best, however, when he expressed his own thoughts in his own voice, even though he based them on the still limited anthropological knowledge of the day.

"I see in every animal an ingenious machine," he wrote, "to which nature has given senses with which to rewind itself and even to protect itself, to a certain point, from all that would tend to destroy or upset it. I find precisely the same things in the human machine, with this difference: that nature alone functions in all the operations of the beast, whereas man concurs in his, in the quality of a free agent. The one chooses or rejects by instinct, and the other by an act of free will. . . ." [4]

It was Hobbes, of all Rousseau's sources, whose *De Cive* he must have read in its original Latin, who had most influenced his thought, as Diderot was brilliantly to point out in his article

Hobbisme, in the *Encyclopédie.* "The philosophy of Monsieur
Rousseau of Geneva is almost the opposite of that of Hobbes.
The one believes the natural man is good; the other, evil. According to the philosopher of Geneva the state of nature is the
state of peace; according to the philosopher of Malmesbury,
it is a state of war. Laws and the organization of society changed
man for the better, if one is to believe Hobbes; no, they
corrupted him, if one is to believe Rousseau. The former was
born in the midst of the tumult of factions; the latter lived in
the world amid the savants. Other times, other circumstances,
other philosophers."

Amid general prudery, Rousseau defended man's natural passions. "Whatever moralists may say, human understanding owes
much to the passions . . . it is through their activity that reason is perfected. We seek to know only because we desire to
enjoy; and it is impossible to conceive why anyone with neither
desires nor fears should give himself the trouble to reason.
The passions, in turn, spring from our necessities, and their
progress from our knowledge; for one can desire or fear things
only through the ideas one may have of them, or from the
simple impulse of nature. Primitive man, deprived of all enlightenment, experiences only passions of this latter kind, his
desires not going beyond his physical needs. The only blessings
he knows in the universe are food, a female and rest. The only
evils he dreads are pain and hunger. I say pain and not
death, for the animal will never know what it is to die. Awareness of death and of its terrors was one of the first acquirements
made by man as he drew farther away from the animal
state. . . ." [5]

Through man's slow hard journey toward civilization, progress and perfectibility Rousseau led his reader. "How many
centuries must have passed before men had advanced enough
to see any other fire than that of heaven. What perils must
they not have gone through to acquire the simplest uses of this
element! How many times must they have let it go out before
they had learned the art of rekindling it! And how often had

each of these secrets died with its discoverer! What shall we say of agriculture, an art which demands such labor and foresight . . . and which evidently is practicable only in a society which has at least made a beginning. . . ." [6]

From man's physical needs Rousseau proceeded to those of his awakening consciousness. "The first language of man, the most universal and compelling, and the only one required before he was obliged to persuade an assemblage, was the cry of nature. As this cry was forced out only by a kind of instinct on pressing occasions, to beg for help in times of peril, or for comfort in violent suffering, it was not often employed in the ordinary course of life, where moderation prevails. . . ." [7]

While dwelling so exhaustively on the general, he was no doubt called to the particular by the thought of his own off-spring, whose first cry on entering life he had never heard, whose face he had never seen. It is likely that at this very time Thérèse was again with child. Whatever the motivations, Rousseau's mind began to ponder another work, one treating the ideal rearing and education of a child from the moment of his birth until young manhood. Years were to pass between the genesis of *Emile* and its fulfillment, but the seed once planted in Rousseau's fertile brain germinated and threw out its hidden shoots and airy tendrils, blending his reflections with external experience.

"Thus in a robust or a delicate temperament," he wrote, years before the publication of *Emile*, "the strength or the weakness dependent upon it often derives from its strong or effeminate upbringing, rather than from the original constitution. It is the same with the powers of the intellect. Not only does education differentiate between cultivated and uncultivated minds, but it augments the former in proportion to its culture; for if a giant and a dwarf walk along the same path, every step each takes will give added advantage to the giant. . . ." [8]

An essential element, love, which he was to treat in a way that was to influence all Europe, also called for consideration. "Where there is no love, what would be the use of beauty?" It was a question that would echo through his creative imagination for a while longer before he answered it with *La nouvelle Héloïse.*

Emile it was, however, that now began to absorb him, Emile, the child born of his conscience and Thérèse's fecund but frustrated maternity. This, of course, he could not avow openly to the world; but he let the thought of the physical, spiritual and moral education of an unspoiled infant engage his profoundest self, as if he were another Supreme Being breathing into the scarcely formed clay the rights, duties and morals of the highest evolution which the human creature had as yet attained. From this exemplar the world might learn and benefit. He was himself overwhelmed by the scope and moral responsibility of such a work and therefore postponed putting pen to paper till he knew himself ripe for the labor. He was still spending his mornings copying music, which brought him enough at least to maintain his intellectual independence; therefore he could afford to wait until he was ready.

Although strangely deficient in fellow feeling, that natural sympathy which makes another's suffering as keen as one's own —this despite his readiness to shed tears—Rousseau had the true artist's Protean ability to become the being he created or, for that matter, the person one expected him to be. He had principles, but they, too, were subject to change. As a youth he had turned Catholic after a solemn abjuration. Now, not long after his *Discours sur l'inégalité,* he abjured again and once more became a Calvinist to regain the Genevan citizenship which suddenly, because of his dedication of the book to his native city, had become imperative. One could question what, actually, was his religion. An enemy would answer: "That which at the moment was the most advantageous." A friend, perhaps more justly, would recall the *Profession de foi du vicaire savoyard* and also the words he was to put into the mouth of the dying Julie at the close of *La nouvelle Héloïse.* He believed in God, a just God, merciful and forgiving. "The God I serve is a clement God, a father; it is His goodness that touches me. . . . His might astounds, His immensity confounds me. . . . He made man weak; since He is just, he is merciful. A vengeful God is the God of the wicked. . . . O God of Peace, God of Goodness—it is You I adore . . . and at the Last Judgment it is You I hope to find, even as You have spoken to my heart during my life. . . ." [9] "He made man weak." That statement, which shifted human weakness to a Higher Power, exculpated man, and therefore Rousseau, for his frailties, past and to come.

In the meantime, while gestating his *Emile,* he threw off little trifles like *"La reine fantasque,"* which certainly must have been suggested by Thérèse in her latest pregnancy, for indeed, the whims and caprices of the expectant queen in the tale are too close to life to be wholly fanciful. Neither is it a humorous or satirical work in the manner of Voltaire's, which, possibly, Rousseau had tried to imitate. It was at best an exercise to keep his genius active and perhaps his temper from exploding at the quirks of Thérèse, "vivacious, headstrong, whimsical, foolish in the head, wise in the heart, good by temperament, bad through caprice." [10]

All this considered, it was understandable that Rousseau should seek the distraction of the salon of Madame d'Epinay, who had recently changed lovers, abandoning Francueil for Grimm. Not that she had ceased to love Francueil. Indeed, she still loved him as much as her cool, calculating nature allowed—but she saw greater advantage for her prestige in Grimm. Before Rousseau had left for Geneva Madame d'Epinay had taken him to see the changes she was making at her chateau of La Chevrette. When they had walked for about a quarter of a mile toward the forest of Montmorency, they came upon a dilapidated cabin with its own small vegetable garden, a secluded place which was called the Hermitage. "Ah, Madame!" cried Rousseau. "What a delightful dwelling that would make!"

Rousseau had already forgotten all about the place when, on taking the same walk with his hostess some time later, he saw a comfortable cottage where the lodge had been. "It is for you, my Bear," said Madame d'Epinay. "Here is your den. You chose it and friendship offers it to you. I hope it will rid you of the cruel idea of parting from me."

Of course the tears of emotion gushed from Rousseau's eyes and moistened the hand that he kissed with gratitude and, at the same time, with misgiving. What of his independence? He had sworn never to sacrifice it. Also, he had always thought of Geneva as his final refuge, though the closer he scanned the Republic the more faults he saw in it—the same inequalities as in lands that were not republics; the same taste for show and luxury that corrupted Paris and other cities. Why not accept Madame d'Epinay's generosity? He was not in love with her—indeed, he could never have fallen in love with a woman who had no breasts—and Madame d'Epinay was as flat as an adolescent boy. Still, he loved the forest of Montmorency and he yearned for solitude. Before long Madame d'Epinay had captured her bear, thanks to tactful little bribes to the *gouverneuses,* who had no love for Geneva.

The winter in town had been cold and uncomfortable. Paris no longer stimulated Rousseau, for in his current mood it had become a place of vice and corruption where virtues, like flowers in an untended garden, were choked by the weeds. At every turn one encountered misery and indifference, even hate. But while deploring the general wretchedness, he pitied more than he condemned, for his heart, taught to respond from childhood to the noble Romans, was incapable of an unworthy emotion. Yet he was not unlike the individual he was to describe in *Emile.* "A certain philosopher loves the Tartars so that he may be dispensed from loving his neighbors." [11]

On the ninth of April, 1756, when in the country snowdrop and violet would be piercing the snows, Rousseau left the noisy rue de Grenelle and ensconced himself in the refurbished cottage. No doubt the faithful nightingale that would sing for him in and out of season, serenaded him the first night he spent in the Hermitage. He was again in the surroundings he loved best, nature and solitude—and now he was also enjoying what he had not often had before, the security of some two thousand francs on the rights to the *Devin du village.*

His working habits remained the same, but perhaps the greatest advantage of his retreat was his being spared the intrigues and literary jealousies of Paris. Alas, he still had his troubles with mother and daughter, the one eager to take as much advantage as possible of the benefactions offered her son-in-law; the other frustrated and embittered by her abysmal ignorance and her frustrated motherhood. She had gradually become an inveterate gossip and a shameless liar, sparing nothing and no one, least of all Rousseau. Even at Geneva she had exploited her union with him, giving Monsieur Deluc such an account of her relations with Rousseau that the poor man's hair fairly stood on end. In the great houses she was tolerated thanks to Rousseau, but she was never really accepted, she and her intriguing mother occupying the position of go-betweens whenever gifts were offered which Rousseau refused.

Rousseau, too, had changed, for despite his own special pleading to his conscience, and his effort at catharsis in the boy Emile, who had begun to haunt his creative imagination, he was becoming moody and suspicious, seeing a trap in the simplest question, an accusation in a look. The secret of his abandoned children was no secret and the remorse for his deed obsessed him. How would he have reared them had he kept them? How would he have resolved the daily problems that came up in every family, even the wealthiest—to judge by the advice Madame de Chenonceaux and other ladies sought from him? Had he kept at least one of his sons how would he have reared him? What would he have taught him? How would he have set about forming his character and awakening his conscience? The problem challenged and inspired him. He had been a tutor, but only of other people's children. Now he had

Emile, the child he had engendered on his creative imagination. He was not yet ready, however, to bring him to life. He had fallen under the spell of a Madame d'Houdetot, young, intelligent, charming and, alas, as inaccessible as she was irresistible—or so he thought.

16. *Sophie, Rousseau and Madame d'Epinay*

The solitude which Rousseau had always sought seemed at last to be his. He arranged his books and papers on the writing table and, disciplined by the habit of years, took up his routine of the day: the morning hours for his copying of music, his afternoons for his own works; the twilight hours for the solitary and fecund walks, during which he pondered his own creations. What pleased him most in his retreat was the privacy he enjoyed against the curiosity of Grimm and the too officious Diderot. He was intoxicated with his own virtue and proud that he had the will power to abide by it.

Like Saint Anthony in the desert, however, he was not without his temptations, the strongest and most intoxicating of them all incarnated in the attractive, sensual, exciting, bold little person of Madame d'Houdetot, who enjoyed the reputation, unusual for those days, of utter fidelity—to her lover, the

Comte de Saint-Lambert, who was at that period with the Army. Her husband, Captain of the Gendarmerie, happened also to be called to duty at the time. Before his departure he had taken care to rent for his wife the pretty little house she was occupying at Eaubonne, in the delightful valley of Montmorency, not too far from the chateau of her sister-in-law, Madame d'Epinay. If the count hoped in this fashion to protect her against the admiration of his sex he must have been extraordinarily naïve. Saint-Lambert, the lover, was if possible even more ingenuous when he urged his mistress to seek the edifying company of the philosopher Rousseau, with whom earlier she had acted in his little comedy, *L'Engagement téméraire—The Bold Venture*. She had also met Thérèse one rainy day when she had come to bring Rousseau news of his friend Gauffecourt. The gracious lady had arrived all wet and muddy, whereupon Thérèse lent her one of her robes, built a great fire and had her warm herself before it. Such intimacy at his own hearth had also had its effect upon Rousseau.

Obeying her lover's wishes, Elizabeth Louise Françoise d'Houdetot sought out the great man, emboldened by her twenty-six years and the virtue of being the mother of three, though she looked as if she had never had any children. Certainly her costume, a man's riding habit, which she adopted for her equestrian exploits, gave her more the air of an amazon than of a matron. She wore her thick long black hair like a mantle flowing down her shoulders or floating in the wind in the speed of her gallops. Though not strictly beautiful—her slightly pockmarked face and her too round eyes detracting from true beauty—she was, however, vivacious, gay, of an angelic temper and exemplary goodness, sufficiently responsive to frailty not to make her a prig. Jean-Jacques, for all his dreaming, had never envisioned anyone like her except in the character of his Julie, who was at that time haunting his imagination. Here was his Julie in the flesh—but ah! he was not Saint-Preux, his noble hero. Madame d'Epinay noted the little drama between the coquettish matron and her "bear" and saw too well whither it was leading. There was so short a distance between discussion of love and love itself.

Meanwhile Rousseau, in the creative fervor of *La nouvelle Héloïse,* blended reality with imagination. "I saw my Julie in Madame d'Houdetot, and soon I saw only Madame d'Houdetot, but invested in all the perfections with which I had just decked the idol of my heart. . . . Finally, without our being aware, she inspired in me toward herself all that she had expressed as feeling toward her lover." [1]

It was all fruitless passion, however, for Madame d'Houdetot, in the role of the faithful mistress, wished to play her part to perfection. She did not hesitate, however, to tease and agitate Rousseau with all the wiles of a woman who knows herself desired but will not yield. One day she arrived at the Hermitage on horseback, dressed as a man. This disguise incited Rousseau more than ever—and this time, he triumphantly declared, there *was* love.

Still, Madame d'Houdetot was too much part of the sophisticated yet often petty circle of her sister-in-law not to be affected by it. There, as in all coteries, she had to accept or reject people and ideas as the group dictated. At the center of the circle was Madame d'Epinay, with Melchior Grimm whom Rousseau considered his archenemy, as supreme dictator and salon philosopher. Fearing the influence of these two upon Madame d'Houdetot, all his suspicions were on the alert and not, as was often the case, without cause. Despite his removal to the country, his health did not improve. He brooded, but unfortunately his thoughts, always unconsciously turning inward, merged the present with memories of the past when love had been an unexplored mystery, a groping in a dim realm of wonder, with companions as inexperienced as himself—Mademoiselle Galley and the lovely Graffenried and, yes, with voluptuousness which fully awakened him as a man, the arts of the incomparable Zulietta. With Thérèse, love and passion, if they had existed, turned to comfortable habit, with no exaltation but also without torment.

Now suddenly he was again feeling the romanticism of youth with all its ecstasies and its anguish. However, he was forty-four years old and, as he believed because of his physical ailments, already marked for the grave. Still, he gloried in his sudden resurgence and, overwhelmed by passion, abandoned himself to it, though not without self-justification. How could he, with such inflammable senses, with a heart that yearned for love—how could he help burning, once at least in his lifetime, for a beautiful woman? He was literally devoured by the need to love and had been for years, without ever having satisfied it. Soon he would be seeing the doors of old age opening before him and he would enter with the tragic knowledge that he would die without ever having lived.

These reflections filled him with a tender pity for himself, a pity that was not without compensation. Fate, he convinced himself, owed him this bliss, which he had not yet experienced. It was then that he began to set down what he remembered having felt in his youth; and while writing he gave full scope to his own yearning for love, which he had never satisfied and which devoured him anew. He wished to experience it fully now, in imaginings which were often more potent than reality. He was Julie, he was Saint-Preux, he was everyone who had ever suffered and been exalted by that noble yet terrible passion. As he wrote, fiction in its inevitable way began to shape reality as Madame d'Houdetot lent soul and body to Julie.

With Madame d'Houdetot he was able to do what he could never have done with Thérèse: he read her passages from the novel as it took life from their love, and in the voice of Saint-Preux he could tell her what would have been but stammering in his own. He let her draw her own conclusions from the responses he wrote for Julie.

Her little notes were casual enough. She addressed him as "Citizen" and invited him to dinner. Yet to one with understanding, they were quite explicit. "You must come next Tuesday to dine with me; I shall be quite alone," she wrote on one occasion. She possessed a number of agreeable talents with which to amuse him. She played the clavecin, she danced, and she even made little verses. She also had social grace and, a virtue which spoke wonders to the Citizen, even her enemies did not have to conceal themselves from her. If only *he* could have said as much! Another of her qualities, and one which the suspicious Rousseau appreciated, was her great magnanimity. He had never heard her speak ill of anyone. As for her honesty, Rousseau was certain that she spoke of her lover to her husband as candidly as she did to loyal friends like himself.

Saint-Lambert was evidently as much a paragon of his sex as Madame d'Houdetot was of hers. The husband, according to the ethics of romanticism, should have left much to be desired, and he complied. Though a man of standing and a gallant soldier, he was rough, a gambler, and not beyond chicanery. Moreover, he had an unamiable disposition, which evidently justified his wife in seeking amiability elsewhere. For Rousseau, especially in his state of infatuation, Madame d'Houdetot was perfection itself. At first, when he had found himself smitten, he was far from being aware of how deeply she had affected him; it was only after her departure that, whenever he pondered on his Julie, he found Madame d'Houdetot in her place. "Then my eyes were unsealed. I felt my misfortune, I sighed over it, but I did not foresee the consequences." [2]

Still, he could not help feeling perplexed. Had he been young and attractive, and had Madame d'Houdetot succumbed, he could have blamed her frailty and that would have been the end of the affair. But since the procedure had been contrary to the rule, and since Madame d'Houdetot was generous as well as prudent, he was at a loss to know how to think or act. Here again that paragon of womanhood came to think and act for him. While pitying his folly, she did not reproach him for it, but sought rather to cure him. Thus in her womanly wisdom she preserved a friend for her lover and a grateful admirer for herself. What a close and beautiful relationship they could all enjoy, she would tell Rousseau, if he would only be reasonable. Even a marble statue would have yielded to such pleading, from such lips—and Rousseau was mere flesh and blood.

His constant alternation between desire and repression did not contribute to his peace of mind, however; but his work gained by it, at any rate in the truth of Saint-Preux's feelings and reactions. Like all lovers Rousseau gave all of himself to the beloved, whom he now called Sophie—for was she not wisdom itself? To her he confided his plans, thoughts, ambitions and ideas for regenerating mankind, so that all might reach the heights that he had attained. She paid him the compliment of listening in wonder and admiration, while unconsciously contributing to the physical frustration which could not but tell upon Rousseau's none too prosperous health.

"I shall dine with you in any case, and I shall bring you a heart entirely new, which will please you," he was writing her in October, 1757. "I have in my pocket an unfailing talisman, which will protect me against you. It required nothing less to make me come to myself. I have done so, that is certain— rather, I am all for the friendship you owe me, which you promised, and of which I am worthy from this moment on." [3] Through it all, however, leers an unpleasant by-play that would have made candid physical surrender a virtue. They became lyrical in their transports as recalled in the notes they exchanged. "You are a lover more tender than I could imagine," she told him. "Never, no, never did any man love as you love." The compliment pleased him so well that he repeated it in his letter to her, lest she had forgotten.

To Saint-Lambert he wrote what would most delight a lover: news of his mistress. She had come to say good-bye to the valley, Rousseau informed him, and he and Sophie had done nothing but talk about him. "Our hearts placed you between them and our eyes were not dry as we talked of you. I told her that her attachment to you was henceforth a virtue. She was so moved that she wished me to write you about it. Yes, my children, may you be joined forever; there are no more souls like yours and you deserve to love each other to the tomb." [4] That last was a favorite phrase of his which Thérèse, who had heard it time and again, had managed to impress upon her otherwise impervious mind as the ultimate in devotion.

Not to be outdone in chivalry, Saint-Lambert urged his too willing mistress to cheer the solitude of their great friend— this despite his knowledge that Rousseau had no lack of intruders of one kind or another. Rousseau, however, received Sophie's visits with delight, for more than ever in his infatuated state he saw her as his heroine. How noble of Saint-Preux, rather, Saint-Lambert, to be so unselfish! Still, it was also a prudent move on his part, for by putting Rousseau and Sophie on their honor he was safeguarding his own. Theirs was a friendship made in Heaven and Rousseau determined to be worthy of it.

In the same letter in which Rousseau had encouraged Saint-Lambert in his love of another man's wife, he also mentioned Madame d'Epinay's impending departure for Geneva. Although the lady had no royal blood in her, she behaved like royalty by reason of her wealth and her marriage to a Farmer-General. Her court, with Rousseau, Holbach, Grimm and others, boasted as much intellect as a king's, if not more, and she was so proud of it that she would not dream of traveling without at least part of it for her improvement and stimulation during the tedium of the journey. Grimm, of course, literally leapt to the saddle in his eagerness, and others followed; but what Madame d'Epinay desired above all else was to enleash her philosopher.

Rousseau, however, was not to be so easily snared. First of all his precarious health—real or imagined—made such an undertaking impossible; but there was something else that weighed far more than such a consideration: the humiliation of his following like a lackey at the heels of a Farmeress-General. Yet knowing all that, his so-called friends, and even Sophie, urged his humiliating compliance. Then, too, what about the money he would be needing for the necessary entertainment on the way? What about the clothes, the linen that he could ill afford and which he certainly did not wish to receive from a woman? No, he refused absolutely to exhibit himself, and in his native Geneva, as one of her lackeys. "My friend, why are you not here?" he wailed to Saint-Lambert. "I would pour out my troubles into your soul; it would understand mine annd would not give to my just pride the vile name of ingratitude. . . . I despise money; I cannot set a price upon my freedom. If Fate should reduce me to choosing between the two vices which I most abhor, my choice is made, and I had rather be an ingrate than a poltroon." [5]

The tempest in a teapot boiled over. Madame d'Epinay would have to leave with her numerous train but without her prize bear. He preferred being put through rather extraordinary paces by Madame d'Houdetot. To her he gave complete dominion and enjoyed his own enslavement. Were they not both burning with love, she for Saint-Lambert and he, Rousseau, for her? They exchanged tender confidences and invariably their tears would mingle, intoxicating them with their own sensibility, which certainly played as much part as their love —if not a greater—in their relationship.

The very violence of Rousseau's passion, however, held it in check, while his obligation to deprive himself, exalted his soul and made of Madame d'Houdetot an inaccessible divinity. It would have been the *grande passion* that he believed it to be, had it not been so commonplace. "I loved her too much to wish to possess her," he rationalized.[6] The truth of it was that the Julie he had chosen in the material world fell far short of his own creation, and so the love that should have been exalted and exalting, only agitated him and kept him in torment. "I dreamed as I walked toward the one I would soon be seeing, of the fond welcome she would give me and of the kiss that awaited me on my arrival. This kiss alone, this fatal kiss, would so fire my blood, even before I received it, that my head reeled, my eyes were dazzled to blindness, and my knees, trembling, gave way, so that I was compelled to stop and sit down. My whole organism suffered an inconceivable disorder. I was on the verge of fainting." [7]

A letter to Madame d'Houdetot, which he drafted but never sent, tells even more. "After those delicious moments during which you made me experience all that a love pitied yet not shared can know of pleasure . . . you have become so dear that I have no longer dared to desire happiness at your expense. . . . You know, you who witnessed my insane passion, if even then I did not hold your person sacred. Never did my ardent desire, never did my tender pleas dare to solicit for an instant the supreme bliss without my stopping short at the inner cries of a terrified soul. . . . I would have given the world for a moment of happiness, but to degrade you, Sophie! Ah, no . . . After such sweet moments the thought of an eternal privation is too terrible for one who grieves that he cannot identify himself with you . . . What! Will my burning lips nevermore lay my soul upon your heart with my kisses? What! Shall I nevermore feel this celestial shudder, this fleet, devouring fire that more rapid than lightning . . . O inexpressible moment! What heart, what man, what God could feel it and renounce you?"

On finally arriving at Eaubonne he would be so weak that he could scarcely stand. Yet the instant he approached Sophie his blood would be fired to the peak of desire—inexhaustible and always unfulfilled. Three months of such constant irritation without release affected his health. At any rate he was to attribute to the frustration of this period the aggravation of a hernia and the genital troubles that manifested themselves at this time.

Madame d'Epinay, half-curious and more than half-jealous of the passion she saw developing between Rousseau and her sister-in-law, began to use improper and yet too common means of getting to the bottom of it all and so expose it. She would scrutinize the lovers whenever they were together, hoping to catch an expression, a glance that would betray them. Worse, she tried to bribe Thérèse to intercept the notes they exchanged, and bring them to her. Since Thérèse would not lend herself to what even her simple mind interpreted as treachery, Madame d'Epinay went so far as to search the bosom of her frock where she carried the letters addressed to Rousseau. On a certain occasion, when Rousseau had invited her and Monsieur de Margency to dinner at the Hermitage, Madame d'Epinay, taking advantage of a walk that the two men wished to take together, persuaded Thérèse and her mother to take her to Rousseau's study, urging and finally bribing them to show her the letters from Madame d'Houdetot. The mother was more than willing to comply, as much to injure her son-in-law as to make a little profit, but Thérèse, insisting in her loyalty that there were no such letters, that he always tore them up, Madame d'Epinay had to leave without satisfying her curiosity. Furious with Thérèse, she flung at her, at parting: "How can you be so blind as not to see that there is a criminal relation between them? If in spite of what's before your eyes you need other proofs, here's what you should do. You say he tears up the letters after he has read them. Well, pick up the pieces and bring them to me; I'll take the trouble to put them together again."

For the moment Madame d'Epinay was frustrated in her designs, but she had a propitious opportunity to bring matters to the light at a grand dinner that she gave, a sort of game of chess with her guests for pieces and herself as the chief manipulator. Everything turned out as she desired, for Madame d'Houdetot, whether from innocence or defiance, arrived escorted both by Rousseau and Saint-Lambert. Gossip was rife of course, to the delight of Madame d'Epinay and to the enrichment of her *Mémoires*. "The Marquis de Croismare," she noted, "would have it that she (Madame d'Houdetot) made her entrance much like a stage princess at the height of the catastrophe. I asked him what he meant by that; he said that he was never responsible for what he said. . . . Saint-Lambert and she looked very much preoccupied, and Rousseau was not much gayer."

She left them, very discreetly, saying that she was badly in need of rest, and the party proceeded without her. Rousseau felt ill at ease before Saint-Lambert, as well he might. Fortunately, like most writers, he had brought with him his latest manuscript. It was a *Letter* he was sending to Voltaire concerning that sage's latest works, his *"poèmes"* on *Natural Law* and on *The Lisbon Earthquake.*

The letter which Rousseau wrote on the eighteenth of August of that year of 1756 was really a very long essay. Indeed, it was a pamphlet of several dozen pages, which had much eloquence and an equal amount of candor. Rousseau praised Voltaire for the works themselves, but he could not forbear speaking out on the sage's treatment of the Lisbon earthquake for, he said, "I expected effects worthy of the humanity which seemed to have inspired it. You reproach Pope and Leibnitz for insulting our ills by maintaining that all is well, and you so overcharge the tableau of our miseries . . . that instead of the consolation I expected to find, I found myself sorely afflicted. One would think that you feared I was not sufficiently aware of my unhappiness and therefore, it seemed, you tried to give me great peace of mind by proving that all is evil. Do not deceive yourself, Sir, for everything is the very opposite of what you suggest. This optimism which you find so cruel, still succeeds in giving me comfort in those same sorrows which you paint as unbearable. Pope's poem soothes my ills and leads me toward patience; yours embitters my suffering, incites me to complain and, taking from me everything but a shattered hope, reduces me to despair. . . . No, I have suffered too much in this life not to expect another," he replied to Voltaire's denial of immortality. "Not all the subtleties of metaphysics can make me doubt for a moment the immortality of the soul and of a benevolent Providence. I feel it; I believe it; I desire and I hope for it and will defend it to my dying breath. Of all the disputations in which I have been involved, this is the only one in which my own interest will not be overlooked." [8]

On and on he proceeded, carried away by his eloquence through the thick sheaf of pages which the unliterary members of the audience eyed with dismay. Saint-Lambert, less inhibited than the rest, fell sound asleep and accompanied the reading with a not too gentle snore. After all, he had little reason to keep awake. Madame d'Houdetot, feeling the eyes of all fixed upon her and Saint-Lambert, when they were not scrutinizing Rousseau, suddenly became aware of her position. It was one thing to be unfaithful to one's husband, but unforgivable to betray one's lover. Her scruples of conscience so wrought upon her sensibilities that she decided then and there to break with Rousseau.

Accordingly her attitude changed. She avoided meeting him. Indeed, she went out of her way to spare herself the pain of seeing his anguished face and accusing look. What had he done to cause such a change in her? Wherein had he failed her? Indeed, he was utterly innocent of any sin of omission or commission. Finding no motive for her sudden coldness he began to suspect the usual plots, with himself as the victim and Madame d'Epinay as the culprit.

Seized with restlessness in the conflict of her emotions, Madame d'Houdetot could not stay long in one place, particularly Eaubonne, where she would constantly be running the danger of seeing the aggrieved face of the lover she had wronged; and therefore she found all kinds of pretexts for going to Paris. There, too, she had no rest, and like the culprit who will revisit the scene of the crime, she would return to Eaubonne.

Rousseau it was, however, who suffered the deepest anguish. He was still desperately in love and still wrestling between his heart and his conscience. In the midst of his torment he was plagued with letters from the officious but well-meaning Diderot, and the equally officious and malevolent Grimm, urging him for whatever reason each saw fit, to accompany Madame d'Epinay on her Genevan journey. Stubbornly but against his interests, he refused, and so Madame d'Epinay finally left without him, but with her shadowy husband, with her son's tutor and a half dozen retainers. Diderot sent Rousseau a reproachful letter, a phrase of which infuriated him and set him brooding. In his opinion Rousseau should have gone with his benefactress, "surcharged as you are by the weight of the obligations you have toward Madame d'Epinay." Rousseau was so incensed about it that he unburdened himself in a long letter to Saint-Lambert. "Whatever happens," he declared, "no one will ever enslave me through favors. I have always guarded against such a thing. I despise money: and I cannot set a price on my liberty. . . ." [9]

In his misanthropic gloom which had begun to assert itself early in the previous year, after he had read Diderot's *Le fils naturel,* which the author had sent him, he looked for pretexts to encourage his mood and, of course, found them. What alerted his sensitiveness was the speech of the heroine, Constance, when she addressed Dorval, the hero: "You have been gifted with the rarest talents and you are accountable for them to society. . . . What! You renounce society? I appeal to your heart. Consult it and it will tell you that the good man lives in society, and it is only the wicked who lives alone."

Rousseau quivered with hurt and anger, convinced that he was Diderot's target, and protested. Diderot, astounded by such an interpretation, tried to quiet Rousseau's suspicions. "You don't share my opinion of hermits," he wrote. "Go on speaking well of them as much as you please. . . . Adieu, O citizen. Still, a hermit is a rather peculiar kind of citizen." [10]

Rousseau had no sooner licked his wounds which *Le fils naturel* had inflicted, than he began to look for other motives for grievance.

17.Julie ou La Nouvelle Héloïse

"I am commencing a correspondence which has had no parallel and which will scarcely be imitated," wrote Rousseau to Madame d'Houdetot on the thirteenth of July, 1758. Modesty had never been one of his virtues, but this time he was stating at least a partial truth. The novel in letters had been done before and very brilliantly in England, especially by Samuel Richardson, of whose works and success Rousseau was well aware. Indeed, if there had been no *Pamela; or Virtue Rewarded*, and more important, no *Clarissa Harlowe*, which was published in successive volumes in 1747-48, there might have been no *Nouvelle Héloïse*—at any rate not in its by then highly popular form of a romance evolved through letters written by the various characters. Rousseau unashamedly adopted the form which by 1758 had already become popular. However, his own creative impulse at the time was equally excited, no doubt, by the twelfth century theologian and philosopher, Pierre Abélard, the story of whose love for Héloïse could be read in stone on their tombs side by side and intertwined with ramblers at the cemetery of Père Lachaise.

Rousseau had much in common with Abélard: his analytical mind and philosophic depth and, in a sense, his physical disability which made him partially impotent, though his difficulty was congenital whereas Abélard's had been inflicted by the cruelty of man. Madame d'Houdetot, the Héloïse who inspired him, had in her much of the world and nothing of the nunnery; but art can accomplish remarkable transformations, according to the myth of Pygmalion. Certainly the impact of Madame d'Houdetot upon Rousseau at their first interview had had that electric thrill for him that comes but once in a lifetime and his recorded account of it, many years later, still had the palpitations of his excitement in its breathless staccato rhythm. *"Elle vint, je la vis: j'étais ivre d'amour sans objet; cette ivresse fascina mes yeaux, cet objet se fixa sur elle; je vis ma Julie en Madame d'Houdetot."* [1] For the artist, throbbing at the sudden materialization of his imaginings, it was the propulsive shock for which he had been waiting. With his Julie before him in the flesh, he began writing his novel in a fever of inspiration. Rather, he communicated that fever to his characters who spoke for themselves: Julie d'Etanges, a well-born girl of eighteen; Saint-Preux, her young tutor, and her cousin of the same age as herself, Claire. There was also an Englishman with the unromantic and unlikely name of Edouard Bomston, together with a number of subsidiary characters and the whole panoply of Rousseau's imagination and experience. One curious fact: when the book was published he, who always affected symbols and mottos, omitted the one he had been using on his previous works: *Vitam impendere vero.* Why this omission? Was he so literal-minded that he expected his readers to find truth, the truth of his own love, in his fiction? For certainly he had nothing to fear from those other facts of his own life and experience which, like all authors, he used as fuel for the fire of his creativeness.

Whatever the reason, possibly the very fact that here his own heart was exposed, compelled his indirect disavowal; but no one minded or took it amiss. The confidences of Julie and Saint-Preux were so genuine, so candidly shocking at times, and so human, with all the frailties, virtues, vices and inconsistencies of nature, that the young saw themselves in the lovers, while the old reminisced on what they had once been. Moreover, a frank realism gave to what might have been one of the many sentimental novels of the period the stark and sometimes vivid sense of life which made the story at once acceptable as truth and its characters as beings no better and no worse than one-self. It had also that sense of daring in its absolute candor which titillated where it did not shock. Certainly no one read with indifference the hero's confession to his Julie of his visit, albeit unwilling, to a brothel, in the company of friends who had taken him there.

"The mistress of the house seemed pretty though somewhat faded; other women of about the same age and looks were with her; their appearance, though brilliant, had more éclat than taste. The initial compliments were exchanged more or less as they are at any gathering . . . This false dignity soon gave way to more natural manners. They began to converse in a low voice . . . whispering and smiling as they looked at me while the Madam interrogated me on the state of my heart. They served; and the familiarity of the table, which seems to merge all classes yet puts everyone in his place without his being aware of it, made me realize where I was. It was too late for me to get out of it. [Now Rousseau himself is surely speaking.] Gaining assurance from my repugnance I consecrated this evening to my function as observer and resolved to employ this unique occasion in my life to the study of this sort of women. My effort bore little fruit. They had so little notion of their actual state, so little prevision of the future and, beyond the jargon of their calling they were in all respects so stupid, that contempt soon canceled the pity I had had for them. As for the pleasure itself, I saw that they were incapable of feeling it. They gave me the impression of being violently avid for anything that might tempt their covetousness. . . . I marveled how respectable people could tolerate such revolting company.

"Meanwhile . . . since love was wanting, wine heated the company. There was no tenderness in the conversation . . . and the women endeavored by their disarray to excite desire. At first all this had the opposite effect upon me and all their efforts to seduce me served only to repel me. Sweet modesty, I would say to myself, what charms a woman loses the moment she renounces you. . . . What a difference, I thought, between the gross impudence, the equivocal behavior of these creatures, and those timid and passionate looks, that talk so full of modesty, of grace and sentiment, which . . . I don't dare go on; I blush at these unworthy comparisons. . . . What a place to think of her who . . . ! Alas, unable to dispel from my heart too dear an image, I struggled to veil it. . . ."

Having brought his reader to the gasping point, Rousseau gave him a moment to catch his breath. Will the hero keep himself pure for his Julie? Will he succumb? Alas for the virtuous Saint-Preux! The women on either side of him gave him no respite from their teasing. His head began to spin, his blood to course fierily through his veins. In vain he tempered his wine with water, which the women obligingly poured into his glass. Its effect was even more disastrous—for too late he discovered that it was white wine. "When I came to," he resumed, "I was surprised to find myself in a private chamber, in the arms of one of those creatures. At that instant despair made me feel the enormity of my guilt . . . O thou from whom I await my punishment, I implore thy severity; I deserve it. Whatever my punishment, it will be less cruel than the memory of my crime." [2]

If Saint-Preux erred he could not be too greatly blamed, for though loving him, Julie was more chary of her charms than a nun. Finally, at their secret rendezvous in a little wood, they kissed, once and once only. "What have you done, O what have you done, my Julie!" cries the enraptured lover. "You wished to reward me but you have caused my ruin. I am drunk—no, mad. My senses reel, all my faculties are troubled by this fatal kiss. You wished to soothe my woes. Cruel one! You have only aggravated them. It is poison that I gathered from your lips; it ferments in my blood, it sets it afire; it is killing me, and your pity makes me die. . . ."

On and on he wrote, for their passion seemed to induce *cacoëthes scribendi*. "One favor!" he cried in passionate despair. "Keep your kisses, I could not bear them. They are too acrid, too penetrating. They pierce, they burn to the very marrow. They would drive me insane. One kiss, one only, has flung me into a daze from which I shall never recover. I am no longer the same. . . . O Julie! Whatever the fate preordained by a transport beyond my control, whatever the treatment your severity imposes, I can no longer live in my present state; and I feel that in the end I must either expire at your feet . . . or in your arms." [3]

To this incandescent epistle Julie replied with the poise and discipline of a schoolmistress—an attitude which, by throwing the lover into greater despair, placed him even more in her power. Just as the age of chivalry had had its established code, the era of sentiment also acquired its formulae. In *La nouvelle Héloïse,* Jean-Jacques Rousseau gave it its bible. Julie, by succumbing to her love of Saint-Preux without the blessing of marriage, had been guilty of no crime, for she injured no one, except possibly herself, while at the same time giving happiness to her lover. She had surrendered through weakness perhaps, and therefore at the very worst, she had committed a fault; but as the gallant Claire, her cousin, saw it, Héloïse's life had been a continual battle during which, even after her surrender, honor and duty struggled for supremacy and were at last victorious. Unconsciously, it was a special pleading for himself and Madame d'Houdetot, and for all who, in the name of love or a *grande passion,* strayed from the thorny path of duty.

After many difficulties and negotiations, Rousseau finally arranged with Rey of Amsterdam for the publication of his novel. Why Rey and not a French house? He knew he had written perhaps his best work of fiction. He felt that it would captivate not only France but Europe. He was living in Paris, however, and he had too much experience of French censorship to wish to expose his book to it. Publication in Amsterdam would to a certain extent protect it. He had worked for several years on his novel. He himself, in his exquisite calligraphy, had made the final manuscript, so beautiful that Madame d'Houdetot and the Maréchal de Luxembourg, a recent friend and protector, had ordered copies for themselves, to which, from old habit, Rousseau devoted his mornings. Rey agreed to pay the author two thousand one hundred and sixty livres for the novel, a sum which Rousseau hoped to put away as a nest egg for Thérèse's future and his own. He was even thinking of selling most of his possessions, including his small library, to add to his capital, but thanks to the success of *La nouvelle Héloïse* he did not.

As the proofs and the vignettes began to arrive for the author's corrections and approval, Rey wished that Rousseau would change his mind and allow him to use his old device—a suggestion which roused Rousseau's suspicions. What did Rey mean by such insistence? No, he would not have it, he wrote the publisher. To begin with, what purpose would such a motto serve in a romance? Besides, it was bad taste to adorn a book of this kind with Latin or Italian. Inwardly Rousseau feared as much as he desired the revelation of the passion which had given such a vivid life to his two lovers. *Vitam impendere vero.* Yes, here, too, he was submitting his life to truth, but he had no wish to advertise it to the world. Let those who had eyes to see and hearts to feel discover his secret.

However, despite his protest against embellishing a romance with quotations from foreign languages, *La nouvelle Héloïse* was full of them, beginning with the title page itself, which bore two lines of Petrarch's:

Non la conobbe il mondo, mentre l'ebbe:
Conobbil' io ch'a pianger qui rimasi.

"The world, while she was of it, knew her not; but I did know her and remained to weep." It was an affecting quotation and also effective in its promise to the reader that here would be matter to move the heart and make the tears flow.

From the moment the first part of *La nouvelle Héloïse* appeared in the spring of 1760, its success was assured. Everybody bought it, everybody talked about it and, with each successive volume rewarded with increasing floods of tears, the fame and popularity of the novel grew. "Ye gods!" Lamartine was to write to Virieu: "What a book! What writing! I am astonished that it does not catch fire."

At last Rousseau had the success he had longed for and not until now achieved. Made prudent by his experience of poverty, he arranged with Rey to place some of his earnings in an account to provide for Thérèse after his death. There was comfort, there was security in the modest household at last; there was even a sense of happiness as Thérèse sewed and chatted with him, while he sat with Turc his dog stretched out at his feet, and the cat, Minette, curled on his lap. He was pondering, as he had been doing for many years, a book quite different from *La nouvelle Héloïse*—a book which, if heeded, might revolutionize and improve all humankind.

It was to be called *Emile* and it would treat of the education of a child from his birth to the age of discretion. For years Rousseau had been obsessed with the memory of the children he had abandoned and for whom he now longed—in vain, as he confessed to those friends who knew his bitter secret. If only he had been successful in tracing one of them, at least. Impossible; he had awakened too late to his duties as a father. "Were there some way of recovering this child," he wrote of his first-born to Madame de Luxembourg, whom he had already made his confidante, "it would mean the happiness of his tender mother; but I despair, and I shall never have this consolation.

The ideas with which my misdeed has filled my mind have contributed to a great extent to making me ponder the treatise on education. . . ." [4] Perhaps the writing of *Emile* would be his explanation as well as his catharsis.

The neglect of his duties as a father may have brought to his conscience his duties as a husband, for in that same letter to Madame de Luxembourg he charged her to look after Thérèse in the event of his death. It also offered an apologia for his not having married her. "A public marriage would have been impossible for us because of the difference of religion; but otherwise I have always loved her and honored her as my wife for her kind heart, her sincere affection, her unexampled selflessness, and her spotless fidelity, of which I have never had occasion to doubt. . . ." [5]

Still, difference of religion had been no barrier to others in a similar situation. Moreover, from a man as independent as he boasted of being, there was no action that would not have been understood, if not condoned. Certainly, rather than hurting him, the legalization of his bonds would have relieved him of mounting guilt in connection with Thérèse, besides elevating her to the rank of wife that she had been to him, instead of the servants' entrance caller that she was in the estimate of some of Rousseau's exalted friends—for he now counted a number of "great houses" among his patrons and admirers.

Nevertheless, in a false humility that deceived himself if no one else, he insisted on posing as a copyist, the poor artisan who managed to earn his living by his daily grind at the writing table. He convinced himself that by such humble work he was aligning himself with the modest laborer and was therefore living what he preached. Nevertheless, his quills laid aside, he would dress and make his calls at the palace of the Maréchal de Luxembourg, his recent patron, whose wife, an intelligent and enterprising woman, had undertaken to handle Rousseau's publishing negotiations with Rey. Soon Rousseau was on an intimate footing with every member of the household, including the Maréchal's young son, with whom he used to throw bread crumbs to the birds. But even here his pathological mistrust found cause for suspicion when the child innocently asked him one day why he did not come as often as before to feed the birds with him.

Lately there had been a subject of a very intimate and profoundly personal nature which had been rising constantly from the depths of memory where he had sought for many years to bury it, and clamored to be given life. It was the evocation of a child, a boy—his first-born?—to whom alone of all his sons he had given an identifying mark before surrendering him to the Enfants-Trouvés. At any rate, day by day, the phantom child took shape in Rousseau's imagination and there, where its creator had his truest being, it took shape and grew.

Meanwhile, thanks to the extraordinary success of *La nouvelle Héloïse*, Rousseau had become a public figure throughout Europe where the book had been translated into almost every language. His correspondence increased, and so did the number of his visitors, most of whom, however, he tried to avoid for their infringement upon his privacy as well as his time. His misanthropy grew apace, as did also his self-esteem. He was all the philosophers, ancient and modern, all the notable novelists rolled into one. His temper and patience also suffered and he decided to rid himself of the burdensome correspondence of admirers as well as of would-be Rousseaus who submitted their manuscripts for his opinion when they did not boldly demand his collaboration. He wrote these authors and *beaux-esprits* an open letter in the *Mercure de France,* begging them not to send him their works, especially by mail, since he was in no position to afford the postal charges, not to mention the time required for answering so many letters.

He also decided to set his own affairs in order, especially with regard to Thérèse, "this poor girl"—though it was not until 1765 that Rousseau's publisher legalized his request that Thérèse, after her husband's death, should receive the four hundred livres per year which Rousseau was now getting—comparative riches in their modest life.

18. Emile

Rousseau's capacity to feel all passions, to be all things, was never so strong as after his removal to Montmorency, where, following his triumphant *Nouvelle Héloïse,* he pondered one idea after another in a fervor of creativeness. He had done justice to the passion of love itself, the love between the sexes. There was also that other love, of one's own blood, the children of one's flesh. That love he had not allowed either himself or his poor Thérèse to experience for reasons which now seemed foolish as well as unnatural. What harm had he not done to "this poor girl." What tender care, which might have been his, had he not foolishly avoided, thinking nonetheless that he had acted wisely. Now he was sick, on the verge of death, as he believed when he wrote to the faithful Moultou on the twenty-third of December, 1761. "It is done, dear Moultou; we shall see each other again only in the realm of the just. My fate was decided by the accident which I mentioned earlier; when the time comes, I shall take counsel of virtue itself, from My Lord Edouard. . . ." [1] What was the accident to which he alluded? It was perhaps the breaking of one of the small pipes or *sondes* with which his bladder now had to be tapped to relieve his chronic retention. And My Lord Edouard? He was a recent friend and patron and benefactor, Edward George Keith, Milord Marshal hereditary of Scotland—or My Lord Marshal, as he was generally known—a handsome, imposing and generous man in a wig of long white curls that hung down his back and draped over his shoulders on either side of his expansive chest. His oval face commanded attention by its fine, large, thoughtful eyes under thick, graying, straight brows. A double chin and a flourishing look of health revealed the bon vivant. The upper lip, well defined and firm, arched with humor, a quality which Rousseau perhaps did not wholly appreciate for his own lack of it. He had been introduced to My Lord Marshal by another recent and influential connection, the Maréchal de Luxembourg who, with Madame la Maréchale his wife, had been extending all kinds of courtesies to him and to Thérèse.

Not long after their meeting, Jean-Jacques, whose malady had grown worse, so that he was constantly in a state of discomfort from the distension of his bladder, had resolved to discard the tight-fitting breeches that were the common mode, in favor of a flowing gown, a sort of caftan—his Armenian costume, as he called it—which he embellished with a wide sash in lieu of a waistcoat. It was certainly a picturesque garment, especially in winter, when he topped it off with a high furred cap. On his first appearing in his caftan before My Lord Marshal, he was greeted with a ceremonious *"Salaam Aleikam!"*

My Lord Marshal himself looked like a pasha and had lived like one in the African colonies which he had governed and which he had helped to populate in the manner of an Eastern potentate. Among his sons he counted Ibrahim, Motchko, Guinée and Stepphen the Kalmuk. He also had an adopted daughter, Emet Ulla, for whom he was going to find a husband in Scotland when he returned there to live. In speaking to Rousseau about it, he painted an ideal republic which he and Rousseau would create with perhaps the help of their friend, David Hume.

My Lord Marshal was powerful and powerfully connected and therefore Rousseau, who in all his relations preferred to be the sensitive vine around the sturdy trunk, found in this Scottish oak the support for his emotional dependence. As it was, My Lord Marshal also became the source of many blessings, not the least of which was his concern for the philosopher's peace of mind and the safety of his person. According to the custom of the day, copies of *Emile* had circulated before it was finally printed. And, strangely enough, Rousseau's innocent, his aspiring, profound yet brilliant treatise on education, the child of his soul and intellect, *Emile*, had turned the Church—indeed, all the institutions of Europe—into inquisitorial courts, banning him from the King's estates and, as the juridical expression quaintly put it, "depriving him of fire and water" wherever he might be.

At first Rousseau had not taken the matter too seriously. How could such a book which strove for the amelioration of mankind—how could a sane curriculum of education that would make intelligent, wise and moral individuals for the brotherhood of nations, stir up both Church and State against him and have him persecuted like the worst of malefactors? His publisher Rey, thrown into a panic by the clamor, advised Rousseau to omit his name from a work that would in all likelihood ruin him, and incidentally himself, Rey. Rousseau held firm and endeavored to make him see the needlessness of his fears. He, Rousseau, had always been respectful toward the Government; he had endeavored to be a good man and a good citizen, abiding by the laws of France like any Frenchman. He could not in all justice be persecuted for loving the human race and for wishing to guide it toward its happiest fulfilment. However, his persecution was exactly what the dominant powers wanted; and when Rousseau saw himself and his innocent Thérèse hounded like criminals and on the verge of ruin, he applied to My Lord Marshal in a letter dated simply July, 1762.

"My Lord," he addressed him, "a poor author banished from France, from his own country and from the Canton of Berne for having expressed what he thought to be useful and good, comes to seek asylum in the King's estates. My Lord, do not grant it to me if I am guilty, for I seek no grace and consider myself in no need of it; but, if I am merely oppressed, it is befitting you and His Majesty not to refuse me the fire and water that they wish to take from me everywhere. I have thought it my duty to declare my retreat and my name, too well known through my misfortunes. Decree my fate and I submit to your orders; but if you command me to leave in my present state, obedience will be impossible, for I would not longer know whither to flee. . . ." [2]

As he wrote, Rousseau felt uneasy since earlier, when he had gone to see him, the Marshal had asked what, in his more than usually suspicious state, Rousseau had considered strange questions. The Marshal, in his interest and his affection for his friend, kept him informed of even the least waves of reaction to his situation. One day, however, an alarming letter came from the Curé of Deuil, who had it on good authority that at the very time of his writing, Rousseau, together with others, had been discussed in the Parlement and had been decreed subject to seizure wherever he might be found within the jurisdiction. The more truculent members had even gone so far as to express the opinion that it was not the offending books that should be burned, but rather the authors themselves.

"What!" Rousseau exploded to Moultou on the twenty-second of June, 1762. "Decreed without being heard! But where is my crime? Where are the proofs? O people of Geneva! If that is your liberty, I find it hardly to be regretted. . . . Learn to play the part of the wolf, my young friend," he advised Moultou, "and never charge headlong against the passions of men when you wish to bring them to reason. Envy and hate against me are now at their peak. They will diminish when, after having long ceased to write, I shall begin to be forgotten by the public and people will no longer fear the truth from me . . . For the moment say nothing," he advised his disciple. "Respect the decision of the magistrates as well as public opinion. Don't abandon me openly, for that would be a cowardly act; but speak little of me. . . . Write to me at rare intervals and, most of all, guard against coming to see me. I forbid it with all the authority of friendship. . . . If you wish to serve me, serve me in my fashion; I know better than you what is best for me. . . ." [3]

He was then staying at Yverdun, with his friend and patron Monsieur Roguin, the uncle of Madame Boy de la Tour. Roguin's large family adored their guest; the children petted and spoiled him. "How I love being loved and caressed," he told Moultou in the same letter. "I seem no longer to be unhappy when people love me; affection is sweet to my heart; it makes up for everything else." [4] Nevertheless, all the affection of such friends, all the loyalty of his well-wishers throughout Europe would probably not suffice to prevent the Parlement of Toulouse from finding him guilty and condemning him to be broken on the wheel—the barbarous death they had inflicted only recently on the Toulouse merchant, Jean Calas, falsely accused of having murdered his son to prevent him from abjuring his Protestant faith.

The Luxembourgs saw the danger to Rousseau and kept him informed of every move; however, what they had feared occurred. Rousseau was reading the Bible one evening and reflecting on the story of the Levite Ephraim, when Thérèse admitted a messenger with a letter from Madame de Luxembourg, which contained a warning from the Prince de Conti. According to the Prince, Rousseau was to be decreed the following day. "You have not a moment to lose to bring your papers and to protect yourself against all possible vexations," wrote Madame de Luxembourg, "for when one has power in his hands he does not always have justice, too. In God's name, come. It is the greatest token of friendship that you can give me. La Roche will tell you why I am sending for you in the middle of the night." [5]

Harassed though he was by the threat to *Emile,* the aging romanticist was still susceptible to Eros. He had sent a copy of his work to Madame de Franqueville who, flattered by the compliment, decided that the author must be in love with her. Like everyone else in her society, she had read *La nouvelle Héloïse,* with the usual result. If she was not exactly Julie, surely she could become that heroine under the guidance and manipulation of the author, who was all too willing. He was already writing to her in the partly audacious, partly poetic style of his epistles to the fair sex; indeed, he was expecting her at a rendezvous which they had already arranged when, alas, *Emile* was seized. Such a procedure meant that the author himself was in danger of a *prise de corps.* The prudent, would-be Julie ceased all correspondence with her all-too-willing Saint-Preux the moment she scented danger and gave him the Job's comfort of her sympathy by saying that, alas, the penal quarries were always to be dreaded for those who dared to speak the truth.

For that matter, everyone about Rousseau, even My Lord Marshal, had a long face in anticipation of the worst, and plied him with solicitous questions, when not betraying fear of the inevitable by long and somber silences. Rousseau seemed by far the least concerned of them all. Had he written in criticism of certain important personages in the *Contrat social?* the Marshal would suddenly ask him. Had he offended any exalted sensibilities? Madame de Boufflers, genuinely concerned for his safety, even suggested his seeking refuge for a time at the Bastille, which at any rate the jurisdiction of the Parlement did not reach.

Rousseau held firm and solaced himself by corresponding with a new and famous acquaintance, the Scottish philosopher David Hume, whose epistolary acquaintance he had made, thanks again to Madame de Boufflers. "The esteem of this unique man effaces all the outrages they heap upon me," Rousseau was to write to her in August of 1762. "Monsieur Hume was a man after my own heart even before I had the pleasure of knowing you, and your feelings toward him have made mine even stronger. He is the truest philosopher I know, and the only historian who has ever written with impartiality. I dare believe that he has never loved truth more than I have; but I have put passion into my search for it, while he has lent only his faculties and his fine genius. . . . I have hated despotism in the guise of republicanism, and intolerance as theism. . . . He has seen in all its aspects what passion allowed me to view from one side only. . . . A hundred times have I longed to see England and I yearn to do so still, both for its sake and to be able to speak with him and cultivate his friendship, of which I feel myself not unworthy. But this project becomes less practicable every day, and the great intervening distance would alone suffice to make it so. . . . What, Madame! I who can no longer suffer without horror the look of a street; I who would pine away with sadness when I could no longer see the meadows, the shrubs, the trees before my window—would I now go to live in the city of London, at my age, in my condition—to seek my fortune at Court and thrust myself in the midst of the crew of valets surrounding the ministers?" [6] He would remain to face whatever happened.

For the powers that be, the book despite its innocent purpose contained enough explosive power to blow up established society. "Civilized man is born to slavery," Rousseau wrote, "and lives and dies in it. At his birth they sew him up in swaddling clothes; at his death they nail him in a bier; while he still keeps his human frame, he is enchained by our institutions. . . .

"It is said that some midwives maintain that by shaping the head of the child they give it a better form; and people put up with it! Our heads would not do in the shape given them by the Author of our being: they must be molded by the midwives without, and by the philosophers within. The Caribbeans are far happier than we. . . . Could not such cruel constraint influence their (the infants') humor as well as their temperament? Their first sentiment is one of pain; they find nothing but obstacles whichever way they have to turn; more unfortunate than a criminal in irons, they struggle in vain, they become irritated, they cry. Their very first sound, you say, is a wail? I well believe it. . . . The first gifts they receive from you are chains; the earliest treatments they experience are torments. Since the only thing they are free to use is their voice, how could they avoid shrieking their complaints? They cry for the harm you do them; were you garroted in that fashion you would shriek even louder than they. . . ." [7]

Whence sprang this unnatural usage? Rousseau answered his question. Mothers simply disregarded their first duty by turning over their infants to mercenary women who, finding themselves the mothers of children not their own, sought only to spare themselves. It would require constant alertness to look after an infant allowed to run loose. But when it was well swaddled it could be flung in a corner to yell as lustily as it pleased. There was furthermore a pertinent question to be asked. Did it make any difference whether the child was nourished by its mother or by its nurse? The doctors, he declared, had answered to please the women. For his part, wrote Rousseau, he preferred having the child suckled by a good, healthy nurse than by a spoiled mother. For that matter, the beasts could furnish the infant with the milk which the mother might refuse; but maternal care, he maintained, could not be supplemented.

He wrote with extraordinary insight, setting down precepts and advice and adumbrating psychological consequences in which the nineteenth century would recognize a new science with the emergence of Sigmund Freud and his followers. It was all dangerous heresy, however, to the ruling powers of Rousseau's day. Suddenly and ruthlessly they took action. *Emile* was seized and the Grande Chambre convened to judge it. At noon of the same day the order for Rousseau's arrest was issued, the court marveling at the author's daring in signing his name to such a work.

The provocations for the Parlement's action were that the author affected to instruct his pupil according to nature, which he made the only guide in shaping the moral man; also that he regarded all religions as equally beneficial. Further, he would have his pupil confine himself to the kind of knowledge which instinct alone prompted him to pursue, since, argued Rousseau, the passions are the principal instruments of man's preservation. He also asserted that man may be saved even if he does not believe in God, on the supposition of an invincible ignorance which some persons may lie under with regard to the Deity and which will excuse their unbelief. According to Rousseau's principles, man should be directed by reason only in the choice of his religion.

Today *Emile* can be read with admiration and profit for its profound thought, its insight, wisdom and common sense, if also for its occasional, unintentional humor. To the eighteenth-century guardians of the public good it spelled, if not outright revolution, at least a challenge to the ruling order. Therefore it was ordered to be torn up and burned in the courtyard of the Palais "by the executor of High Justice . . . while the said Jean-Jacques Rousseau should be seized and apprehended bodily and conducted to the prison of the Conciergerie du Palais."

Weighing the gravity of his danger, Rousseau wisely decided on flight. He sent for Thérèse who came to say good-bye to him at the chateau, and as their tears mingled he promised that he would have her join him wherever he might be. He left in grand style, for after all he was no criminal fleeing justice, but Jean-Jacques Rousseau, who had already made a number of valuable contributions not only to the present but to posterity, through the power of sentiment, intellect and reason. His books might be burned, as indeed they were in the Palace courtyard, as promised; but he was already out of reach of tyranny. Indeed, tyranny itself, rather tyranny's henchmen, respected him; for he was certain that the four soberly dressed men in a carriage whom he met between Montmorency and Deuil were the ushers sent to arrest him. Instead, they greeted him civilly and let him go on his way amid the pride of his post chaise, his postillion and his fine horses. When, after four days' riding in the chaise, during which he pondered and partly composed the long poem, *The Levite Ephraim,* he reached Yverdun, he flung himself down upon his knees and kissed the soil.

From Yverdun, on the seventeenth of June, he wrote to Madame de Luxembourg: "You have wished it, Madame la Maréchale. Here am I, exiled from all that bound me to life. Is it worthwhile to preserve it at this price? . . . On passing through Dijon I was obliged to give my name, but having taken up the pen to substitute that of my mother . . . it was impossible for me to do so; my hand trembled so that I was twice constrained to put it down; finally the name of Rousseau was the only one I could write, and all my subterfuge consisted in my omitting one of the J's of my two first names." [8]

The experience nonetheless unnerved him, for all through the journey he imagined he heard the gallop of his pursuers at his heels, "What must the torments of crime be, if oppressed innocence can feel the like?" he questioned.[9]

He had become so attached to Thérèse that he could not bear to be without her. He did not wish to force her to a decision, however, and in his letter on the subject to the Maréchal de Luxembourg, he begged him to sound her out cautiously, for under no circumstances would he wish Thérèse to do anything that might be repugnant to her. His desire to have her with him was only secondary; his first concern was that she should be happy and contented. "If she will not come," he wrote, "I shall miss her my life long . . . Another thing holds me in suspense—the fate of the small belongings I left behind. If they're still left to me . . . those that could be easily transported could be wrapped or crated. . . . But if the Parlement thinks it *à propos* to confiscate everything and enrich itself with my poor rags, I must manage to provide myself little by little with what is absolutely indispensable. . . ." [10]

He wrote the same day to Thérèse. "My dear child, you will be pleased to learn that I am safe. May I hear from you soon that you are well and that you still love me. I made plans for you on leaving and during my journey; at present I am concerned with our reunion. See what you wish to do and follow your own inclination; for no matter how repugnant I find the idea of parting with you after the long time we have lived together, I can do it without inconvenience, though with regret. . . . Think it over then, my dear child, and see if you can stand my exile. If you come, I shall endeavor to make it agreeable, and I shall even try to make it possible for you to fulfill the duties of your religion as often as you wish. Still, if you prefer to stay where you are, do so without any scruple, and I shall still endeavor as much as lies within my power to make your life comfortable and agreeable. . . ." [11]

He had no idea of what was happening but he expected the worst from the Parlement—imprisonment, exile perhaps. "Do not despise me, my child, because of my wretchedness," he pleaded in the same letter. "Men may make me unhappy, but they will never make me wicked or unjust; and you know better than any that I have never done anything contrary to the laws. . . ." [12]

He advised her, in the event of the worst, to consult his friends on how to dispose of his goods. The large pieces of furniture and the books were to be sold. His personal belongings should be placed in a trunk together with hers, and brought along when she joined him. Things were very expensive at Yverdun, he warned her, and it would take much more than they had to try to reëstablish themselves. His meticulous conscience impressed it upon her that the spinet and a number of books belonged to his friend Mathas, and should be restored to him. Also the woodman and the barber had to be paid. "You'll find in the lid of the bonbon box three or four écus, which should be enough to pay the woodman." [13]

He sounded rational in his letters and in conversation with his friends, but his suffering and mental anguish gradually told upon him till it was obvious to his few intimates that he was in an exaltation akin to madness. His suspicion was congenital, but now everything served to awaken it. An expression, a word, a glance or a smile he would instantly interpret as an insult. He felt persecuted, as indeed he was, but his imaginings exceeded reality. On the ninth of July, however, he had an unexpected blow—the warning that on the following day he would be served with an order from Berne to leave the territory of the Swiss Republic within a fortnight. Before this order could arrive at Yverdun, he had already left Berne and taken refuge at Motiers-Travers. "I have been here since yesterday," he wrote to the faithful Moultou on the eleventh, "and I am catching my breath till it pleases Messieurs de Voltaire and Tronchin to pursue me and have me cast out—which no doubt will soon happen. . . . My situation forces me to consent that you write of me," he agreed on the solicitation of Moultou, who had long cherished that ambition, "provided you do so in a manner befitting you and myself, without anger, without satire and, above all, without praise but with moderation and dignity, with strength and wisdom, in short in a way that befits a friend of justice, rather than of the oppressed. For the rest, I do not wish to see this work. I must warn you, however, that if you execute it as I imagine, it will immortalize your name (for you must use your name or not write at all); but you will be a lost man. Think about it. . . ." [14]

He needed the comfort of someone close to him in all his troubles and he could hardly wait for Thérèse to join him. She had answered his letters urging her departure, and in her own peculiar spelling told him *"geunatan que leu moman pour vous reu goindre et vous sanbraces du fon de mon quer"* (In French she was saying: *"Je n'attends que le moment pour vous rejoindre et vous embrasse du fond de mon coeur. . . ."*) Certainly his heart had no difficulty in translating into its own language Thérèse's willingness to come to him and her assurance that her love belonged wholly to him; and that if there were seas to cross or precipices to climb, he had only to call her and she would come at once. "It is my heart that speaks, not my lips," she said, adding as usual that their love would end only with the tomb. Somehow there was something infinitely touching in this scarcely decipherable, illiterate scribble to a man who had written some of the best French prose of the century.

Thérèse arrived, bringing with her a supply of bandages and bougies, as Rousseau had requested, but best of all, the simple familiarity of her comforting presence. Unfortunately her status as an unwedded wife, or one wedded according to the notions of her husband, exposed her to the snubs and insults of the conservative population of the little town, to which she seemed no better than a harlot.

However, Rousseau, now in the principality of Neuchâtel, was under the jurisdiction of his admirer and friend, the King of Prussia, and thus in a sense protected against the prejudice and hate of his own people and the unremitting enmity of Voltaire. Nonetheless Voltaire managed to accomplish his mysterious and nefarious purposes, according to Rousseau, even going so far as to interrogate one of his own laborers from the county of Neuchâtel. Scrupulously Rousseau had written down the dialogue as it had been reported to him.

Voltaire: Is it true you're from the county of Neuchâtel?
Workman: Yes, Monsieur.
Voltaire: Are you from Neuchâtel itself?
Workman: No, Monsieur. I am from the village of Butte in the valley of Travers.
Voltaire: Butte! That's not far from Motiers?
Workman: One short league.
Voltaire: You have there a certain character who's been up to all kinds of tricks.
Workman: Who can that be, Monsieur?
Voltaire: A certain Jean-Jacques Rousseau. Do you know him?
Workman: Yes, sir, I saw him one day at Butte, in the carriage

of Monsieur de Montmollin who was driving with him.

Voltaire: What! That flatfoot in a carriage? That must have set him up, no doubt.

Workman: Oh, Monsieur, he also goes a lot on foot. He dashes about like a lean cat and goes scrambling up our mountains.

Voltaire: One of these days he many be scrambling up a ladder. He would have been hanged in Paris if he had not run away.

Workman: Hanged, Monsieur! He looks like such a good man. *Mon Dieu!* What could he have done?

Voltaire: He writes abominable books. He is an impious man, an atheist.

Workman: That's strange! He goes to church every Sunday.

Voltaire: The hypocrite! But what do people say of him in the village? Is there anyone at all who would wish to see him?

Workman: Everybody, Monsieur. They all seek him out and they say that Milord is very good to him.

Voltaire: That's because Milord doesn't know him, and neither do you. Wait two or three months and you'll know your man. Why, the people of Montmorency, where he lived, sent up fireworks when he ran away to escape the rope. He is a man without faith, honor or religion.

Workman: Without religion, Monsieur! But they say you haven't very much of it yourself.

Voltaire: Who? I? Good God! Who could possibly say such a thing!

Workman: Everybody, Monsieur.

Voltaire: What a terrible calumny! I, who studied with the Jesuits! I have spoken of God better than all the theologians . . . ! [15]

Another dialogue, reported by Moultou after an encounter with Voltaire, pleased Rousseau better. According to Moultou, Voltaire had said: "Jean-Jacques will come back. The Syndics will say to him, 'Monsieur Rousseau, you have done ill to write what you have written. Promise to respect the religion of the country in the future.' Jean-Jacques will give his word and perhaps he will say that the printer added certain words to his book." "No, Monsieur," replied Moultou, "Jean-Jacques does not put his name on his works in order to disavow them."

Part Five

19. *The rising of the storm*

In spite of his letter to Madame de Boufflers, the prospect of a visit to England tempted Rousseau, especially since the antagonism of the people of Motiers-Travers, nourished by prejudice, increased against him after the publication of *Emile*. Even his friend, Dr. Tronchin, had a barb to cast in his direction when he commented that Rousseau could well be pleased with himself for stabbing humanity while pretending to embrace it. Yes, he, Tronchin, could wish him dead, for these last two works of his would certainly do great harm to humanity. Not only Tronchin, but even Pastor Jacob Vernes with whom Rousseau had begun to correspond in October, 1754, while he was still in Paris, now took umbrage at his views. It seemed that by broadcasting his ideas he was sowing himself enemies everywhere. Fortunately his good friend, My Lord Marshal, stood as firm as the rocks of Dover and daily gave him some proof of his protective friendship. Rousseau, however, faced with the growing resentment against him, both near and far, thought it wise to propitiate power, in case of future need.

"Sire, I have spoken much ill of you," he wrote boldly to Frederick II, King of Prussia, in September, 1762. "I shall probably do so again. Nevertheless, banished from France, from Geneva, from the Canton of Berne, I come to seek asylum in your estates. My fault lies perhaps in my not having started out from there: and this praise is among the praises of which you are worthy. Sire, I have deserved no grace from you, and I request none; but I thought it my duty to declare to Your Majesty that I am in your power, and that I would have it so. Your Majesty may dispose of me according to Your Majesty's pleasure."[1]

His qualms of conscience with regard to the Prussian monarch stemmed from the fact that at Montmorency he had had among his framed prints a portrait of Frederick with a couplet under it, the second line of which read: "He thinks as a philosopher but he behaves as king." Moreover, if Frederick had read *Emile,* he would have recognized himself as Adraste, King of the Daunians—a portrait which had not escaped Madame de Boufflers and which certainly would have been obvious to the original. But what was done was done and Rousseau would alter no word if by so doing he would subvert the truth. Meanwhile letters were reaching him from readers throughout Europe, and among the usual correspondence from idle women in search of intrigue and from young men who, as philosophers *en herbe,* sought the master's guidance and advice, came also ponderous epistles from fellow philosophers, like the German Hirzel, who thought him more courageous than Socrates for not having fled and sought asylum in a friendly state.

The world seemed to have grown brighter for that lover of emotional crepuscules, but the person who literally enriched his life was the generous My Lord Marshal, on whose vast bosom, like that of an earthly Abraham, Rousseau saw himself depositing all his cares. The Marshal was well on in years, none of which he had failed to enrich through knowledge of the world and the ways of men. He had not permitted that world, however, to alter him to its own design and thus he preserved his ideals, his integrity and, an invaluable asset, his sense of humor, a quality in which his protégé was notably wanting. Immediately Rousseau snuggled against that tower of strength, which was all the more secure for having known the storms and passions of the world.

Rousseau still had his scruples, however, about accepting favors from a king, and his republican pride therefore gagged at the prospect of bread offered by a royal hand. While reaching out for the gifts—Frederick had subsequently sent him flour, wine and wood, thinking to spare him the embarrassment of accepting money—Rousseau did so with an inverted pride that came close to arrogance. "You wish to give me bread," he wrote the monarch. "Is there none of your subjects who is in need of it? Take away from before my eyes this sword that dazzles and wounds me; it has more than done its duty, and the scepter is abandoned. There is a great career for kings of your mettle, and you are still far from your term. . . . Could I but behold Frederick the Just, the Redoubtable, covering his estates with a vast populace of which he would be the father! Then Jean-Jacques would go to die at the foot of his throne."[2] He had written a sentence in his original draft which he omitted in the letter: "This, Sire, is what I had to say to you: it is given to few kings to hear it, and it is given to none to hear it twice." Young Frederick was well served, if only privately, for his generosity.

In the meantime the pastors of Neuchâtel had succeeded in having both *Emile* and *The Social Contract* banned, detecting heresy in the one and the tocsin of revolution in the other. What! A society organized on democratic principles? What of the prerogatives of the privileged classes? Would *they* have to bow to the will of that amorphous monster called "the people"? Others before Rousseau had thought of social amelioration. Indeed the *philosophes* were even now writing tearful treatises on social injustice; but while bemoaning the disease, which by now was chronic, they were offering panaceas as harmless and ineffectual as the electuaries prescribed by the medical quacks. True, their caution was not unfounded. People were thrown daily into dungeons for their thoughts, while the rope and the wheel took care of unregenerate rebels.

Rousseau had been stirring dangerous ashes in his *Discourse on the Origin and Foundations of Inequality*. He was now playing with fire. He was troubled, as well he might be, by the banning of his books, but he found consolation in the pastor of Motiers, Monsieur de Montmollin, who did not exclude him from the Holy Services, though he knew that Thérèse worshiped in the little Catholic church of a neighboring town and that his fellow ministers disapproved his leniency toward the infidel, as they deemed Rousseau.

Still, he yearned for a peace that always eluded him. He had found it, long ago, in the bosom of Maman. He might have found it in Thérèse, had she not always allowed herself to be influenced by her family and succumbed to "the Roman idolatry" which to the Genevans was anathema. In the midst of his troubles and in the scarcity of commissions for his services as music copyist, he took to employing his idle time—rather, his leisure for lucubration—in making corset laces with the aid of a spool and silk cord. These he would give away to young mothers who promised to suckle their infants. He was a strange figure in his long tunic—"more than half woman," as he said. He longed for rest but instead he was suddenly thrown into the den of controversy. If only he could have accepted the invitation of Monsieur de Conzié, who urged him to spend a few days in his beloved Charmettes, with the memory of Maman, now laid to rest, and the simple pleasures of the pastoral life—a tiny cell, fresh milk, excellent fruit, good chestnuts and great peace.

He yearned for that peace all the more now that he found himself in the midst of contention, in spite of himself, with Monsieur de Beaumont, Archbishop of Paris, who had incited him by charging in an attack full of personalities, that from

the bosom of error had sprung a man full of talk and philosophy, but no philosopher; a man endowed with much learning,
which had not enlightened him but had, on the contrary,
shrouded other minds in darkness; a character given up to
paradoxical opinion and equally paradoxical conduct; a man
who allied simple morals with luxurious thoughts; who was
zealous for ancient maxims while seeking to establish his
novelties; who vaunted his love of retirement while striving to
be noticed by the world. . . . A man, indeed, who extolled
the beauty of virtue while quenching it in the souls of his
readers . . . a man who in a work on inequality of social
conditions had debased man to the level of the beasts. Worse, in
a more recent production, the Archbishop declared, Rousseau
had infiltrated the poison of sensuality while seeming to pro-
scribe it. In the present work, *Emile,* he had seized upon man
from the moment of birth in order to establish irreligion.

Rousseau, facing such imputations, had no choice but to
answer them. His had to be a considered retort, however, as his
reputation both as author and, particularly as moral leader,
depended upon his rebuttal of the Archbishop's charges. Ailing
and discouraged as he was, he began his *Lettre de Jean-Jacques
Rousseau, Citoyen de Genève à Christophe de Beaumont,
Archevêque de Paris.* In it he wrote of himself, man and citizen, and the self-portrait was as important an item in his defense as were his facts and arguments. In a sense this *Lettre*
was a portrayal, indeed, a preliminary sketch of the full-length
portrait which was to evolve in the *Confessions,* whose first
introduction has much in common with the epistle.

His new device now was *Intus et in cute*—In and under the
skin—which more than exemplified his current state. "Why,
Monseigneur, should I have anything to say to you?" he opened
the epistle. "What common language can we speak? How can
we understand each other? And what is there between you and
me? Still I must answer you; it is you who force me to it. . . .
I was born with a certain amount of talent; the public has so
judged it; nevertheless I passed my youth in happy obscurity

from which I did not seek to emerge. . . . On approaching forty I had, instead of a fortune, which I have always despised, and a renown which has cost me very dear—I had peace and friends. . . . Mobs of adversaries then attacked me without giving me a hearing. . . . I defended myself, and from dispute to dispute I was caught in my career, almost without thinking about it. I thus found myself an author at an age when one ceases to be one, and a man of letters because of my very contempt for this state. From then on I was something in the world; but with that, peace and friends disappeared. . . . I had to swallow my pains; repute had to compensate for everything. . . .

"I have written on various subjects, but always with the same principles; always with the same morale, the same belief, the same maxims . . . Meanwhile they have brought judgments opposed to my books, rather, to the author of my books, because they have judged me on the matters treated, much more than on my sentiments. After my first *Discourse,* I was a man of paradoxes. . . . After my *Letter on French Music,* I was the declared enemy of the nation and I was almost treated as a conspirator. One might have thought that the fate of the monarchy was allied with the glory of the Opéra; after my *Discourse on Inequality,* I was an atheist and a misanthrope; after the *Letter to Monsieur d'Alembert,* I was the defender of Christian morals; after *Héloïse,* I was sweet and tender. Now I am impious; soon, perhaps, I shall be a bigot. . . ." [3]

From this beginning Rousseau embarked on a defense that filled more than one hundred and fifteen pages of small print, leaving no ground uncovered which would have allowed a prickly rebuttal to sprout. "I feel my soul!" he explained as proof of his religion; but so personal a reaction convinced nobody, least of all those who would have had him declare his faith in miracles, his belief in the Trinity and in Christ's redemption of mankind. Surely it was himself speaking in the Savoyard Vicar who said: "I wished that God had said to me what He had not said to others." In the conflict within him

megalomania and paranoia seemed to take turns speaking in
his letter to the Archbishop. There was not a hurt that he did
not recall. "A Genevan has a book published in Holland and,
by a decree of the Parlement of Paris, this book is burned with
no regard for the sovereign whose privilege it bears. . . . This
same Parlement, always so careful of its procedures with regard
to the French, neglects them all when it is merely a question of
a poor foreigner. . . . I know not how consonant this is with
the rights of the people, but I do know that by such procedures
the liberty and perhaps the life of every individual are at the
mercy of every printer. . . ." [4]

At the time that he was preoccupied with this grave situation, he was having one of his vapid and chiefly epistolary
amours, into which he had fallen, oddly enough, as the result
of a note he had placed in the *Mercure de France* in April of
1762, begging all authors and *beaux esprits* to stop sending
him letters and, particularly, manuscripts by post, even if they
were franked, not only because he was in no condition to afford
the expense, but because he could not spare any time for such
labor. A young woman, Madame Marianne de la Tour, persisted. She was briefly rewarded but at that time there was little satisfaction in the relationship, for the man, already a figure
in the world, was nonetheless alone and lonely.

With the new year, 1763, after sending his new manuscript
to Rey, though with many misgivings, Rousseau, feeling more
than ever persecuted, thought seriously of changing his name,
but My Lord Marshal, with his sound sense, dissuaded him.
As if the Citizen of Geneva would not immediately be detected
by his views and his style! Meanwhile, with almost every post
Rousseau received some refutation, or at least a comment on
his *Profession de foi,* for everyone, it seemed, had turned defender of the established faith. At bottom the argument had
rested on the dogma of original sin, which Rousseau refused to
accept, adhering as he did to his axiom that the first impulses
of nature are always right, and that there was never any original evil in the human heart.

In the view of the dogmatic his error lay in his failure to distinguish the cause of Man from the cause of God and therefore they, like Monsieur de Beaumont, Archbishop of Paris, refused to heed his plea: "I am a Christian, Monseigneur, sincerely Christian, according to the doctrine of the *Evangile*. I am a Christian, not as a disciple of the priests but as a disciple of Jesus Christ. My Master subtilized little on the dogma but insisted much on duties; He prescribed fewer articles of faith than good works; He commanded one to believe only what was necessary to make one good . . . and He told me Himself, and through His apostles, that he who loves his brother has fulfilled the law . . . But when unjust priests, arrogating rights which they do not possess, would make themselves arbiters of my faith, and would come arrogantly to tell me, 'Retract, disguise yourself, explain this, disavow that'—their superiority would not impose upon me; they would not make me lie for orthodoxy, nor would they make me say what I do not think in order to please them. If my veracity offends them and they wish to cut me off from the Church, I shall have little fear of this threat, as its execution is not within their power. They cannot prevent me from being united at heart with the faithful; they cannot remove me from the roll of the elect if I am there inscribed. They may deprive me of the consolations of this life, but not of the hope in the life to come; for it is there that my most ardent, my most sincere hope is to have Jesus Christ Himself as arbiter and judge between themselves and me. . . ." [5]

Such, he declared, were his true sentiments, which he did not seek to impose upon anyone as a rule of life and which he would retain as long as it pleased not man but God, the sole Master of his heart and reason. He also expressed his gratitude toward the pastor who, resisting the general clamor against him, and judging solely by the truth, did not exclude from his Church a defender of the cause of God. For the rest he had no fear. Let them argue at their ease, these men vested in their dignity. As they recognized no rights nor laws except those they had imposed, they could be neither just nor human, their abuses costing them no more than their aggressions.

"I have found in religion the same falseness as in politics," he boldly proceeded, "and I have been much more indignant about it: for a vice in the government can only render its subjects unhappy on earth; but who knows how far errors of conscience may harm unfortunate mortality? . . . It seems nevertheless certain, I admit, that if a man is made for society, then the truest religion is also the most social and most human; for God would have us be as He made us; and if it were true that He made us evil, it would be disobedient to Him if we wished to cease being evil. . . . I do not say that there is no good religion on earth: but I do say, and it is only too true, that there is not a single one among those which are or have been dominant that has not inflicted cruel wounds upon humanity. All parties have tortured their brothers; all offered to God sacrifices of human blood. What is the source of these contradictions? For they do exist. Is it a crime to wish to remove them? Charity is not murderous; love of one's neighbor does not impel one to massacre. . . . The less reasonable a cult, the more one seeks to establish it by force. . . . Reason then becomes the greatest of crimes; no matter what the cost, one must take it away from others, because one is ashamed to appear lacking in their eyes. . . . Most new cults are established by fanaticism and are maintained by hypocrisy; thus it happens that they shock reason and fail to lead to virtue. Enthusiasm and delirium do not reason; while they last, everything goes. . . . But whatever one may do, fanaticism is a state of crisis which cannot last forever; it has its accesses of greater or lesser duration. . . . It has also its periods of relaxation. . . . It is then that, coming to oneself, one is surprised to see oneself bound by so many absurdities. Meanwhile the cult is regulated, the forms are prescribed, the laws are established and the transgressions punished. Is one lone individual going to protest, reject the laws of his country and abjure the religion of his father? Who would dare? One submits in silence." [6]

He had not submitted in silence. He had dared. More than that, he had inaugurated the new year of 1763 by sending *La Lettre à Monsieur de Beaumont,* or *The Letter to the Archbishop,* as it was called, to his publisher Rey and awaited the storm. Everywhere *La profession de foi du vicaire savoyard* was still being disputed. *The Letter to the Archbishop,* published in March, raised the storm to a hurricane. Rousseau read, pondered and sometimes answered the attacks on his ideas. So far his *Vicaire savoyard* had brought him a great sheaf. Many more would be arriving for the new work, judging by the responses he had received. They came from the most unlikely sources, from sophists to dancing masters. Rousseau amused himself by answering them.

He was most curious to know how his fellow Genevans would take the latest work. His enemies, according to Moultou, were disconcerted, but the sale of the book was not prohibited, as Rousseau had feared. However, the Résident de France had forbidden its reissue in Geneva. The cowed Petit Conseil submitted. On the twelfth of May, 1763, Rousseau sent a calm, well-considered letter to the Premier Magistrate of Geneva, abdicating in perpetuity his right as bourgeois and Citizen of the City and Republic of Geneva. "I have endeavored to honor the name of Genevan," he wrote. "I have tenderly loved my compatriots; I have overlooked nothing to gain their love: one could not have had worse success. I would be complaisant to them even in their hate; the final sacrifice left me to make is that of a title which has been very dear to me. Still, Monsieur, my country, while becoming a stranger to me, cannot become indifferent; I shall remain attached to it by tender memories, and I shall forget only its outrages . . . May it always prosper and its glory increase. May it abound in better citizens and, most of all, in happier ones than myself. . . ."[7]

It was not an unexpected move. The Genevan citizenry that had followed the wrangling between the philosopher and the Petit Conseil knew that a decision must be made. They were relieved. Rousseau, relinquishing his citizenship of Geneva, would perhaps be less of a troublemaker. He, however, saw beyond the moment, to the significance of his persecution— proof, if he needed one, that like all heralds of new gospels, he must have his share of suffering.

He found balm for the wounds inflicted by his own countrymen in the admiration of such men as My Lord Marshal and his new friend David Hume, who through their correspondence had kept him from wholly despairing of the human species. The correspondence then lapsed for a while but it was renewed after Rousseau's retreat to what he hoped would be the peace of Motiers-Travers, thanks to the friendship of his friend and Hume's, Madame Boy de la Tour. His former place had become impossible what with the people's misunderstanding of his habits and their ignorant superstition which made them look upon him as a sort of sorcerer who would surely end by doing them some mischief. Together with the resentment of the populace, there was also his hounding by the clergy, whom nothing would pacify. It was while talking to Madame Boy de la Tour of his many hardships that he sighed and said he wished that he could find asylum in England, whose laws and government he admired. My Lord Marshal, he added, had advised him to take that step and to place himself under David Hume's protection.

Madame Boy de la Tour lost no time in communicating Rousseau's desire to Hume himself, who was at the time charged with the affairs of England in the Court of France. "As I had the prospect of soon returning to London," wrote Hume, "I would not reject a proposal made to me under such circumstances by a man so celebrated for his genius and misfortunes. . . ." [8]

For once Rousseau was not exaggerating his adversities. Besides his old and established enemies, the Holbach and Grimm clique, there was also Voltaire, whose barbed wit went deeper and took some of Rousseau's living flesh with it. Against such enemies Rousseau had only a few faithful, well-meaning but not always wise friends. He relied mostly on his young disciple,

Paul Moultou, who had already proved his loyalty and devotion. Thus, in January, 1763, Rousseau had asked him to undertake the editing of his works after his death. He was obviously concerned about what would happen to his writings, published posthumously, judging by the way his Paris editors, Néaulme and Formey, were mutilating *Emile,* on which they would have the audacity to put his name, after having rendered the book as vapid as themselves, he complained.

His annoyance was quickly dissipated on his receiving a letter in September, 1764, from the Corsican revolutionist aptly named Buttafoco, Firethrower, inviting him in the name of the leader, Paoli, to deign to become the legislator of their renovated nation. The news reached all Europe and, of course, the salons, where Grimm made capital of it by commenting on the irony of such an invitation to a man who at that very time was acting the part of an incendiary with regard to his own country.

Rousseau, however, knew exaltation. "It is superfluous, Monsieur, to seek to excite my zeal for the enterprise you propose. The very idea elevates my soul and transports me," he opened his letter. "I would deem my remaining days most nobly, most virtuously and most happily employed; I would even think I had redeemed the futility of my past days could I but render the sorry remainder good for something on behalf of your brave compatriots, by some counsel useful to the views of their worthy chief and of yourself. Have confidence in me on that score. My life and my heart are yours. . . . Were I in fair health I would say to myself: I shall go to Corsica. Six months spent on the spot would teach me more than a hundred volumes. . . . Would they let me pass? A thousand obstacles would stop me on going, and the sea air would kill me before my return. . . . I know that under such a leader as they have today, the Corsicans have nothing to fear from Genoa. . . . But, Sir, the independence of your country is not yet assured while it is unrecognized by any Power. . . ." [9]

In this same autumn of 1764 Tronchin, the Procuror General

of Geneva published his *Lettres de la campagne—Letters from the Country*—which offered a well-reasoned and skillful defense of the oligarchy. Rousseau responded with his *Lettres de la montagne,* bringing to a crisis the mounting zeal of opposing forces. Standing by his principles Rousseau, in a series of essays that ultimately formed a substantial book and with a logic which, had he employed it in his daily life, would have made him a lord of the universe, expounded his theories and beliefs on the competence of the civil Tribunal to judge him. He had reason for his protest. First of all, without warning, without an inquest, the Tribunal had branded his books. Then, with no regard for his misfortunes, his ailments and his condition, its members had decreed his person. They had not even spared him the epithets generally employed for criminals. These gentlemen had not been indulgent. Had they at least been just?

"My books are impious, scandalous, daring and full of blasphemy and calumnies against religion," he quoted. "Under the cloak of doubt the author assembles all that could tend to sap, undermine and destroy the principal foundations of the revealed Christian religion. They attack all governments. These books are all the more dangerous and reprehensible for being written in French in the most seductive style, and for appearing under the name and designation of a Citizen of Geneva. . . . In judging these books it has not been possible for the Council to avoid casting a look in the direction of the man presumed to be the author. . . ." [10]

In vain Rousseau objected that the Council had judged without preliminary formalities; that Article LXXXVIII of the Ecclesiastical ordinance had been violated in this judgment; that the procedure of 1562 against a certain Jean Morelli, under this act, had set an example in jurisprudence which should not have been ignored; and that this novel procedure was contrary to the fundamental right admitted by all societies, which demands that no man should be condemned without a hearing.

"I am a man; I have written books; I have therefore made mistakes," he admitted. "I am myself aware of a great number, and I have no doubt that others will discover many more. . . . But what author has not been in the same case, or could dare flatter himself that he would never be? . . . A man is not guilty for doing harm while purposing to do good. . . . To become an author one must be inspired by the Holy Ghost, and he should have only men inspired by the Holy Ghost as his judges. . . ." [11]

At the height of his crisis came an interlude which he was in little humor to appreciate. He had just received a letter, in French, in which the writer introduced himself as James Boswell, a Scots gentleman of ancient family. "I am twenty-four years old," he wrote. "I am traveling with a genuine desire to improve myself. . . . I have heard, Sir, that you are very difficult, that you have refused the visits of several people of the first distinction. For that, Sir, I respect you the more. . . . I present myself, Sir, as a man of singular merit, as a man with a feeling heart, a lively but melancholy spirit. Ah, if all that I have suffered does not give me a singular merit in the eyes of Monsieur Rousseau, why was I made as I am? . . . O dear Saint-Preux! Enlightened Mentor! Eloquent and amiable Rousseau! I have a presentiment that a noble friendship will be born today. . . ." [12]

Whether it was the allusion to Saint-Preux, or the appeal of James Boswell's suffering invented for the occasion, Rousseau consented to the visit, provided he made it short. Boswell set out with alacrity. "I found at the street door Mademoiselle le Vasseur. . . . She was a little, lively, neat French girl who did not increase my fear. . . ." Since at that time Thérèse was forty-four years old, Boswell's description speaks well for her appearance. "At length his door opened and I beheld him, a genteel black man. . . ." It was an odd description, since Jean-Jacques was not particularly dark, though his eyes were black.

No doubt Boswell's elegant coat and waistcoat of scarlet and gold lace, his greatcoat of camlet lined with fox and his other adornments annoyed the ailing Rousseau, whose own youth had had its extravagances. After they had talked for a while of their common friend, My Lord Marshal, Rousseau said: "I love the Scots. Not because My Lord Marshal is one of them but because he praises them. You are irksome to me . . . Go away." [13]

Boswell did not take offense. As Thérèse accompanied him to the door she said: "I have been twenty-two years with Monsieur Rousseau. I would not give up my place to be Queen of France." [14] Affected as he always was by the great, Boswell paid another visit to Rousseau, and this time asked him: "Will you, Sir, assume direction of me?" Such a question must have startled one whose direction of himself could hardly have been called exemplary. "I cannot," he answered. "I can be responsible only for myself." [15] The irrepressible Scot thereupon sent Rousseau an account of his affair with a married woman, but the philosopher soon had a more important, if less amusing, matter to occupy him.

The *Lettres de la montagne* had scarcely appeared when, in January, 1765, a booklet was launched, *Le sentiment des citoyens,* attacking Rousseau's person and ideas, as well as his morals. Rousseau and the public in general attributed it to Voltaire, who indeed had been its instigating spirit, but it had also had the collaboration of the young pastor, Jacob Vernes, who had paid Rousseau frequent visits during his stay in Geneva, and in whom the unwary author had confided. All the libels against him had found their way into the pamphlet, as well as the fact that he had exposed his children at the Enfants-Trouvés (which he now found it convenient to deny) and the false assertion that he had caused the death of Thérèse's mother, who happened to be very much alive and as unscrupulous and rapacious as ever.

In the beginning of the friendship Vernes had ingratiated himself by his enthusiasm for Helvetius, whose book, *De l'Esprit,* had appeared in 1758. Rousseau had not yet read it, but when he did he was so shocked that he would have refuted it publicly, had not its hapless author roused his sympathy by the misery and persecution the book had loosed upon him. He was disappointed, however, that his disciple, a pastor, could admire the materialistic theories of Helvetius. He soon had other reasons for mistrusting him when he learned that through Tronchin, Vernes had discovered the secrets of his, Rousseau's, private life; furthermore, he was making capital of them. Rousseau's disenchantment was complete when Vernes took it upon himself to refute *Emile,* which he had completely misunderstood; worse, he accused the author of not being a Christian, and of undermining religion. Certainly, after the publication of Rousseau's *Letter to the Archbishop,* Verne's, or Voltaire's, pamphlet was more than inopportune. It was malicious.

For a while the friendship between Rousseau and Moultou cooled, each nursing his grievance, each too proud to be the first to reach out his hand. Finally Moultou wrote to him. Rousseau replied, grateful yet haughty: "Your withdrawal rent me; if you come back sincerely, your return will restore life to me. Unhappily I find in your letter more praise than feeling. I have no use for your praises, but I would give my blood for your friendship." [16]

As might be expected, the feeling against Rousseau roused by *Le sentiment des citoyens,* which swept like a storm over Geneva, intensified to a hurricane in Motiers. People were shocked by the revelation that he and Thérèse had exposed their children, which Rousseau denied having done, salving his conscience by using the more accurate word, abandoned. Whether exposed or abandoned, the children, he staunchly maintained, had been better served and reared than they would have been, had they shared their unhappy father's precarious existence. People, however, particularly when united by a common feeling, react to emotion more than to reason. The philosopher and his mate could not help noting the enmity against them increasing from day to day. How else could the unsophisticated citizens of Motiers have reacted to such allegations as they read in black and white in the pamphlet that accused

Rousseau of attacking Jesus Christ and His ministers? "Let us see who treats them thus," they read. "Is it a *savant,* disputing with other *savants?* No. It is the author of an opera and of two comedies hissed off the stage. Is it a man of good will who, deceived by mistaken zeal, lays indiscreet charges against virtuous men? We admit in pain, and flushing with shame, that it is a man who still bears the fatal marks of his debauches and who, disguised as a mountebank, trails after him from village to village and from mountain to mountain the unfortunate woman . . . whose children he exposed at the door of a hospital . . . abjuring all the sentiments of Nature as he despoils those of Honor and Religion." The mountebank disguise was an allusion to his Armenian costume.

At this juncture Rousseau made arrangements with some businessmen of Neuchâtel for a collected edition of his works, and a printer of Lyon, somehow or other, joined the venture. The contract had been drawn up and lacked only the signatures when the fracas over *Les lettres de la montagne* exploded. Together with it the plan for the collected edition blew up.

Rousseau tranquilly went his way, despite the persecution and the decrees against him and, harking back to a pleasure of long ago with Madame de Warens, found distraction by botanizing on his walks. Such respites, however, were not infrequently made hazardous by a stone hurled at him by an ambushed enemy, or by some satellite of those in power.

On the night of the Motiers fair, which was held in the beginning of September, Rousseau and Thérèse went to bed as usual, perhaps with a sense of relief that the good folk of the town were too pleasantly occupied to think of any new mischief. Suddenly, in the middle of the night, Rousseau started up at the rattle of a hail of stones hurled against the window and the door at the back of the house. The noise was so great that the dog, which slept in the gallery, began to bark, but terrified by the din, ran to a corner and began scratching the boards in a panic. Rousseau leapt out of bed and was going into the kitchen when a stone hurtling through the window flung open the bedroom door and crashed at his feet. He leapt into the kitchen where Thérèse, trembling with terror, threw herself in his arms. Together they hugged the wall, out of range of the stones that were still flying through the window. They dared not go out, knowing it would mean certain death. Luckily a neighbor's servant nearby raised an outcry, and the Guard, which was making the rounds, came to their rescue. On seeing the stones that had piled up in the gallery, the chatelaine cried out: *"Mon Dieu! It is a quarry!"*

Though in his reminiscence Rousseau may have exaggerated the demonstration, it was nonetheless all too indicative of the feeling against him. He seemed destined not to find peace anywhere. It was at this juncture that the Marquise, Madame de Verdelin, came to his rescue, though he had no liking for her and had resented her many kindnesses to him during his infatuation with Madame d'Houdetot. She had then offered him a key to her garden, where he and Madame d'Houdetot could walk and talk in privacy. Now she was dangling before him the possibility of a refuge offered him across the Channel by a certain Monsieur Walpole, whom she called My Lord.

Rousseau had always wished to see England and Scotland, but now that the accomplishment of his desire was offered him, he yearned for the little island of St. Pierre, in the middle of the Lake of Bienne, which belonged to the people of Berne— his enemies. He discussed his wish and his fears with My Lord Marshal who, with the patience of a saint, talked with the Bernese, sounded them out on Rousseau and, discovering that they were eager to propitiate him after their earlier ill-treatment of him, obtained their permission for Rousseau to live on the island.

It was small, only about half a league in circumference, but nonetheless a complete little world, with tall trees, among them poplars, with meadows, brooks and woods, and the yellow *genièvre* shrubs that had given Geneva its name. In this haven of peace he felt separated from mankind, protected against their outrages, forgotten by them. His financial security was also assured, thanks to My Lord Marshal, who had recovered all his goods and now fixed a pension on Rousseau, who gallantly had it transferred to Thérèse. This money, together with the pension of his publisher, Rey, would secure her against want—indeed, it would keep her in comfort. Rousseau was now taking a sort of leave of his times and his contemporaries, as he said.

20. *How two philosophers can misunderstand each other*

Soon Rousseau was deep in an epistolary friendship with the philosopher David Hume, to whom he had first written in February, 1763, and who suddenly attained paramount importance for him when My Lord Marshal suggested to him that he place himself under the Scot's protection, since Hume was then still charged with the affairs of England in the Court of France. Hume wrote to him from Paris, making an offer of his services, to which Rousseau replied from Strasbourg on the fourth of December, 1765. "Sir, your goodness affects me as much as it does me honor," he began. "The best reply I can make to your offers is to accept them, which I do. I shall set out in five or six days to throw myself into your arms. Such is the advice of My Lord Marshal, my protector, friend and father . . . I may say it is the advice of my own heart, which takes pleasure in being indebted to the most illustrious of my contemporaries, to a man whose goodness exceeds his glory. . . ." [1]

Hume, however, gave Rousseau no encouragement to join him at that time. In the spring of that year, while Rousseau was compiling his *Dictionnaire de musique,* Hume had been of inestimable help to him by persuading the publisher to give him more money—an accomplishment approaching a miracle in Rousseau's eyes. But unfortunately the agent who was to have put through the deal died suddenly, and the promised increase failed to materialize.

As Hume learned to know his friend better, his canny Scots shrewdness penetrated more deeply into his character than Rousseau would have cared to allow. True, Rousseau had had more than the average share of hardship and suffering, but he was neither the martyr nor the pauper that he pretended to be. When, therefore, he alluded once too often to "the torrent of misfortunes that overwhelm me," after the publishers failed to give him the additional sum he expected, Hume commented on the letter: "It is with reluctance I say it; but I am compelled to it. I know now for a certainty that this affectation of extreme poverty and distress was a mere pretense, a petty kind of imposture which Mr. Rousseau successfully employed to excite the compassion of the public; but I was then far from suspecting any artifice. . . . I felt on this occasion an emotion of pity, mixed with indignation, to think that a man of letters of such eminent merit should be reduced, in spite of the simplicity of his manner of living, to such extreme indigence; and that this unhappy state should be rendered more intolerable by sickness, by the approach of old age, and the implacable rage of persecution. I knew that many persons imputed the wretchedness of Mr. Rousseau to his excessive pride, which induced him to refuse the assistance of his friend; but I thought this fault, if it were a fault, was a very respectable one. . . ." [2]

At about this time Rousseau was thrown into a state of dejection by the death of his friend and patron, the Maréchal de Luxembourg. He, too, had once been young, like himself, and at once he thought back upon his happy childhood, his strange forced youth with its errors and its beauty, too. Then there was that deeper, truer life within him, engendered by his acutely vibrant perceptions and his emotions, quivering and responsive to every breath, like the most sensitive aeolian harp. He had lived joyfully and also usefully, if not always trustingly, in a world full of pitfalls; and he had sought for his fellows as for himself the common rights and privileges of decent men in an equitable society. He had hurt no one with intent, and he had sought to do good. Still, many misunderstood him; some hated, others reviled him. There was also *Le sentiment des citoyens* which, whether by Voltaire or Vernes, blackened him in the eyes of posterity, on which living fame depends. Who knew the truth about Jean-Jacques better than himself? Who could present him as he was, with all his faults and idiosyncrasies, his weaknesses, but also his greatness? He thought of his friend Duclos, who had written him in November, 1764, after the agitation in Geneva over *Les lettres de la montagne*: "I have always wished that you would write your personal memoirs; it seems to me that you have begun them." Rousseau had answered him that it would be difficult to write them without compromising certain individuals. Nevertheless, he did not say no. Indeed, on one of the large sheets of paper which he used for his writing, he set down the words: *The Confessions of Jean-Jacques Rousseau containing the details of the events of his life and his private sentiments in all the situations in which he found himself.* The seed had been planted; the fruit would come.

At present he was still full of excitement over the prospect of his going to England, for Hume, with the help of his friends, John Stewart and Sir Gilbert Eliot, who would soon be returning to London from Paris, was already looking out for some honest discreet farmer in his neighborhood in the country "who would be willing to lodge and board Mr. Rousseau and his *gouvernante* in a very decent and plentiful manner, at a pension which Mr. Stewart might settle at fifty or sixty pounds a year; the farmer agreeing to keep such agreement a profound secret and to receive from Mr. Rousseau only twenty or twenty-five pounds a year, I engaging to supply the difference." [3]

No sooner were the arrangements made than Rousseau arrived with the passport which his friends had obtained for him. Thérèse was to join him later. Soon Hume learned that the man Rousseau was quite different from Rousseau the philosopher. For two months after they reached England, Hume and his friends, who shared his admiration for the visitor, gave way to all his caprices, excused the many singularities that began to crop up and indulged him in his humors. "Neither time nor trouble was spared to procure him what he desired," noted Hume, "and notwithstanding he rejected several of the projects I had laid out for him, yet I thought myself sufficiently recompensed . . . by the gratitude and affection with which he appeared to repay my solicitude. . . ." [4]

The close of January and most of February of 1766, Rousseau spent in Chiswick where he was generously entertained, but as usual he was soon voicing his discontent. Knowing his love of nature, Hume introduced his difficult guest to Mr. Davenport, a gentleman of family, worth and fortune, as he described him, who offered Rousseau a house at Wooton, in the County of Derby. As Rousseau and Hume had agreed in advance not to lay each other under any restraint by a continued correspondence, for a while Hume was free of his guest.

One evening, before their departure from Calais, where their vessel had been detained by contrary winds, Hume had asked Rousseau if he would accept a pension from the King of England, if His Majesty should be pleased to grant him one. It was a difficult matter to resolve, Rousseau had answered, adding that he would be entirely directed by the advice of My Lord Marshal.

Taking the reply as an affirmative, Hume lost no time about seeing General Conway, Secretary of State, and General Graeme, Secretary Chamberlain to the Queen, to institute the proper proceedings. George III graciously consented, asking only that the affair should not be made public, to which Rousseau agreed. Meanwhile, General Conway having fallen ill, the matter was for a time left in suspense. Knowing Rousseau's natural restlessness of mind, as well as his brooding imagination, Hume lived in daily expectation of a storm, and was relieved when the days passed with nothing to mar them. There had been flashes of hidden tempests which he had glimpsed the day after they had left Paris. He had also noted with what suspicion Rousseau had followed him with his eyes on the occasion when he, Hume, had taken a letter of his from one of the domestics, that he might expedite it himself. Little did he know what sinister plots and fantasies Rousseau had built on that and on other equally innocent actions. Hume, he was certain, would unseal the letter, make it serve his malevolent purposes, seal it again, and send it to its destination.

His suspicions aroused, memory and an ever wakeful imagination did the rest. Every act of Hume's since their meeting was revived, rehearsed, reinterpreted. There was that first night at Senlis—Rousseau mistakenly says Roye—after they had left Paris, which struck him, in his present state, with the force of revelation. They were sharing the same room at the inn when, in the middle of the night, Hume cried out in his sleep: *"Je tiens Jean-Jacques Rousseau! Je tiens Jean-Jacques Rousseau!"* Several times he reiterated the cry with extraordinary emphasis. What could it mean, this exultation that he *had* Jean-Jacques Rousseau? It could have but one interpretation— that Rousseau was his prisoner, his creature, to do with as he pleased. That suspicion was all Rousseau needed to set his imagination ablaze. He now saw sinister purposes in every act of his host, in his every look—his look especially. The impression of this look haunted and disquieted him, yet also filled him with remorse for his suspicions.

One day while they were together and Rousseau felt Hume's gaze upon him, he was suddenly seized with shame for his unworthy suspicions and leaping upon the solemn Scot, he flung his arms about him and, choking with sobs and drowned in tears, cried out: "No! No! David Hume is no traitor! Were he not the best of men, he would be the blackest of them all!" Though startled, Hume nevertheless politely returned Rousseau's embraces and kept repeating, while tapping him gently on the back: "How now, my dear Sir! Ah, my dear Sir! What now, my dear Sir!" That was all. Rousseau felt his heart shrivel. He went to bed. The following day he was installed at Chiswick, on the Thames, in lodgings that would be suitable for Thérèse, who would soon be joining him under the chaperonage of that decorative young man, Boswell, whom he now liked a little better.

Dumbfounded by the whole mad affair, Hume could only declare: "I cannot answer for anything I may say in my sleep, and much less am I conscious whether or not I dream in French. But pray, as Mr. Rousseau did not know whether I was asleep or awake, when I pronounced those terrible words, with such a terrible voice, how is he certain that he himself was awake when he heard them?" [5] He now began to think that perhaps he had been wrong not to heed the warning of Holbach who, on hearing of his friendship with Rousseau, had warned him: "My dear Monsieur Hume, I am sorry to deprive you of flattering hopes and illusions, but I predict that it will not be long before you find yourself sadly deceived. You don't know the man. I tell you frankly that you are warming a snake in your bosom." [6] It was not the only warning Hume had received, for the *philosophes* of Paris predicted that he would not conduct Rousseau to Calais without a quarrel.

As it was, Rousseau now became the celebrity of the hour. There was nothing he said or did that failed to find its echo in the newspapers and in society, which was anxious to make much of him. The climax of his popularity came when the King's own brother-in-law sought him out. He could not go anywhere without attracting attention. One evening, when it was known that he would be going to a gala performance in his honor, of Garrick's satirical comedy, *Lethe,* with the great actor himself performing, Their Majesties themselves attended, more out of curiosity to see Rousseau than the play. Their exalted Majesties would have been scandalized, no doubt, had they known that Rousseau had very nearly failed to put in an appearance out of anxiety for his dog, Sultan, who more than once had given him cause for alarm by straying away, allured no doubt by some inviting English canine.

Time passed agreeably while he waited for Thérèse. There were visits to return to English friends, to fellow Genevans who had established themselves in London, among them a cousin, Jean Rousseau. He went also to call on Daniel Malthus in Surrey, to return a visit that Malthus had paid him at Motiers. Did he also see the son, Thomas Robert Malthus, whose *Essay on the Principle of Population* was to raise such a storm when it appeared in 1798 and which, like his own works, was to aid the cause of the French Revolution?

Thérèse, with Sultan, in the wake of the resplendent Boswell, arrived in London on the twenty-third of February, 1766. As Rousseau's present quarters could not accommodate them both, the long-suffering Hume was again in quest of adequate lodgings—more difficult to find this time, since Jean-Jacques insisted that his *gouvernante* dine with him at his host's table, an unheard-of arrangement, according to the mores of the day. Rousseau might have had to surrender his principles had not the wealthy old squire and property owner, Mr. Davenport, come unexpectedly to the studio of the painter, Ramsay, while Rousseau was sitting for his portrait. When the subject of lodgings was brought up, Mr. Davenport mentioned a property he had at Wooton in Derbyshire, some fifty leagues from London, and out of regard and admiration for the philosopher, offered it to him at a ridiculously low rental—thirty pounds a year. Whether or not Rousseau saw through the generosity of Davenport, he lamely protested but let him have his way.

On the twenty-second of March, a day glistening with a fresh snowfall, he, Thérèse and Sultan were comfortably ensconced at Wooton. But peace was not long with Rousseau, as Hume had foreseen. Nor was Thérèse content, even though all their needs were provided for in a house which by their own admission was beautiful, pleasant and comfortable. One of their difficulties was their failure to make their wants understood by the servants, so inalienably British that even the efforts of Thérèse in dumbshow failed to make an impression. "I find even a certain compensation in my ignorance," wrote Rousseau to Hume on the twenty-ninth of March, 1766, "and that is, keeping the idle at a distance by boring them. Yesterday I had a visit from the minister, who, seeing that I spoke to him only in French, chose not to speak English, so that our interview ended with our scarcely uttering a word . . . It was much like the ruse of the monkeys who, say the Negroes, don't want to speak, though they know how, for fear that they'll be put to work." [7]

Thérèse, who far from her gossips had no one with whom to exchange the ill-natured little comments that for the most part formed her acidulous conversation, amused herself with tormenting Mr. Davenport's ninety-year-old housekeeper, Mrs. Cooper, by spilling ashes into her soup. Age and her life with her famous husband, together with her awareness of her own inadequacies, had embittered her. The news of her mother's death completed the process.

Meanwhile in Rousseau's mind a storm was brewing. In the solitude of Wooton he imagined all sorts of snares and pitfalls laid for him by his enemies in London. What was he doing, in this obscure province, cut off from all his friends? What plots were hatching in the perilous metropolis? Why was he here, at Wooton, where he might die without anybody's ever being aware of his death? What was all this talk about a pension from the King of England? Was it true, or were the wits making sport of him? What if the population of Wooton should rise up against him, as at Motiers, on that terrible night? He was concerned also about the safety of his papers, of the memoirs that he had begun to jot down at Strasbourg. One of the parcels was missing from the material that Thérèse had brought with her from Paris.

Rousseau had unbosomed himself to Hume about his memoirs while they were voyaging from Paris to London, when Hume had chanced to ask him whether he had ever thought of writing them. "At present it may be affirmed that nobody knows me perfectly, any more than himself. But I shall describe myself in such plain colors that henceforth everyone may boast that he knows himself and Jean-Jacques Rousseau." [8]

On the eighteenth of January Hume had mentioned to Rousseau that a letter, said to have been written to Rousseau by Frederick of Prussia, was going the rounds in Paris. Rousseau immediately wrote for further information to Madame de Boufflers, pretending, however, to be indifferent to such fabrications. Nonetheless, he was anxious to know what it was all about. He learned soon enough when the *Saint-James Chronicle* published the letter in the issue of April, 1766. "My dear John-James," it began, "you have renounced Geneva, your native soil. You have been driven from Switzerland, a country of which you have made such boast in your writings. In France you are outlawed. Come to me. . . . I admire your talents, I am amused by your reveries, which, let it be said in passing, take up too much of your time. . . ." Let Rousseau show his foes that he was sometimes capable of common sense, the letter advised, for that would annoy them without doing him any harm. His, Frederick's estates, offered Rousseau a peaceful retreat. If he refused, he, Frederick, would tell no one. However, if Rousseau still persisted in delving within himself for new sources of misery, let him find suitable ones. He, Frederick, was a king and could furnish him with such as suited his wishes. Moreover he, Frederick, would cease to persecute him when he, Rousseau, would cease to take pride in being persecuted.

On the very face of it the letter was a fabrication and Rousseau protested, demanding that his denial be published. The *Saint-James Chronicle* accordingly did so. "I apprise you that this letter was concocted in Paris and, what afflicts and rends my heart, is the fact that the impostor has accomplices in England. You owe it to the King of Prussia, to truth and to myself, to publish the letter which I write you and which I sign, in reparation for a mistake for which you would certainly reproach yourselves if you knew to what evils you lend yourselves."

At the same time he wrote to the Marquise de Verdelin, who had counseled moderation: "You advise me to go with what you call my grievances to My Lord Marshal for judgment: My Lord Marshal is too wise to think that from where he is he sees more clearly than I do from where I am. When a man, standing face to face with me, keeps thrusting a dagger into my breast, I don't have to ask others to find out if has wounded me. Let us put an end to this subject once for all, I beg you. . . . If I knew that Monsieur Hume would not be exposed before his death, I would have difficulty in still believing in Providence." [9]

Though he begged the Marquise de Verdelin to drop the subject, he himself kept it alive by picking up, and commenting on, every bit of gossip, such as his being the son of a musician and of his owing his passport and other privileges to Hume. He could not forgive Hume, most of all, for having allied himself with Tronchin and his son, avowed enemies to himself, Rousseau. The catalogue of injuries went on and on. To Madame de Boufflers he wrote: "All my letters so far have passed through his hands, for he has always been very eager to see them and to have them . . . Nearly all those sent to me have been opened. . . ." [10]

To My Lord Strafford he sent a letter of protest on his treatment in England. "What! My Lord! Will anonymous defamations that should produce a just horror for the cunning scoundrels who spread them suffice to destroy the effect of fifty honorable years? . . . No, the countries that know me well will not judge me by your badly instructed public. All Europe will render me the justice which they refuse me in England . . . Last year they circulated in Geneva a horrible pamphlet on my conduct in Paris. My only retort was to have this *libelle* printed in Paris itself. It was received as it deserved. . . . You will say, My Lord, that they know me in Paris and that they do not know me in London. . . . One does not deprive a man of honor of the public esteem he enjoys without knowing him, and without giving him a hearing . . . My Lord, the unfortunate are luckless everywhere. In France they decree them, in Switzerland they stone them, in England they dishonor them: it is indeed a high price to pay for their hospitality." [11]

Hume had no choice but to answer, and he did. "I was sorry to see Mr. Rousseau display such an excess of sensibility, on account of so simple and unavoidable an incident as the publication of this pretended letter from the King of Prussia. But I should have accused myself of a most black and malevolent disposition if I had imagined that Mr. Rousseau could have suspected me to have been the editor of it; or that he had intentionally directed his resentment against me. . . . Just eight days before I had received a letter written in the most amicable terms imaginable. . . . I am, of a sudden, the first man not only suspected but certainly concluded to be the publisher; I am, without further inquiry or explication, intentionally installed in a public paper; I am, from the dearest friend, converted into a treacherous and malignant enemy; and all my present and past services are at one stroke very artfully cancelled. Were I not ridiculous to employ reason on such a subject, and with such a man, I might ask Mr. Rousseau, Why am I supposed to have any malignity against him? My actions in a hundred instances have sufficiently demonstrated the contrary. . . ." [12]

Rousseau felt persecuted and he would have it no other way. "As to the deep distress which he mentions to General Conway and which, he says, deprives him even of the use of reason," continues Hume, "I was set very much at ease on that head by receiving a letter from Mr. Davenport, who told me that his guest was at that very time extremely happy, easy, cheerful and even sociable. I saw plainly in this event the usual infirmity of my friend who wishes to interest the world in his favor by passing for sickly and persecuted, and distressed and unfortunate beyond all measure, even while he is the most happy and contented. His pretenses of an extreme sensibility had been too frequently repeated to have any effect on a man who was so well acquainted with them." [13] Indeed, while lamenting his fate he was enjoying the pleasure of botanizing with the Duchess of Portland, who had engaged him to help her collect specimens for a herbal.

Hume waited in vain for a reply from Rousseau but nevertheless continued his good offices toward him with His Majesty. "As I have not received any answer from you," he wrote Rousseau on the nineteenth of June, 1776, "I conclude that you persevere in the same resolution of refusing all marks of His Majesty's goodness, as long as they must remain secret. I have therefore applied to General Conway to have this condition removed. . . . It will only be requisite, said he, that we know previously from Mr. Rousseau whether he would accept a pension publicly granted him, that His Majesty may not be exposed to a second refusal. . . . I beg to hear your resolution as soon as possible. If you give me your consent, which I earnestly intreat you to do, I know that I could depend upon the good office of the Duke of Richmond to second General Conway's application; so that I have no doubt of success." [14]

With saintly patience and extraordinary magnanimity Hume, after consulting Rousseau and, at his suggestion, My Lord Marshal, applied to King George III for an annual pension of a hundred pounds for him. On the second of May, 1766, Hume announced to him joyfully that the pension had been granted. Would Rousseau notify General Conway, the Minister, of his acceptance of His Majesty's generosity? Rousseau wrote Conway to thank him. "Noble and generous acts always carry with them their own reward. It is as natural, Sir, to congratulate you for making them, as it is flattering to me to be their object . . . There is in me something worthier of your esteem than my mediocre talents, which would be less known had they brought me fewer ills . . ." [15]

As for Hume, after despairing of ever hearing again from Rousseau, he received the following reply, dated June 23, 1766: "I imagined, Sir, that my silence, truly interpreted by your own conscience, had said enough; but since you have some design in not understanding me, I shall speak. You have but ill disguised yourself. I know you, and you are not ignorant of it. Before we had any personal connections, quarrels or disputes, while we knew each other only by literary reputation, you affectionately made me the offer of the good offices of yourself and friends. Affected by this generosity, I threw myself in your arms; you brought me to England apparently to procure me an asylum, but in fact to bring me to dishonor. You applied to this noble work with a zeal worthy of your heart and a success worthy of your abilities. You need not have taken so much pains; you live and converse with the world; I with myself in solitude. The public love to be deceived, and you are formed to deceive them. I know one man, however, whom you can not deceive; I mean yourself. You know with what horror my heart rejected the first suspicion of your designs. You know I embraced you with tears in my eyes, and told you, if you were not the best of men, you would be the blackest of mankind. . . . I leave you and your friends to carry on your schemes as you please; giving up to you without regret my reputation during life, certain that sooner or later justice will be done to that of both. As to your good offices in matters of interest, which you have made use of as a mask, I thank you for them, and shall dispense with profiting by them. I ought not to hold a correspondence with you any longer nor to accept of it to my advantage in any affair in which you are to be the mediator. Adieu, Sir, I wish you the truest happiness; but as we ought not to have anything to say to each other for the future, this is the last letter you will receive from me." [16]

Of course the correspondence did not end there, for the allegations in Rousseau's letter obliged Hume to defend himself, appalled though he was by the way everything he had said or done had been twisted by Rousseau's perverse fantasy. He nonetheless managed to be temperate. "As I am conscious of ever having acted toward you the most friendly part, of having always given the most tender, the most active proofs of sincere affection, you may judge of my extreme surprise. . . . Such violent accusations, confined altogether to generals, it is impossible to answer, as it is impossible to comprehend them. . . . I shall charitably suppose that some infamous calumniator has belied me to you. . . . You say that I myself know that I have been false to you, but I say it loudly, and will say it to the whole world that I know the contrary, that I know my friendship towards you has been unbounded and uninterrupted, and that though instances of it have been very generally remarked both in France and in England, the smallest part of it only has yet come to the knowledge of the public. I demand that you will produce me the man who will assert the contrary; and above all, I demand, that he will mention any one particular in which I have been wanting to you. You owe this to me; you owe it to yourself; you owe it to truth and honour and justice, and to everything that can be deemed sacred among men. As an innocent man; I will not say as your friend; I will not say as your benefactor; but, I repeat it, as an innocent man, I claim the privilege of proving my innocence, and of refuting any scandalous lie which may have been invented against me. . . . Happily I have preserved the letter you wrote me after your arrival at Wooton; and you there express in the strongest terms, indeed, in terms too strong, your satisfaction in my poor endeavors to serve you. . . . Tell me, what has since given you offence? . . ." [17]

To this earnest and reasonable exposition Rousseau replied with his "enormous letter" of July 19, 1766, as Hume described it. It was indeed enormous, taking up twenty-eight pages of fine print in the *Collected Works* of 1801. It began with an indirect bid for pity. "I am sick, Monsieur, and in little condition to be writing; but since you desire an explanation,

it must be given you. . . . I do not live in the world; I am
ignorant of what goes on; I have no party, no associate, no intrigue. They tell me nothing. I know only what I feel; but
as they make me feel it deeply, I know it deeply. . . . You
demand very self-confidently that one name your accuser. This
accuser, Sir, is the only man in the world who, testifying
against you, could have been listened to by me: it is yourself." [18]

From this point of departure Rousseau began a catalogue of
grievances that justify Hume in exclaiming: "How strange are
the effects of a disordered imagination! Mr. Rousseau tells us
he is ignorant of what passes in the world, and yet talks of
the enemies he has in England. How does he know this? Where
did he see them? He hath received nothing but marks of
beneficence and hospitality. Mr. Walpole is the only person who
hath thrown out a little piece of raillery against him, but is not
therefore his enemy. If Mr. Rousseau could have seen things
exactly as they are, he would have seen that he had no other
friend in England but me, and no other enemy but himself." [19]

Rousseau thought otherwise. In Paris Mr. Hume had noted
the welcome he, Rousseau, had received from a great prince
and from the public, and had taken umbrage. "He should have
been moved, as I was." Rousseau could not forgive him this lack
of feeling. When, on arriving at Dover he, Rousseau, after kissing the ground had leapt on his neck and covered his face with
tears and kisses, he had elicited no response from the Scot. The
man of feeling had been grieved and unhappy. True, Hume
introduced him to all his friends and even had his portrait
painted, *en grande*. But he, Rousseau, would gladly have dispensed with such favors for some warmth of affection on
Hume's part.

Somehow, whether through the mediation of friends or because Rousseau finally saw his injustice to Hume, they made up
their quarrel on the eve of Rousseau's departure. They were
sitting together, Hume trying to make conversation while
Rousseau remained sullen and silent, when he did not reply

peevishly. He then got up and took a turn or two about the room. Suddenly he bounded upon Hume's knee, to the Scot's great surprise, and throwing his arms about his neck kissed him fervently and bedewed his face with tears.

"My dear friend! Can you pardon this folly?" he cried. "After all the pains you have taken to serve me, here I reward you with this ill-humor and sullenness. But your forgiveness of me will be a new instance of your friendship; and I hope you will find at bottom, that my heart is not unworthy of it. . . . Though you have many better titles to recommend you to posterity, yet perhaps your uncommon attachment and friendship to a poor, unhappy, persecuted man should not be altogether overlooked." [20]

"I was very much affected, I own," confessed the sober Scot, "and I believe there passed a very tender scene between us." [21]

Dr. Johnson, in London, had his own views of philosophers in general and of Hume in particular. "Hume and other sceptical innovators are vain men," he pronounced, "and will gratify themselves at any expense. Truth will not afford sufficient food for their vanity; so they have betaken themselves to error. Truth, Sir, is a cow which will yield such people no more milk, and so they are gone to milk the bull." [22]

21. *The wanderings of Monsieur Renou*

Rousseau would have been restored to his senses and his quarrel with Hume forgotten, had not their correspondence been made public by T. Becket and P. A. De Hondt, in 1766, under the title: *A Concise and Genuine Account of the Dispute between Mr. Hume and Mr. Rousseau.* To a certain extent Hume, a sane, clear-minded man, had been at fault not to recognize that in Rousseau he had been dealing at that time not with a madman of genius, but simply with a madman. Therefore in defending himself against what he believed to be conscious malevolence and worse, he had resorted to the press for justification. The Holbach coterie at once made capital of the imbroglio and prided itself on having prophesied correctly that the two philosophers, despite their vaunted friendship, would end by quarreling most unphilosophically.

The noise of the feud reverberated throughout Europe, and at Monsieur Necker's own house a letter to Holbach was read in which the writer roundly declared: "Jean-Jacques is a scoundrel." On all sides Hume found himself urged to publish an account of the whole matter, since it was bruited about that Rousseau was at work on his *Confessions*. Even Voltaire was impelled to put in a word on the subject, which he did in the famous *Letter to Pansophe,* so virulent that it shocked even Jean-Jacques' ancient enemy, Grimm.

"Why do you say . . . that a sensible State would have raised up monuments to the author of *Emile?*" Dr. Pansophe is asked. "For the author of *Emile* is like a child who, after blowing up soap bubbles or made circles by spitting in a well, thinks himself a very important man. Why is my friend Jean-Jacques constantly extolling his virtue, his merit and his talents? It is because man's pride can become as hard as the hump on the camels of Idomenea . . . They tell me, Dr. Pansophe, that you're going to England. . . . The English will laugh when you will tell them that you think women are merely female animals, who should be busy cooking for their husbands, patching their shirts and, in the bosom of virtuous ignorance, providing them pleasure and children. . . ."

Rousseau's suspicions were intensified. Now he was certain another plot was brewing: that, having learned he was at work on his *Confessions,* his enemies were scheming to get hold of them and destroy them. He thought of escaping, of returning to the Continent, for even My Lord Marshal seemed to have cooled toward him. This time Thérèse approved her husband's plans. Since learning of her mother's death, she thought of nothing but of their return home. As 1767 approached, Rousseau, to lighten the burden of his material goods, sold his books and his collection of prints, keeping only one, an engraving of the King, whose pension he would at last do His Majesty the honor of really accepting.

No sooner was it known that Rousseau intended to leave England than letters came from all over Europe, offering him hospitality. The Marquis de Mirabeau put at his disposal any one of his many possessions, at Mirabeau itself, at Angoumois,

Montargis and Villers-Cotterêts, not to mention at least a dozen other alluring places. Rousseau, deeply moved, thanked *"l'ami des hommes"* for this consolation to the afflicted, mentioning particularly the noble sentiment that inspired it, the noble hand that wrote it, and the unfortunate one to whom it was addressed. "How beautiful it would be that the Friend of Man should give asylum to the Friend of Equality!" But there were too many reasons against it. First of all, Rousseau could not brave the Parlement of Paris and force it to admit its injustice. "Thus, Monsieur, in order not to expose myself to other storms, I adhere to the only decision that could assure the peace of my last days. . . . I have not had, Monsieur, for your works, the indifference of Monsieur Hume, and I could speak so well of them that, with two treatises on botany, they are the only books that I have brought back with me in my trunk. . . ." [1]

Madame de Verdelin, too, invited him to take refuge in the Limousin district, in the southwest of France, where the Parlement could not reach him. She could arrange to buy a little house for him, for which he would only have to pay a modest rental; but he said that he did not wish to be tied down and then embarked on a long tirade of unsolicited advice. Why did she not remarry? She was still young. If she remained as she was, she would have difficulty in marrying off her daughters, despite their birth and their dowry. "Have faith, have faith in your friend, the friend of all honorable things. Marry, since your age and your heart both require it; your daughters' interest will not stand in the way. Your children, on both sides, will have the inheritance of their father . . . besides the mutual attachment which you will inspire in them. . . ." [2]

Invitations kept coming from everywhere. Peyrou then told him of a compatriot, the Swiss De Cerjeat, who was living in Spalding, Lincolnshire. Rousseau did not wait to be told twice. Writing a note for Davenport, he laid it on a table. Then he and Thérèse, packing their few things, left the Davenport house to seek refuge with De Cerjeat. For this trip Rousseau dispensed with his gown and his caftan, which Thérèse gave away to the servants. Somehow with the help of some coachmen they reached Spalding, but their stay was not long, possibly because Rousseau had not been made as welcome as he expected. At any rate, within a week he was writing to Davenport that he preferred being confined in *his* house. That long-suffering and generous man sent a carriage to fetch him back, but it could not keep pace with Rousseau's unpredictable flights. By the sixth of May, 1767, in a great storm, Rousseau and Thérèse arrived in Dover. The vessel was ready for the crossing to Calais, but the wind and the rain made it impossible, so it waited, moored.

Rousseau felt the panic of an animal suddenly released from a cage only to find itself in a trap. A gentleman, noting his trouble, invited him and Thérèse to dine with him. For a while Rousseau sat with his host, eating; but suddenly he bounded up, ran out to where the vessel was moored on the sands and, clambering up, tore into a cabin and locked the door behind him. In vain he was urged and coaxed to come out. It was only when Thérèse expanded her lungs in a few proletarian yells that her husband reappeared and sheepishly came out to join her. He was a haunted, frightened man, the prey of a few real and many imagined enemies. Even the weather was in the plot and, thinking of plots, he evoked some plotters. God only knew by what lures he had been led to England, he wrote to General Conway; but now, it seemed, they did not wish him to leave—and he *must* either get out of England or out of life. Let him only leave in peace and he would pledge his honor never again to utter a word about his sufferings in England, about Hume, about his enemies. If necessary, he would even renounce writing his *Confessions*. "Until now," he wrote, "I had always thought of leaving some memoirs behind me which would inform posterity of the true events of my life: I began them, entrusted them to other hands, and from then on abandoned them. This last blow makes me see the impossibility of executing this plan. . . ." [3] He saw his last hour preparing and resolved either to seek it and die, or else be free. There was no other way.

On the twenty-first of May the weather cleared and toward sunset the vessel at last set sail, to deposit him the following morning on the blessed soil of Calais which, surely, he greeted with his ritual genuflection and a kiss for his recovered liberty. But was it liberty? He was still an outlaw in France. To conceal his identity he called himself Monsieur Renou, adopting the maiden name of Thérèse's mother, who, now being dead, could have no objection. But another phobia seized him, to join the already established and understandable fear of "lapidation"—the dread of being secretly poisoned. He had no doubt about the plot: they would kill him with hemlock, he confided to Du Peyrou. Indeed, he said, they had already given him some in England, he declared. They had put it into a salad, all cut up so that it looked like parsley; but fortunately it had not had the effect his enemies anticipated. Then suddenly, in his overwrought mind, he would change from the accuser to the accused. Certainly there was no other way of interpreting the words and looks of the gravely ill Du Peyrou in his delirium, except as an accusation that he, Rousseau, had tried to poison him. The very attitude of the sick man proved it. Why, even his valet looked suspiciously at him, Rousseau! Seized with remorse for a crime he had not committed, he suddenly flung himself upon the invalid's breast and pressing his cheek against Du Peyrou's, drenched it with tears. The poor man, in no state to appreciate such emotion, failed in the proper response and even gently reproved him. That was the end of Rousseau's nursing as of his friendship, which was extinguished, he said, to the last spark.

With England and Switzerland closed to him, he still counted on the magnanimity of France. Would it too be denied him? He decided to find out. At Amiens he could not have had a warmer welcome. His heart expanded and his fears left him, particularly after he met Cresset, the author of the popular *Vert-Vert,* who like himself had had a set-to with Voltaire.

In pleased silence Rousseau heard him talk, then finally he said, to excuse his taciturnity: "You see, Monsieur, it's far less easy to make a bear talk than a parrot"—possibly his only instance of spontaneous wit.

However, while he was delivering his witticism, his friends were in terror of what might happen to him, and the Prince de Conti warned him that he was in great danger, for it would take just one malevolent person to denounce him. Somehow Rousseau and Thérèse managed to reach Saint-Denis. They stopped off at the Trois-Mallets, from where Mirabeau had them escorted to Fleury-sous-Meudon. The Prince de Conti heaved a sigh of relief, only to discover to his great alarm that his charge was roaming about the streets and the park of Meudon, as unconcerned as if he were in his private garden. Should they put him in the Château de Vincennes? That would seem too much like imprisonment, said the Prince. Monsieur Renou and Mademoiselle, his "sister," were a greater problem than the prince had anticipated.

The guests had their troubles too, however. The valets and servants, with their acute snobbery, had quickly sized up their charges as being no more aristocratic than themselves—people from whom they could expect no kind of bounty—and so they openly resented the exigencies of Thérèse, who made the most of her situation, and had their thoughts about the odd Monsieur Renou. It was inevitable under the circumstances that Thérèse share the treatment accorded her husband. It was a consolation to them both to welcome their dog, Sultan, finally arrived from England. The petty irritations, however, continued; for Rousseau, the insignificant little man, boasted no decoration after all, no ribbon, no sword; and they, the servants, judged their masters by their adornments.

To fill the empty days Rousseau went back to his unfailing consolation, botany, and, wandering off by himself, he collected his leaves and blossoms, thinking of the Duchess of Portland with whom he had herborized in England and with whom he corresponded. In writing to her his stilted, respectful letters, he occasionally signed himself "Herborist to the Duchess of Portland." At least while he was gathering his specimens his thoughts could wander to happier days and his beloved Chambéry where, with Maman, he had pounded herbs and brewed marvelous elixirs—how many years ago! Such thoughts, however, gave way to his unfounded yet tormenting guilt, to imagined accusations which he read clearly in the eyes of Du Peyrou's servant. With the logic of unreason he convinced himself that his enemies had come to learn that Du Peyrou was the depositary of all his secrets, all his papers, and the confidant of all his projects. What could they not make of the situation if Du Peyrou should die? He, Rousseau, would assuredly be accused of having killed him. Fortunately for Rousseau's sanity Du Peyrou recovered.

Something, however, seemed to have died in Rousseau. Nothing he did now gave any joy to the man who had loved life and lived it so joyously. He heard that his *Devin du village* had been revived in Paris; that his *Dictionnaire de musique* was at last published and put on sale, with extraordinary success. He felt no pleasure at the news and applied to his own case the lines of Metastasio:

Sentirsi, O Dio morir,
E non poter mai dir—
Morir mi sento.

O God, to feel oneself dying
And yet to be unable to say—
I feel death coming.

Yet there were about him sympathetic ears to listen to his complaint that he was dying. The fact was, however, that though like all sensitive souls he often felt "the tears of things," his health was no worse than it had ever been.

At the year's close he prepared himself for Du Peyrou's departure but saw him leave without regret. Was his heart, that quivering, responsive instrument of his sensibility atrophying?

His phobia of the plot to poison him gave his mind no rest. Why was he so hated—he who always sought to do good? Where were his defenders in the intrigues that were ruining his reputation and undermining his reason?

As early as the twenty-sixth of July, 1766, he had written to the one man he trusted, My Lord Marshal, confiding his many troubles. But he was happy, he said, in his botany. "You would not believe what pleasure the study of plants lends my solitary rambles. I have had the good fortune to preserve a heart still whole enough to be pleased with the simplest amusements. On rainy days, frequent in this country, my occupation is to write my life; not my external life, like the rest, but my real life, the life of my soul, the history of my most secret sentiments. I shall do what no man has done before me, and which in all likelihood no one else will do in the future. I shall tell all, the good, the bad, everything; I feel within me a soul which can reveal itself. . . ." [4]

He was to show that soul in a letter to "M.D.," which the *Political Register* published in its issue of August, 1767. It has still, of course, to do with Hume. "His philosophic spirit was visible in his writings; but his heart, his generous heart, was by no means so. He wanted a victim. He found it in a man persecuted for truth; and under pretense of procuring me a false asylum, he made me serve the purpose of his ridiculous vanity. . . . Thus, my dear friend, into your bosom I pour out my heart. . . . Pity, the first of all social virtues, tender pity, is natural to you: You can compassionate an unhappy man who hath fallen a victim to the knavery of the wicked. They have leagued against me; they have attacked me with more than common fury. Everyone hath shot his bolt at me. The first flash appeared in the heart of my ungrateful country; the thunder burst in France; the lightning reached as far as England. What has been the consequence of all this combustion? A smoke which my patience hath dissipated. The three-fold brass of Horace hath defended me against all the strokes, which must otherwise have overwhelmed me. The struggle has caused me some sighs in secret; but my heart was never dejected."

He was occupied with his future *Confessions*. As always with Rousseau, whatever he undertook he must believe to be unique. Saint Augustine had confessed long before him and had told all. But what did that matter? It was now Jean-Jacques Rousseau, *his* life, that would be brought before the judgment of the world. The sooner he revealed himself as he was, the better for his memory, perhaps even for him during the years remaining him on earth. His solitude was becoming insupportable, with Thérèse, incapable of intellectual growth, descending more and more to the level of a nurse, if not a servant, to the souring of her disposition. Rousseau always addressed her now as his *chère soeur,* and indeed his feelings for her were chiefly fraternal. To all but old friends she was known as Mademoiselle Renou.

For a few weeks time passed quietly, when all of a sudden Rousseau was thrown into a panic by the death of the castle keeper, Deschamps, whom he had often gone to visit with little gifts of wine, sweets, or some delicacy that Thérèse had prepared. To behold his despair one might have thought he had lost his dearest friend. But no, he was in a frenzy of terror because he feared that he and Thérèse, because of their gifts of food, particularly some fish recently, would be accused of having poisoned him. Soon he was reading the accusation in everyone's eyes, hearing it in the most innocent words. Nothing would do but for him to prove his innocence. But how could he do it? Deschamps was dead and could not speak for him. He therefore demanded that the body be opened to prove that Deschamps had died of natural causes. He was so insistent that an autopsy had actually to be performed before he was satisfied that his innocence had been proved.

From now on he left the castle infrequently and finally restricted his walks to its little garden, the prisoner of his fears, going round and round the circle of his torment. Refusing to admit his derangement, he saw insanity in everyone else, chiefly in the long-suffering Du Peyrou, though others joined the circle of his suspicions.

Then one day, in June, 1768, he addressed a note to the Prince de Conti. "Monseigneur, those who compose your household (and I except no one) are little capable of knowing me; whether they take me for a spy, whether they believe me a man of honor, all must equally fear my looks. Moreover, Monseigneur, they have spared nothing, and will spare nothing . . . to render me hateful and despicable in all eyes, and to force me out of your castle. In that, Monseigneur, I must, indeed I wish, to satisfy them. The graces with which your Serene Highness has overwhelmed me suffice to comfort me for all the misfortunes which await me when I leave this asylum, where glory and opprobrium have shared my stay. My life and my heart are yours, but my honor belongs to me. Permit me to obey its voice which commands that I leave tomorrow. . . ." [5]

He left, and this time his fugue became a pilgrimage of love and sentiment, though perhaps it had not started as such. Whatever the need that made him leave the Chateau, there was another, too deep to come to the surface, which had given him the strongest impulsion. He had been forced to turn his thoughts into himself in writing the *Confessions,* and may have been reminiscing on his early adolescence and his meeting with Maman. At any rate, after a flying visit to Paris and an equally brief stay at Lyon, which as the seat of the Parlement de Paris spelled danger for him, he went herborizing at the Grande Chartreuse with four fellow botanists. July 13th found him at Grenoble, where to his tearful gratitude he saw himself made much of, not as Renou, but as Jean-Jacques Rousseau. On the twenty-fifth, that July of 1768, at three o'clock in the morning, he wrote to Thérèse; but whatever exaltation he may have felt at his welcome had been canceled by his pessimism. In an hour from the time of his writing, he would be leaving for Chambéry, he told her. If he accomplished his journey without impediment, thanks to his passports, he would be returning to Grenoble before the end of the week. "If in a week you have no news of me, don't wait for any more, but place yourself under the protection of those whom I trust, and who will not forsake you. You know where our effects are. Everything is yours. I am confident that the honorable persons who have them in trust will betray neither my intentions nor my hopes. . . . Adieu, dear sister; I embrace you as brother and friend." 6

He made a good part of the journey to Chambéry on foot, in an incessant rain. He saw again Monsieur de Conzié, to whom he had taught music long ago and to whom he had been bound in friendship; but he was much changed. The warmth of their early sympathy was no longer there. Alas, Rousseau concluded, he had seen too much of Monsieur de Choiseul, his own enemy, who had surely turned his old friend against him.

Sadly he learned from Monsieur de Conzié that Madame de Warens had died three months earlier, in the extremest poverty, in a faubourg of Lémenc. To the end, he said, she had talked of him, Rousseau. The royal financiers, under the pretext of an *aubaine,* said Monsieur de Conzié, had placed the seals on her cottage. It had been a pure loss, however, for they found nothing there worth claiming.

Slowly Rousseau made the uphill climb to the little cemetery of Lémenc, and found her grave with difficulty since, uncared for, it was already so overgrown with weeds that he could barely read the inscription. What had become of the beautiful chatelaine who had dazzled him with her youth and beauty when as a boy he had first seen her—Maman, who had had her share of the faults of humanity, but more than the usual allotment of virtue in understanding, kindness, tolerance and generosity. He had never forgotten those enchanted years with her, and the memory of them was to recur not long before his death.

22. *It would not be proper to call me brother*

On returning from Chambéry to Grenoble Rousseau found modest lodgings in the rue des Vieux Jésuites and, with a lawyer, Claude Bovier, an amateur botanist whom he had met through friends, he pursued his favorite pastime. Bovier, an unassuming man, was overawed by the reputation of his companion and trailed about in his wake, noting with respectful silence everything he said or did. One day they had collected a supply of specimens when Rousseau paused before a small, thorny tree laden with fruit, and while Bovier was debating whether or not to warn his celebrated companion that they were poisonous, Rousseau had already plucked and eaten several. On their return Bovier, torn by anguish and guilt, expected him at any moment to contort himself in agony and die before his eyes. However, they reached home without mishap. The following day the incautious botanist was as spry as ever, and glorying in his little drama.

He liked Grenoble and would have lingered there a while

when, surely for some sinister purpose according to his timorous conscience, he learned that the professor of philosophy at the college was planning to discuss the philosophers of the day. A further complication developed when a certain Thévenin, an utter stranger, claimed to recognize him as the man to whom, ten years earlier, he had lent nine francs which he now vociferously reclaimed. In vain Rousseau swore he had never seen him, that he had never been at Verdières-de-Jonc where the transaction ostensibly had taken place. An element of comedy entered in when Thévenin added that he, Rousseau, at that time had given him a number of letters of recommendation to various important personages, which he had signed Le Voyageur Perpetuel.

Despite the ludicrousness of the situation, not to mention the fraud, Rousseau had nevertheless to appear before the Comte de Tonnere at Grenoble to face his accuser until, after weeks of testimony, it was finally established that Thévenin was what Rousseau had taken him to be, an impostor who had already served a sentence at the galleys.

Nevertheless, Rousseau fled the place in a panic, and in such haste that he left his dressing gown behind and forgot to deliver the keys. There could be no doubt about it. His enemies were again unleashed and would soon be on his trail. Where to, now that so many places were forbidden him?

Panting with terror he hurried to the nearest *messagerie* and took a place on the first coach to set out. It was going no farther than Bourgoin, but what did that matter? It was taking him away from the place of danger. When he arrived, Bourgoin was preparing for the patron saint's procession, a few days later. The celebrated Rousseau, recognized by the municipal heads, was made much of and invited to adorn their banquet. Easily shifting from one emotion to another, the desperate fugitive became in no time the gayest of the party. Indeed, he liked Bourgoin so well that he engaged an apartment at the Inn of the Fontaine d'Or and wrote Thérèse to join him there, though he admitted that she would be better off where she was than sharing the terrible rigors that fate destined for him and from which he would have no respite to his dying day. It did not seem proper to him, he said, that she call him brother at Bourgoin. Let them pose simply as friends or relatives while waiting for "something better." What that "something better" was, he did not say.

While waiting for Thérèse, who dutifully left Trie and was on her way to join him, he tacked on his door at the inn a strange manifesto:

"Sentiment of the public on my account in the various estates which compose it:

"The Kings and the Great do not say what they think, but they will always treat me generously.

"The true nobility, which loves glory and knows that I know something about it, honors me and says nothing.

"The magistrates hate me because of the wrong they have done me.

"The philosophers, whom I have unmasked, wish at all cost to destroy me, and they will succeed.

"The bishops, proud of their birth and of their estate, esteem me without fearing me and honor themselves while demonstrating their regard.

"The priests, sold out to the philosophers, bark at my heels to pay them court.

"The wits take vengeance by insulting me for my superiority which they feel.

"The people, once my idol, see in me only a badly combed wig and a man decreed.

"The women, dupes of two *pisse-froid* who hold them in contempt, betray the man who deserved the best from them.

"The Swiss will never forgive me for the harm they have done me.

"The Magistrate of Geneva feels his injustices, knows that I forgive them, and would redeem them if he could.

"The heads of the people, hoisted upon my shoulders, would like to conceal me so well that only they could be seen.

"Authors pilfer and accuse me; rogues curse me; the *canaille* give me the hue and cry.

"People of good will, if there are any left, lament my fate quietly while I—I bless it if some day it may instruct humanity.

"Voltaire, whom I keep from sleeping, will parody these lines. His gross outrages are homage which he is forced to render me in spite of himself."

Here was a man who had been deeply hurt, revealing to the world the extent of his injuries. He was also another Luther nailing his manifesto, not to a church door, but the door of an inn. However, if he expected any response other than the puzzled wrinkling of brows, he was disappointed. However, he soon had other, more personal concerns to occupy him with the arrival of Thérèse on the twenty-sixth of August. To provide for her comfort and for the new status she would henceforth publicly enjoy, he exchanged his room for another, with a double bed.

The whole affair was quietly arranged. Three days later, on the twenty-ninth of the month, that year of 1768, Thérèse and Rousseau, accoutered in their best, were awaiting the guests they had invited to dinner—the Mayor, Monsieur de Champagneux, and another gentleman, the Mayor's cousin. In their presence Rousseau and Thérèse married each other according to the rite of *solo consensu*. They clasped each other, deeply moved. Rousseau then slipped the wedding ring on Thérèse's finger, and the two bound themselves to each other till death should part them. They then led their guests to the dining room where a banquet awaited. Overflowing with emotion, and looking happier than his friends had ever seen him, Rousseau conversed gaily during the feast and then sang several couplets which he had composed for the occasion. Would his friends forgive him, he asked, for having deceived them by passing off Thérèse as his sister?

Marriages of *solo consensu* were recognized as valid and legal. Indeed, the Parlement of Rouen invariably refused to annul them, or to separate husband and wife, or to declare illegitimate the children born of such unions, arguing on the principle of the canon law which provided that it was sufficient for two individuals to declare themselves married and to live together as man and wife, to validate their bonds. Rousseau's marriage, therefore, which many contemporaries and some later writers sought to ridicule, was nevertheless legal, particularly since Rousseau immediately made it public not only through a written declaration, but by the witnesses he had procured.

Most of the people of his day accepted it. It was recognized by the Court of England, and, later, by the French Convention. An extraordinary fact: Rousseau evidently married Thérèse under the name of Renou, which he had adopted; for he wrote to Du Peyrou on October 2, 1768: "I don't understand why you should imagine I had abandoned the name I bear (Renou) in order to marry; it is not names that marry, but persons; and when in this simple and holy ceremony names come in as a constituent part, the one I bear should suffice, as I recognize none other. If it were a question of fortune or goods which had to be safeguarded, that would be another matter; but you know perfectly well that neither she nor myself is in that situation. . . ." [1]

On the tenth of October he wrote again to Moultou. "You surely know that my *gouvernante* and my friend and my sister, and my all, has at last become my wife. Since she has chosen to follow my fate and share all the miseries of my life, I have had to arrange that at least it will be with honor. Twenty-five years of a union of hearts have finally brought about that of the persons. Esteem and faith have forged this link. If others were more often formed under the same auspices, there would be fewer unhappy individuals. Madame Renou will never be the ornament of a circle, and fine ladies will laugh at her without her minding; but to the end of my days she will be the tenderest, perhaps the only consolation, of a man who has the greatest need of it." [2]

He was now indulging in dreams of an exploratory botanical mission of the Archipelago—he did not specify which—perhaps offered him by the Court of England, or perhaps of France. He dreamed of unspoiled, virgin islands, like those of Otahiti, where he might educate a race of Emiles. There was Cyprus the golden—there was also Minorca near at hand. But after indulging his romantic imagination for a few weeks he abandoned the idea and, strangely enough, yearned to return to Wooton. Indeed, he not only wrote to Moultou, telling him of his resolve, but also to the British Ambassador asking whether he, Rousseau, could not find refuge in England or perhaps in Minorca. He had no sooner expedited these letters than Moultou sent him so alluring a description of Cévennes that Rousseau regretted ever having sent them.

At about that time he had received a new supply of notebooks, larger than those he usually employed. On one of them he wrote: "I have resolved to make my readers take another step toward the knowledge of man, by drawing them if possible from the unique and mistaken rule of always judging another's heart by one's own. . . ." For true self-knowledge one needed someone else with whom to compare onself. "That other will be myself," he wrote, "for to this day I know of no man who has dared to do what I propose to do." [3]

Before long he had covered twelve pages of one of the notebooks with a sort of soliloquy on what he sought to achieve; on the criticism and inevitable persecution he must face. Earlier he had written for his pleasure, to occupy his time and to instruct mankind. He had striven for beauty and truth. Now he proposed to paint a man, his life in the world, the deeper life of his thoughts and aspirations, his joys, his passion and his pain. He would be no symbolic Everyman, this man, but a unique individual—himself, in all the truth of nature, his own nature, with nothing good or bad withheld. If he was no better than others, he was at least different. It was that difference, which made him Jean-Jacques Rousseau, that he would paint in perhaps his most significant work, *Les Confessions*.

He was writing the book as much to provide an example to mankind as to justify his life, so much misunderstood in his day, and in danger of being even more perverted by his enemies after his death; for he was now obsessed with the fate of his reputation once he was no longer present to defend it. Still, he cherished the vision of himself as a martyr, for all true greatness must have its martyrdom, and so he wrote to Thérèse, instructing her on her behavior after his death. "Let them tranquilly execute their plots against your husband; don't torment yourself at all about justifying his outraged memory. Content yourself with honoring the truth . . . and let Providence and time do their work; for sooner or later this will be done." [4]

As it was, Thérèse, the future trustee of his memory, had had little concern for his reputation or, for that matter, her own, on occasion, though probably her indiscretions did not go beyond rough jests with the stablemen and couriers at the various inns to which Rousseau's wandering life had so often led him. They were now installed at Monquin, half a mile from Bourgoin, in a farm belonging to the Marquise de Césarges, where they had gone to live on the first day of February, 1769. The site could not have been better chosen for the lover of nature's splendors. Though but an old country house, it was magnificently situated on a height with, in clear weather, a noble view of Mont Blanc's hoary majesty and the Dent du Chat. The Rhône wound its way in the distance, made grand and mysterious by the phantom shapes of the Jura Mountains.

The house itself still boasted ancient frescos, faded, peeling, yet eloquent with imaged texts drawn from the Bible. A sundial in the garden marked the passage of the sun. Outside Rousseau's chamber window, and soon within his room, the swallows shrilled and fluttered familiarly. Whenever he gazed out, he could see spread on the far horizon, the Dauphiné and Savoy. He might have been happy, or at least contented, but he was not. Thérèse had changed; Thérèse was no longer happy with him alone. She disliked the country and longed for the spicy *commérages* of Paris.

He knew that she had ceased to love him. He had known it for some time but had not spoken. Before their removal to Monquin he had left a note for her on a table, not daring to utter aloud what he had to write. He had always striven to make her happy, he said; yet not only had she ceased to take pleasure in his company, but she seemed to find it a burden to be with him even for a few minutes. If she were happy with him he would be content, but he could see clearly that she was not, and that was what pained him. He had not changed. He still loved her and still longed to end his days with her in the most perfect union, "and to have but one bed when we shall have but one soul." Perhaps she should go on a retreat in some convent and look into her heart, though he warned: "Don't let any monk meddle in our affairs in any way whatever. I do not say this through jealousy, and I am certain they have no designs on your body; but that is not the point. Profit by this advice or be sure you'll attract nothing but dishonor and calamity for the rest of your life."

Whatever the scandal to which he may have alluded, it somehow leaked out for on the fifteenth of July, 1770, the scandalmonger Grimm was making capital of it in his correspondence. "Jean-Jacques Rousseau has been back in Paris for about a month with his *gouvernante,* Mademoiselle le Vasseur whom he has finally made his wife. He has cast off his Armenian cassock and resumed the French garb. They have concocted for this occasion an impertinent story which calumniates the virtue of Madame Jean-Jacques, and still more the taste of the one who sinned with her. They would have it that her husband, surprising her *in flagrante* with a monk, instantly cast off his Armenian garb, saying that till then he had wished to distinguish himself from others by his appearance, since he did not think of himself as an ordinary man, but now he saw too well that he was mistaken, and that he belonged to the common class." [5]

While he was suffering the slings of malice and ridicule at

Monquin, he thought back on the time, now made magical by his imagination, which he had spent in England. *There* everybody had loved him. *There* he had friends and was appreciated. In vain he endeavored to emerge from his dark mood by composing at the spinet which Madame Boy de la Tour had had brought to him, carried on the backs of two men, all the way from Lyon. In vain he catalogued his herbs and flowers. The solitude deepened as autumn passed and winter came. In his cold room that even blazing fires, constantly fed, could not warm, he continued to relive his past, dwelling on what most tormented him—the children he had abandoned to the mercies of a foundling hospital. The *Confessions* grew, in secrecy and solitude, for he knew that many feared what he would have to write. Everywhere he suspected enemies. The ceilings had eyes; the walls had ears. Malevolent, ever watchful spies surrounded him. It was at this time that he began heading all his letters with a quatrain imploring heaven to unmask all deceivers and force barbarous hearts to reveal themselves.

> *Pauvres aveugles que nous sommes!*
> *Ciel, démasque les imposteurs,*
> *Et force leurs barbares coeurs*
> *A s'ouvrir aux regards des hommes.*

The snows continued falling; the winter seemed endless. In his morbid mood he found no pleasure in anything and even the fine new edition of his works which Rey had brought out only increased his ill-humor for the flaws—chiefly nonexistent —which he found in it. It was the same old story—the plot against him so adroitly, so relentlessly carried out by his secret enemies. He saw it everywhere, in everything. Pierre-Laurent Du Belloy had just published his *Bayard*. Rousseau read it and, coming upon two innocent lines in it, at once saw himself attacked.

> *Que de vertu brillait dans son faux repentir;*
> *Peut-on si bien la peindre, et ne pas la sentir?*

What virtue in his false repenting glowed;
Can one then feign it without being moved?

Of course it was aimed at *his* reformation, called false by his enemies. Of course it was Jean-Jacques Rousseau who was being publicly excoriated. He had no friends on this side of the Channel. Ah, for England where he had been honored and loved! He must renew his cordial relations with Earl Harcourt, Chamberlain to the Queen's Household, a sympathetic, generous man to whom he could reveal his circumstances, his sufferings, and be understood. Help could come from that quarter, if from nowhere else.

He was not mistaken, for Harcourt wrote to Palmerston, then at Admiralty House, a letter which would have softened a stone. Rousseau, the great Rousseau, was in the direst circumstances. His wife had for a long time been in an ill state of health and incapable of taking care of their small ménage, and he had been her nurse. "But his advanced age will no longer permit him to perform that office; besides, not being able alone to clean the house, to go to market and to dress the victuals, he made an effort to keep a servant-maid, but after eight months' experience, found he could not afford it . . . All they wish is to board in some small family in the country . . . and they earnestly desire to return to England; but their miserable income is not sufficient . . . unless his pension is paid to him. . . ." [6] Young Palmerston himself, inbued with the sentiment of the age, translated into neat English couplets a four-line epitaph of Rousseau's.

Ci gisent deux amans, l'un pour l'autre ils vécurent
L'un pour l'autre ils sont morts, et les loix en murmurent;
La simple pitié n'y trouve qu'un forfait
Le sentiment admire, et la raison se tait.

Here rest a pair who by misfortune tried,
Liv'd for each other, for each other died.

Harsh laws and stern religion blame their loves;
Reason is silent but the heart approves.

Such a compliment would have cheered the philosopher, even in his most atrabiliar mood, had he but known of it. Spring, however, succeeded winter and fair weather the snows, and Rousseau emerged from his hibernation, ready to take to the road. He set out with Thérèse, who had little love of wandering, but this time the inducement was Paris—Paris, to which they were returning, as Thérèse now hoped, forever. Life there would be more expensive than at Monquin, but their means would be adequate, what with Rousseau's English royalties from his works and the allowance which My Lord Marshal continued to send him, tactfully, through Du Peyrou. As for Thérèse, there was the income of three hundred francs which came to her through Rey, and would continue coming to her as long as she lived, according to the arrangement Rousseau had made with him.

Perhaps out of sentiment, perhaps from habit, the two returned to their old rue Plâtrières, and took their few belongings to an apartment of two rooms on the fourth floor. The spinet, of course, had the place of honor in the room that served as a salon. The portrait of King George III of England, which Rousseau had not sold with his collection of prints, hung on the wall. A canary sang in its cage at the window, to which the swallows came for the crumbs they picked at from Rousseau's hand. He copied his music, he composed songs—*Consolations des misères de ma vie* he was to call them—and he secretly, very secretly, began writing his *Dialogues: Rousseau, juge de Jean-Jacques—Rousseau, Judge of Jean-Jacques.*

He had his reasons for the secrecy. First of all, the merest rumor that he was at work on something new roused suspicion, fear and rancor in the many who, justifiably or not, felt that they would be attacked or made the butt of his criticism. He had personal reasons as well: "I have often said that if one had given me, of another man, the ideas that have been given

of me to my contemporaries, I would not have conducted myself toward him as they do toward me." All had seen fit to
judge him in accordance with the hue and cry of his enemies.
He would now show them Jean-Jacques, judged by Jean-
Jacques, who certainly knew him better than anyone else in
the world. For the purpose, he chose as interlocutor a man he
called simply the Frenchman.

True, he had promised the authorities not to publish anything more in his lifetime. He had not promised, however, not
to write. So, by means of this not too subtle but justifiable ruse,
he was able to give voice to his grievances, big and little: from
the rumor which had started at the height of his triumph, that
he was neither the author nor the composer of the *Devin du
village* nor, for that matter, the creator of all the books published under his name. Had the Frenchman read any of Rousseau's works? Of course not! Not a line of anything that bore that
odious name! Rousseau was nothing but a plagiarist who
helped himself right and left to whatever was at hand.

"I submit there must be two Jean-Jacques, and that the author of those books and the perpetrator of those crimes could
not be the same man. It is a feeling so deeply rooted in my
heart that nothing could ever eradicate it."

"Nevertheless, you're mistaken, and another proof that he
has written books and is still writing them."

"That's something I did not know. They told me, on the
other hand, that for some years he has been busy with just
copying music."

"Copying music indeed!" cried the Frenchman. "He only
pretends, so as to give the appearance of being poor, though
he is rich . . . but nobody hereabout is taken in and you must
have come from very far to have fallen into the trap. . . ."

It was obviously a *dédoublement* in Rousseau, a split of the
personality which nonetheless gave such an appearance of sanity in its mad logic as to be frightening. Physically, however,
he had never been better, for even his bladder seemed at last
to have behaved. Erratic in many respects, he nevertheless

observed a rigorous routine for work as well as play. Rising early from old habit, he would go at once to his writing table and the labor of copying. He would then leave it briefly for breakfast and return to the task, working till mid-afternoon, after which he would set out on his walks.

At times, for a treat, he would go out with Thérèse to dine, as on a Sunday when they had gone to the Porte Maillot. Sometimes at La Muette they would sit on the grass like other good bourgeois, enjoying the sunshine and the breezes and watching the life about them. One day a nun had conducted a group of little girls on an outing. An *oublieur,* a vender of cone-shaped pastries called *oublies,* came around with his tempting merchandise, offering to let the children take chances on them. The girls, all laughter and excitement, surrounded him. Rousseau managed to take him aside and held a brief conversation with him. The girls tried their luck. One after the other, they won at every chance, and even the nun received her share. The childless couple returned home, happy in the happiness they had given—and yet, surely, more than a little sad in their loneliness.

23. *The solitary sage*

While Rousseau continued writing his *Dialogues* his burdened
conscience found release, but his misanthropy deepened. There
was not a soul whom he now would trust. He became more
than ever secretive, suspicious, and scarcely admitted anyone to
his parlor-bedroom, with its spinet, its two little beds with
their coverlets of striped white-and-blue calico, its small table,
bureau and chairs. It was a very modest place that His Majesty,
King George III, looked down upon from his frame. Very
seldom did Rousseau receive company, since he had made it a
duty to break with almost everyone he knew. But though he
refused to meet the world, the world was more than ever eager
to see him, and Grimm, making capital of the situation, spread
amusing stories about the recluse who was to be seen everywhere. One day, according to Grimm, a vast crowd collected on
the square of the Palais-Royal.

"What is the occasion?" the people were asked.

"We're here to see Jean-Jacques," came the answer.

"Who or what is this Jean-Jacques?"

"We don't know, but he's going to pass this way."

Though Rousseau never made such public appearances, he would on occasion, to please his patronesses, give a reading from his works, arguing doubtless that he was within his rights, for the interdiction was only against publication. Accordingly he requested the Abbess of Gomerfontaine, to whom he had consigned the manuscript of his *Confessions,* to return it to him for a while. He put it to good use, giving readings at various noble houses. One session, according to the poet, Dorat, lasted from early morning until long past midnight. Rousseau omitted nothing in the readings, both from that honesty of which he prided himself and for the catharsis of public humiliation at the confession of sins that others would have concealed. When he would come to the abandonment of his children, many—the women in particular—would lower their eyes to conceal their horror, or their tears.

He had more than audiences of women for his writings, however. Crowned heads consulted him; legislators wrote to him for advice, or even came to see him, like that Polish nobleman De Wielhorski, who in the midst of his country's political troubles came to Rousseau for a remedy. Rousseau gave it in his *Considérations sur le gouvernement de Pologne,* which from an essay grew into a book of fifteen chapters wherein he ranged from the ancient institutions of such sages as Moses, Lycurgus and Numa, to the three orders, the knights, the senators and the king, that governed Poland. The legislation, he pointed out, was divided. With patient wisdom he prescribed the remedy—privately, however, since he was still forbidden publication. National institutions formed the genius, the character, the taste and the morals of a people, he maintained; yet there were really no Frenchmen, no Germans, no Spaniards, no Britons, but only Europeans. All had the same tastes, passions, morals. "What matters it to them what master they serve, what country's laws they obey? Provided they find money to steal and women to corrupt, every land is their country," he declared bitterly. "Give another direction to the passions of your Poles and you will give their souls a national character which will distinguish them from the rest. . . . Loving their country, they will serve it zealously with all their heart. Even if their legislation were bad, this sentiment alone would make them good citizens; for it is only good citizens who create the strength and the prosperity of a state." [1] This work remained a secret, shared only by Monsieur de Wielhorski, for it would not do to give further fuel to the malice of his enemies.

He had now changed his motto to the hopeful *Post tenebras lux,* seeing that he had sufficiently submitted his life to truth though, he must have reflected, to little avail. His bitterness and mistrust increased. He refused to see any but old friends, and even then, churlishly. If he believed in his motto, that after darkness light would follow, he gave no indication of it. He wondered what to do about the *Dialogues,* now that they were written. He could not publish them because of the interdiction. He had no friend in France whom he trusted sufficiently to appoint as their custodian. He took them, nevertheless, to the Abbé de Condillac, wise and full of years; but he gave the old man no indication of what he desired. The abbé, for all the good intentions he might have had, could not have found the work in sympathy with the classical restraint and moderation which he himself advocated, and therefore he limited himself to matters of style. "As if it were a literary work!" Rousseau exclaimed in disappointment, after reclaiming his manuscript.

Suddenly, whom should he meet in Paris but the young Englishman, Brooke Boothby, Davenport's neighbor at Wooton. Surely Boothby was God's own messenger, sent him just in time. He gave Boothby the first *Dialogue,* because he had not yet made fair copies of the rest. Evidently Rousseau considered no one else he knew worthy of the trust.

When the work was completed the problem arose once more, since Boothby had left Paris. Again Rousseau sought in vain among his acquaintances for another custodian when suddenly light dawned upon him. One day he made a packet of the *Dialogues* and on the wrapper wrote: Consignment remitted to Providence. He then added the invocation: "Protector of the oppressed, God of Justice and of Truth, receive this trust which I place upon Thine altar, and confide to Thy providence an unfortunate stranger, alone, without support, with no defender on earth, outraged, mocked, defamed, betrayed by a whole generation, and for the past fifteen years delivered up to treatment worse than death, to indignities unheard of till now among human beings—and all without my learning the reason. All explanation is refused me; I am deprived of all communication. I no longer expect from men, embittered by their own injustice, anything but affronts, lies and deceit. . . . Deign to take my consignment into Thy keeping and let it fall into young and faithful hands, which will transmit it without fraud to a better generation, that it may learn while deploring my fate, how a man without rancor, without deceit, an enemy of injustice yet patient in bearing it, was treated. . . . If my work . . . should be delivered to my enemies and by them destroyed or disfigured, which seems inevitable . . . I shall count no less upon it. I rest upon Thy justice and resign myself to Thy will."

It was early afternoon, the day before Christmas, 1776, when he set out for the Cathedral of Notre Dame. He would lay his work on the altar, at the feet of God himself. He hurried to the great edifice, a little man neatly dressed, his round wig a little askew and his fine eyes glowing. He crossed the cobbled square to the Cathedral, passed between the carved portals and strode up the Nave toward the altar. The grille, which he remembered as always open, was this day closed. His body swayed; his head reeled in one of those strange attacks which had been occurring of late. Even Heaven was against him.

Dazed, he wandered about the streets, following no particular direction but simply keeping his body in motion. At home he sat down at his writing table and took up his copying, which brought him ten sols per page and enabled him to keep his true work, the *Confessions*, the *Dialogues*, the *Rêveries* untainted by mercenary concerns. It was all work of superlative quality, with fine clarity and logic and, in the *Rêveries*, filled with a serene music which one would never have imagined could come from so vexed a mind. Perhaps his strange psychic dichotomy had reared a protective wall between the insane man—for there is no doubt of his insanity at this period—and the ever sensitive and lucid creative artist.

At this time the madman prevailed, for it could only have been the impulse of one driven mad by a real or a fictive sense of injury that made him write a sort of manifesto addressed "To all Frenchmen who still love Justice and Truth," and distribute copies of it to the passers-by.

"Frenchmen! O nation once gentle and amiable, what have you become?" it read. "How you have changed toward an unfortunate stranger, alone, and at your mercy. . . . Why such engineering, such ruses, such deceitfulness, such lies to conceal from the guilty, crimes of which he must be as aware as anyone, if it is true that he committed them? Why, for reasons beyond my understanding, and by persisting to take from me a right of which no criminal has ever been denied—why have you resolved to drown the rest of my unhappy days in anguish, derision and shame, without my knowing why, without your listening to my grievances, my reasons, my complaints—without even permitting me to speak? For all defense I shall raise to Heaven a heart innocent of deceit and hands clean of all evil, imploring—no, not your punishment and my revenge—but that It grant to my old age a refuge where your insults will not reach me." [2]

He spoke to deaf ears. No one would take a copy of the address, even gratis, some excusing themselves naïvely by saying it was not meant for them, since they had done him no harm.

Meanwhile Brooke Boothby had left for England, and God had given no sign to him, Rousseau. that He had taken His work into His custody. Nothing changed in the world about him. Nobody seemed to care whether he, or anyone else, for that matter, lived or died. There was no love any more—no love for one's fellow man, no love for truth or justice except perhaps among the few, foolishly idealistic, like himself. *His* heart was bursting with love of mankind—in the abstract. *His* soul yearned toward the souls of his fellows whom he sought to arouse to their duty of loving others as themselves. They would not hear.

As he roamed about he ruminated on his works, on mankind, on himself, so absorbed that he took little notice of the world about him. One day, late in October, 1776, he was wandering about Ménilmontant, amid the autumnal landscape, when a carriage came rushing along with a huge Great Dane bounding behind it. Rousseau had time to avoid the carriage, but not the dog which hurtled against him and flung him headlong to the ground, stunning him. For hours he lay unconscious, his upper lip split and bleeding, his whole body aching. Somehow he managed to drag himself home. When Thérèse saw his bloody face she roused the whole neighborhood with her screams. The Lieutenant of Police came to make inquiries. The papers were filled with the news, slanting it toward tragedy or ridicule according to the views of the editor. One sentence in particular was repeated with relish by his joyful enemies: "Rousseau is crushed by dogs!"

It was certainly no atmosphere for peace of mind. Nevertheless, once recovered from the shock and the bruises, Rousseau took up his labors as usual, finding in them the life that was really his, especially now when in his *Rêveries* he was approaching that period of his youth when he had lived fully and joyously, loving and knowing himself beloved. The magic haze of time enhanced what had been its beauties and softened its few sorrows. He also wrote of it at length in the *Confessions*—telling his *"petite histoire,"* as he called it, half in tenderness, half in apology for unveiling to the world things in which it could have little interest, though so dear to him. Still, there might be souls in another age, long after his death, who would read and recognize themselves in Jean-Jacques and, sighing, perhaps would say: "Here was a man like me, no better yet no worse, who has had the courage to reveal himself as he was."

Winter, which had kept him much at home gave way to spring, but he now seldom left the house. There was so much that he still had to say. Would he have the time to say it? It was Palm Sunday, the twelfth of April, 1778, and the pealing of the church bells awakened him early in the morning. With the sound, memory too stirred to life, and the heart, which also remembered, quickened. He got up, the pealing recalling other bells, long ago, on another Palm Sunday. He went to the writing table and began the "Tenth Promenade" of the *Rêveries*.

"Today, Palm Sunday, it will be exactly fifty years since I first met Madame de Warens. She was then only twenty-eight years old, having been born with the century. I was not yet seventeen and my burgeoning temperament, which was still strange to me, gave a new warmth to a heart naturally full of life. If it was not surprising that she should conceive a friendly interest in a lively youth, who was yet gentle and modest and with a fairly agreeable face, it was still less so that a charming woman full of wit and grace should have inspired in me, together with gratitude, tenderer sentiments, which I did not distinguish from it. But what is less usual is that this first moment decided the rest of my life for me. My soul, whose most precious faculties my organs had not yet developed, still had no determined shape. With a kind of impatience it was awaiting the moment that would provide it: yet that moment, accelerated by this meeting, did not come so quickly. . . . She had sent me away. Everything called me back to her. I had to come back. This return settled my destiny. . . . Ah, if only I had sufficed her heart, as she had sufficed mine! What peaceful and delightful days would we have spent together. . . . Not a day passes but that I recall with joy and tenderness this unique and brief period of my life when I was completely myself . . . and when I can truly say that I had lived. Much like that prefect . . . who falling into disgrace under Vespasian, went to end his days peacefully in the country, I can say: 'I have passed seventy years on earth, and I have lived only seven of them. . . .' " [3]

Easter came and went. April gave way to May and May to June, when Rousseau, who was then staying with the Marquis de Girardin at Ermenonville, learned of the death of Voltaire. His face clouded with grief, which astonished the Marquis, who had long known of the antagonism between the two men. Rousseau explained to him: "It is because my existence was linked with his. He is dead, and I shall not be long in following him." Despite the difference in their lives, they had been kindred spirits, each carrying the torch that was to illumine the era of enlightenment.

Rousseau seldom went out now, but his few faithful came to see him. On the first day of July, 1778, the devoted Moultou arrived to see the friend he cherished but also the genius he venerated. He had met with difficulties, however, since, whether for Rousseau's sake, or out of spite, Thérèse had sought to prevent the visit—at least so Moultou implied in a letter to his wife: "I sought out Rousseau in his wretched house. His wife did not recognize me and told me he was not to be seen. I told her who I was; she said he had gone out and that I might see him some other day. If I am prevented a second time, I'll never go back there again. . . ." [4]

The *Confessions,* too dangerous to publish while their author lived, were finished. Rousseau had made his final copy of them, since he wished them to appear after he was dead. That copy he gave to Moultou.

The next day he rose with the sun and by five o'clock was out in the country gathering plants for the herbal he was preparing for the twelve-year-old son of the Marquis de Girardin. Toward eight o'clock he returned complaining of fatigue and of a strange prickling sensation in the soles of his feet. He had his coffee with Thérèse and the servant, but they could see that all was not well. Now and then he would clasp his head in his hands, saying that he felt as if it were splitting and as if an icy fluid were being poured down his spinal column. Nevertheless, he said he would go to the Girardins' to give a music lesson to the Marquis' young daughter. "Don't forget to pay the locksmith and don't argue about the bill," he said to Thérèse, "for he's an honest man."

Thérèse went out to pay the locksmith, leaving Rousseau sitting in his chair. On her return, as she was going up the stairs, she could hear her husband groaning in agony. "I feel pinpricks in my chest and a frightful blow in my head. It is as if they were tearing it apart with pincers." It was about eleven o'clock in the morning and the day was bright. He said he wished to look out on the foliage in the sunlight. Humoring him, Thérèse helped him up and supported him as he painfully stumbled toward the window. "Being of Beings, God!" he said. "How clear the sky! There is not a single cloud. God awaits me. . . ." The next moment his life was extinguished in a sigh. The age had lost its conscience and its guide.

The following day Ermenonville became a place of pilgrimage for those who had heard of Rousseau's death. Among them came the young but already famous sculptor, Jean-Antoine Houdon, to make a cast of that extraordinary head. The doctors had gathered, too, since Rousseau had left his express wishes that an autopsy be performed upon his body. Inevitably rumors were already spreading: that he had met with foul play, that Thérèse had murdered him; but the most persistent one was that he had killed himself. Medical consensus declared that his chronic retention had produced an arteriosclerosis of the kidneys, which eventually had brought about cerebral congestion. Rumor of foul play, however, continued to persist long after he had been laid to rest in the peaceful Island of the Poplars that he loved so well.

With the inception of the French Revolution, Rousseau became one of its idols, and in consequence Thérèse, though she had married a domestic in the household of the Marquis de Girardin, was also made much of. Since, in the fervor of revolution, everything that even remotely suggested royalty had to be destroyed, there was nothing that escaped the zeal of the Revolutionists, not even playing cards, whose kings and queens gave offense to the sons and daughters of liberty. The old decks were therefore eliminated and new decks designed. Now sages took the place of kings and virtues of queens. Hence in a deck issued during the first year of the Republic, the sages on the cards were Solon, replacing the King of Hearts; Brutus, the King of Spades; Cato, the King of Diamonds; and Jean-Jacques Rousseau, the King of Clubs. He is shown in his round wig; he is clothed in a flowing caftan of orange, red and green, and he holds in his right hand a copy of the *Contrat Social*. Here was fame indeed.

Rousseau's ashes were not allowed to rest in their peaceful island, for the Convention had them transported to the Panthéon where for some years they lay beside those of his mortal enemy, Voltaire. In December of 1897, the coffin was reopened and, strangely, at the same time as Voltaire's. According to the report then issued, Rousseau's skeleton was undisturbed, as when he had been laid to rest, his arms crossed upon his chest, his head, now only a skull, leaning slightly to the left as if in sleep. The old rumor that he might have been shot was definitely exploded.

Thérèse, made much of during the Revolution, but misunderstood and often maligned by Rousseau's partisans, must be allowed to speak for herself. "What!" she exclaimed in a letter preserved in the Bibliothèque of Geneva. "Because Rousseau did a poor girl who did not know how to read or write, the honor of having her wash his linen and cook his soup and at times share his bed—must this poor girl be turned into a heroine?" In her way she had loved him, served him, and no doubt by her care prolonged his life. More than wife, she had been what that strange, lonely genius had most needed, the "Companion of Rousseau," as the inscription on her gravestone describes her.

Notes

Chapter 1

1. Jean-Jacques was mistakenly to declare that he had been born on July 4.
2. Jean-Jacques Rousseau, *Confessions*, p. 4.
3. *Ibid.*, p. 2.
4. *Ibid.*, p. 6.
5. *Ibid.*, p. 3.
6. *Ibid.*, p. 3.
7. *Ibid.*, p. 11.
8. Rousseau was then ten years old.
9. *Confessions*, p. 12.

Chapter 2

1. *Confessions*, p. 23.
2. *Ibid.*, p. 31.

3. *Ibid.*, p. 43.
4. Rousseau, *Oeuvres complètes*, XVIII, 3-4.
5. *Ibid.*, p. 4.
6. *Confessions*, p. 47.
7. *Ibid.*, p. 48.
8. *Ibid.*, p. 49.
9. *Ibid.*, p. 51.

Chapter 3

1. *Confessions*, p. 53.
2. *Ibid.*, p. 60.
3. *Ibid.*, p. 61.
4. Gaberel, *Histoire de l'église de Genève*, III, 224.
5. *Confessions*, p. 75.
6. *Ibid.*, p. 79.

Chapter 4

1. *Confessions*, p. 84.
2. *Ibid.*, p. 86.
3. *Ibid.*, p. 94.
4. Jean Guéhenno, *Jean-Jacques: En marge des "Confessions,"* p. 72.
5. *Confessions*, p. 118.

Chapter 5

1. *Confessions*, pp. 132-133.
2. *Ibid.*, p. 138.
3. *Ibid.*, p. 144.
4. *Ibid.*, p. 145.

Chapter 6

1. *Confessions*, p. 147.
2. Guéhenno, *Jean-Jacques: En marge des "Confessions,"* p. 62.
3. *Confessions*, p. 150.
4. *Ibid.*, p. 151.
5. *Ibid.*, p. 158.
6. *Ibid.*, p. 160.
7. *Ibid.*
8. *Ibid.*
9. The authenticity of this letter has been questioned. If Jean-Jacques did not write it, he had a genius for an imitator.

Chapter 7

1. Comte de Saint-Germain, from a manuscript, now in Geneva, published in his *Oeuvres complètes*.
2. *Confessions*, pp. 212-213.
3. *Ibid.*, p. 214.
4. Rousseau, *Correspondance*, *Oeuvres*, XVIII, 35.
5. *Ibid.*, p. 36.

6. *Ibid.*
7. *Confessions*, p. 237.

Chapter 8

1. *Oeuvres*, XVIII, 36-37.
2. *Ibid.*, pp. 37-38.
3. *Confessions*, p. 245.
4. *Ibid.*, p. 245.
5. *Ibid.*, p. 182.
6. *Ibid.*, p. 165.
7. In this translation the author has tried to capture the callowness of the young poet and his rhetorical flourishes.
8. Translation by the author.
9. *Correspondance, Oeuvres*, XVIII, 50.
10. Rousseau, *Annales de J. J. Rousseau*, IX.

Chapter 9

1. *Oeuvres*, XVIII, 93-96.
2. *Ibid.*, X, 117-118.
3. *Confessions*, p. 259.
4. *Ibid.*, p. 260.
5. *Ibid.*
6. *Ibid.*, p. 262.
7. *Ibid.*, p. 263.

Chapter 10

1. Jean-Jacques says the Opéra in the *Confessions*.
2. George Sand, *Histoire de ma vie*, I, 12.
3. From a brochure, discovered in 1910 by Monsieur P. p. Plan at the Bibliothèque Nationale, entitled *Le Nouveau Dédale, ouvrage inédit de Jean-Jacques Rousseau et copié sur son manuscrit original daté de 1742*.

Chapter *11*

1. *Oeuvres*, XVIII, 61.
2. *Confessions*, p. 299.

Chapter *12*

1. *Oeuvres*, XVIII, 63-64.
2. *Ibid.*, p. 65.
3. *Confessions*, p. 304.
4. *Ibid.*, p. 305.
5. *Ibid.*, p. 385.
6. *Ibid.*, p. 306.
7. *Oeuvres*, XVIII, 68-69.
8. *Confessions*, p. 314.
9. *Oeuvres*, XVIII, 314.
10. *Confessions*, p. 332.
11. *Ibid.*

Chapter *13*

1. *Oeuvres*, XVIII, 78-79.
2. *Confessions*, p. 326.
3. René Trintzius, *La vie privée de J. J. Rousseau*, p. 135.
4. Rousseau, *Discours sur les arts et sciences, Oeuvres*, XIII, 5-37.
5. *Ibid.*, pp. 17-18.
6. *Ibid.*, pp. 22-23.
7. *Ibid.*, pp. 5-37.
8. *Ibid.*, p. 37.
9. *Confessions*, p. 330.
10. *Ibid.*, p. 331.

Chapter *14*

1. *Confessions*, p. 336.
2. *Ibid.*, p. 337.
3. Since Charles Burney, a contemporary of Rousseau, made an excellent translation of Rousseau's opera, the author has taken the liberty of quoting his English text. Angel Records has done a recording

of *Le devin du village* (Angel 34521).
4. *Confessions*, p. 351.
5. *Ibid.*, p. 352.
6. *Ibid.*, p. 359.
7. Denis Diderot, *Oeuvres complètes*, I, 179-180.

Chapter *15*

1. *Correspondance, Oeuvres*, XVIII, 96.
2. *Confessions*, p. 364.
3. Trintzius, *La vie privée de J. J. Rousseau*, p. 150.
4. Rousseau, *Discours sur l'origine de l'inégalité* . . . , I, 48.
5. *Ibid.*, p. 51.
6. *Ibid.*, p. 52.
7. *Ibid.*, p. 57.
8. *Ibid.*, p. 73.
9. *Oeuvres*, V, 236-237.
10. *Ibid.*, VIII, 299.
11. *Ibid.*, VI, 14.

Chapter *16*

1. *Confessions*, pp. 410-411.
2. *Ibid.*
3. *Oeuvres*, XVIII, 199.
4. *Ibid.*, p. 200.
5. *Ibid.*, p. 202.
6. *Confessions*, p. 414.
7. *Ibid.*, p. 415.
8. *Oeuvres*, XVIII, 150, 170.
9. *Ibid.*, p. 202.
10. Diderot, *Oeuvres*, VII, 65.

Chapter *17*

1. *Confessions*, p. 110.
2. Rousseau, *La nouvelle Héloïse, Oeuvres*, pp. 395-397.
3. *Ibid.*, p. 86.

4. *Oeuvres,* XVIII, 313-314.
5. *Ibid.*

Chapter 18

1. *Oeuvres,* XVIII, 344.
2. *Ibid.,* p. 404.
3. *Ibid.,* p. 394.
4. *Ibid.,* pp. 394-395.
5. Guéhenno, *Grandeur et misère* . . . , p. 102.
6. *Oeuvres,* XVIII, 421-422.
7. Rousseau, *Emile, Oeuvres,* VI, book I, 22.
8. *Oeuvres,* XVIII, 386.
9. *Ibid.*
10. *Ibid.,* p. 389.
11. *Ibid.,* p. 390.
12. *Ibid.,* pp. 390-391.
13. *Ibid.,* p. 393.
14. *Ibid.,* p. 400.
15. *Ibid.,* p. 441-443.

Chapter 19

1. *Oeuvres,* XVIII, 431.
2. *Ibid.,* p. 444.
3. *Ibid.,* VIII, 3-5.
4. *Ibid.,* p. 7.
5. *La Lettre à Monsieur de Beaumont, Oeuvres,* VIII, 48-49.
6. *Ibid.,* p. 63.
7. *Oeuvres,* XVIII, 375.
8. David Hume, *A Concise Account of the Dispute Between Mr. Hume and Mr. Rousseau* . . . Printed for T. Becket and P. A. De Hondt, near Surry Street in the Strand, London, 1766.
9. *Oeuvres,* II, pp. 282-283.
10. *Lettres de la montagne, Oeuvres,* VIII, 120-121.
11. *Ibid.,* pp. 123-124.
12. *Boswell on the Grand Tour,* ed. Frederick A. Pottle, pp. 218-220.

13. *Ibid.,* p. 229.
14. *Ibid.*
15. *Ibid.,* p. 231.
16. *Oeuvres,* XIX, 140.

Chapter 20

1. Hume, *A Concise Account of the Dispute Between Mr. Hume and Mr. Rousseau* . . .
2. *Ibid.*
3. *Ibid.*
4. *Ibid.*
5. *Ibid.*
6. André Morellet, *Mémoires,* p. 109.
7. *Oeuvres,* XIX, 398.
8. Hume in his letter to Madame de Boufflers, January 19, 1766.
9. *Oeuvres,* XIX, 484-485.
10. *Ibid.,* p. 408.
11. *Ibid.,* pp. 414-415.
12. Hume, *A Concise Account of the Dispute Between Mr. Hume and Mr. Rousseau* . . .
13. *Ibid.*
14. *Ibid.*
15. *Oeuvres,* XX, 42.
16. *Ibid.*
17. *Ibid.*
18. *Ibid.,* XIX, 447.
19. Hume, *A Concise Account of the Dispute Between Mr. Hume and Mr. Rousseau* . . .
20. *Ibid.*
21. *Ibid.*
22. Boswell, James, *Life of Samuel Johnson,* I, 294, London and New York, MCMI.

Chapter 21

1. *Oeuvres,* XX, 6-7.
2. *Ibid.,* XIX, 485.

3. Hermine de Saussure, *Rousseau et les manuscrits des "Confessions,"* p. 149.
4. *Correspondance, Oeuvres,* XIX, 476.
5. *Ibid.,* XX, 128.
6. *Ibid.,* 131-132.

Chapter 22

1. *Oeuvres,* XX, 154.
2. *Ibid.,* p. 162.
3. Saussure de, *Rousseau et les manuscrits des "Confessions,"* pp. 191-192.
4. Letter to Thérèse le Vasseur, August 12, 1769.
5. Friedrich Melchior von Grimm, *Correspondance littéraire, philosophique et critique,* IX, 91.
6. *Portrait of a Golden Age: Intimate Papers of the Second Viscount Palmerston, Courtier under George III,* compiled and ed. Brian Connell, p. 99.

Chapter 23

1. Rousseau, *Considération sur le gouvernement de Pologne, Oeuvres,* II, 173.
2. *Ibid.,* XVI, 409-411.
3. *Ibid.,* XVII, 161-162.
4. Saussure de, *Rousseau et les manuscrits des "Confessions,"* p. 337.

Bibliography

Benrubi, J., *Les idées morales de J. J. Rousseau*, Paris, 1940
Bertrand, Alexis, *Le texte primitif du "Contrat Social,"* Paris, 1891
Boehm, B., *Sokrates im achtzehnten Jahrhundert*, Leipzig, 1929
Boswell, James, Esq., *The Life of Samuel Johnson*, L.L.D., 3 vols., Dent and Co.,
London, MCMI
Burgelin, Pierre, *La philosophie de l'existence de J. J. Rousseau*, Paris, 1952
Carcassonne, E., *Nature et moralité dans la pensée de Rousseau, Recherches
philosophiques*, 1931-1932
Chinard, G., *L'Amérique et le rêve exotique dans la littérature française au XVIIe
et XVIIIe siècles*, Paris, 1913
Cobban, A., *Rousseau and the Modern State*, London, 1934
Connell, Brian, ed., *Portrait of a Golden Age, Intimate Papers of the Second
Viscount Palmerston, Courtier under George III*, Houghton Mifflin, Boston,
1958
Cuendet, W., *La philosophie religieuse de J. J. Rousseau*, Geneva, 1916
Demole, V., *Rôle du tempérament et des idées délirantes de Rousseau dans la
genèse de ses principales théories, Annales médico-psychologiques*, 1922
Derathé, R., *Le rationalisme de Rousseau*, Paris, 1948; *Rousseau et le Christian-
isme, Revue de Métaphysique et de morale*, 1948; *Rousseau et les idées
politiques de son temps*, Paris, 1950
Epinay, Madame d', *Mémoires*, Paris, 1863

Faguet, E., *Rousseau, le penseur*, Paris, 1912

Gaiffe, F., J. J. *Rousseau et les rêveries du promeneur solitaire*, Paris, 1936

Guéhenno, Jean, *Jean-Jacques: En marge des "Confessions,"* Paris, 1948; *Jean-Jacques*, Paris, 1948-1950; *Grandeur et misère d'un esprit . . .* , Paris, 1952

Guillemin, H., *Cette affaire inférnale*, Paris, 1942

Gurvitch, G., *L'idée de droit social*, Paris, 1932

Havens, G. R., *The Theory of Natural Goodness in Rousseau's "Nouvelle Héloïse,"* Modern Language Notes, Baltimore, 1921

Hearnshaw, F. J. C., *The Social and Political Ideas of Some French Thinkers of the Age of Reason*, London, 1930

Heidenheim, A., J.-J. *Rousseau: Persönlichkeit, Philosophie und Psychose*, Munich, 1924

Hendel, C. W., *Jean-Jacques Rousseau, Moralist*, London, 1934

Höffding, H., *Jean-Jacques Rousseau et sa philosophie*, Paris, 1911

Hubert, R., *Les sciences sociales dans l'Encyclopédie*, Paris, 1923; *Rousseau et l'Encyclopédie*, Paris, 1928

Lovejoy, A. D., *The Supposed Primitivism of Rousseau's Discourse on Inequality*, Modern Philology, Chicago, 1923

Luppol, I. K., *Diderot*, Paris, 1936

Macdonald, Mrs. Frederika, *Jean-Jacques Rousseau*, London, 1906

Marck, S., *Grundbegriffe der Rousseauschen Staatsphilosophie*, Kantstudien, 1922

Maritain, J., *Trois réformateurs*, Paris, 1925

Marmontel, *Oeuvres*, Paris, 1804

Masson, P.-M., *La religion de Jean-Jacques Rousseau*, Paris, 1916; *Rousseau expliqué par Jean-Jacques*, Revue des cours et conférences, II, 1908

Monglond, A., *Vies préromantiques*, Paris, 1925

Morley, Viscount John, *Rousseau*, London, 1886

Mornet, D., *Les Sciences et la nature en France au XVIIIᵉ siècle*, Paris, 1911

Musset-Pathay, V. D., *Histoire de la vie et des ouvrages de Jean-Jacques Rousseau*, Paris, 1821

Nemo, Maxime, *L'Homme nouveau, Jean-Jacques Rousseau*, Paris, 1957

Pottle, Frederick A., ed., *Boswell on the Grand Tour: Germany and Switzerland*, New York, 1953

Proal, L., *La psychologie de J.-J. Rousseau*, Paris, 1930

Reiche, E., *Rousseau und das Naturrecht*, Berlin, 1935

Rendu-Moreau, *L'idée de la bonté naturelle chez J. J. Rousseau*, Paris, 1929

Roddier, H., J. J. *Rousseau en Angleterre au XVIIIᵉ siècle*, Paris, 1950

Rousseau, J. J., *Les Confessions*, Garnier Frères, Paris, n.d.

Rousseau, J. J., *Correspondance générale*, ed. Dufour *et* Plan, Paris, 1924-1934

Rousseau, J. J., *Oeuvres de Jean Jacques Rousseau, Citoyen de Genève*, 20 vols., Paris, 1801

Saint-Germain, Comte de, *Oeuvres complètes*, Lefèvre, Paris, 1819-1820

Saint-Pierre, Bernardin de, *La Vie et les Ouvrages de Rousseau*, Paris, 1907

Sand, George, *Histoire de ma vie*, Michel Levy, Frères, Paris, 1856

Saussure, Hermine de, *Rousseau et les manuscrits des "Confessions,"* Paris, 1958

Schinz, A., *La pensée de Jean-Jacques Rousseau*, Paris, 1929

Schinz, P., *Rousseau, Forerunner of Pragmatism*, Chicago, 1909

Seillière, E., *Jean-Jacques Rousseau,* Paris, 1921

Spink, J. S., *Jean Jacques Rousseau et Genève,* Paris, 1934

Streckeisen-Moultou, M. G., *Oeuvres et corréspondance inédites,* Paris, 1861

Tiersot, J., *Les Maîtres de la musique,* Paris, 1911

Trahard, P., *Les Maîtres de la Sensibilité française au XVIII⁰ siècle,* Paris, 1931-1933

Trintzius, René, *La vie privée de J. J. Rousseau,* Hachette, Paris, 1938

Villeneuve-Guibert, ed., *Le Portefeuille de Madame Dupin,* Paris, 1884

Villey, P., *L'Influence de Montaigne sur les idées pédagogiques de Locke et de Rousseau,* Paris, 1911

Wahl, J., *Tableau de la Philosophie Française,* Paris, 1946

Index

357 : *Index*

ABOUT THE AUTHOR

FRANCES WINWAR was born in Taormina, Sicily and came to this country as a child. She was educated at New York City colleges and at Columbia University. Her first poems and articles appeared in magazines, and she soon joined the reviewing staff of the New York *World,* under Laurence Stallings. Her most exciting newspaper coup was the publication of an obituary piece she had written on Joseph Conrad, when his death found the *World* groping for material.

Though Miss Winwar has written and published seven novels, she is best known for her biographies, which have produced high critical acclaim here and abroad. *Poor Splendid Wings,* first of eleven such works, dealt with the English Pre-Raphaelites and won her the Atlantic Monthly Non-Fiction Prize for 1933. In successive volumes she portrayed the lives of Coleridge and the Wordsworths; Byron, Shelley and Keats; and Oscar Wilde. Taken together, these four books form a cultural history of the nineteenth century in England.

Her other "lives" have included Walt Whitman, George Sand, the Brownings and Joan of Arc. *Wingless Victory* (Gabriele d'Annunzio and Eleonora Duse) and *The Haunted Palace* (Edgar Allan Poe) are the most recent. Of the latter André Maurois said: "It is an excellent book, the best she has written. A biography after my own heart . . ."

Miss Winwar's translation of the *Decameron,* commissioned by the Limited Editions Club, has been called the best available in English, and is now in the Modern Library. Apart from writing, she has attained stature as a literary critic and lecturer. She has also been a visiting professor at the University of Kansas City. Today she lives in New York City and has a summer home in Vermont.

D